Tom Gamboa

Tom Gamboa

My Life in Baseball

TOM GAMBOA
with DAVID RUSSELL
Foreword by DOUG GLANVILLE

McFarland & Company, Inc., Publishers
Jefferson, North Carolina

All photographs are from the Tom Gamboa collection
unless otherwise indicated.

LIBRARY OF CONGRESS CATALOGUING-IN-PUBLICATION DATA

Names: Gamboa, Tom, author. | Russell, David, 1992– author.
Title: Tom Gamboa : my life in baseball / Tom Gamboa,
with David Russell ; foreword by Doug Glanville.
Description: Jefferson, North Carolina : McFarland & Company, Inc.,
Publishers, 2018 | Includes index.
Identifiers: LCCN 2017048277 | ISBN 9781476667416
(softcover : acid free paper) ∞
Subjects: LCSH: Gamboa, Tom. | Baseball players—
United States—Biography.
Classification: LCC GV865.G259 A3 2018 |
DDC 796.357092 [B] —dc23
LC record available at https://lccn.loc.gov/2017048277

BRITISH LIBRARY CATALOGUING DATA ARE AVAILABLE

ISBN (print) 978-1-4766-6741-6
ISBN (ebook) 978-1-4766-2871-4

Front cover: Mayaguez Manager Tom Gamboa, 1988 (author's photograph)

Printed in the United States of America

McFarland & Company, Inc., Publishers
Box 611, Jefferson, North Carolina 28640
www.mcfarlandpub.com

To my mom,
Pauline Elaine Connor Fink Gamboa Smith,
who loved me with all her heart.
To my dad (stepdad),
who taught me how to play baseball
at the age of 10 and from where I found my life's passion.
And for my family and friends
who are a constant inspiration for me.
After all, isn't that what life is all about?
The relationships we cultivate
with family and friends throughout our life.
—Tom Gamboa

For my parents
—David Russell

Table of Contents

Acknowledgments

I want to thank my five kids and my many close friends for the inspiration to write a book. About 25 years ago, one of the gifts my kids gave me for Christmas was a blank book with a note that I should really write a book on the many stories that they would hear me talk to my friends about or that they would hear about that occurred during the season. The thought was there. I've often stated that anybody that has spent a life in baseball could write a very interesting book if they had the presence of mind to keep a journal. Being born with a photographic memory made it easier for me.

Ed Sprague, who was a pitcher with the Reds, was a pitching coach in the Milwaukee organization when I was there. He didn't need the money but baseball has a magnet that keeps you in it. When I managed Paintsville, I didn't have a pitching coach other than a rover who would come in, and Sprague came in for three weeks at the end of the season. After we won the championship, we were having dinner one night with somebody else in the organization and Sprague made a joking comment about how I could probably tell him about all of the 72 games. I looked at him and said, "Well of course I could." He told me that he was joking because nobody could remember all the games. I said that I could remember the score of every one of them. Sprague said that it was impossible and took out the notes, and I went through all the games and gave 71 of the 72 right scores. I missed one 8–5 win that I thought was 7–6. To this day, Sprague tells that story and still can't believe it. He's a great guy but is the type of guy that can't remember what he had for breakfast yesterday.

Another inspiration was Don DeRosa, who I met in a golf tournament that I'm in each year with the same 28 people. He's a twice-over retired college president. He's a friend of Sprague's and a big baseball fan. After a night of golfing, he would prompt me to tell him stories. Here's a retired college president who told me every year at this tournament that I would have to write a book someday.

I felt like my family and friends would like the stories but no one outside my inner circle would be interested, but that always stuck in my mind. The final inspiration was the chance meeting of David Russell and his persistence even though I said no on several occasions. He told me he was surprised I never wrote a book and I thought, "Here's another guy telling me what I've heard many times over." He, like Don DeRosa, felt like people would be interested outside my inner circle.

Foreword by Doug Glanville

When you are embraced in the aura of Tom Gamboa, the most positive person in the world will appear to be a pessimist next to him. He is the breath of fresh air that reminds you of what is important, that life is to be cherished as a gift, a passionate journey where time is your most precious currency. Gamby, as we lovingly call him, is infectious, which sets him apart from inspirational flashes in the pan. When you get a taste of his energy, of his undeniable sense of confidence, it changes you. You no longer let doubt enter your thoughts, you see what he calls "destiny" as a tangible goal, and no one can get in the way but you.

And it applies way beyond baseball.

I recall playing for a manager in Triple-A who did not see my baseball future as optimistically as I saw it. At the time, I thought of him as an enemy, someone who wanted me to fail and spent a lot of time and energy to accomplish this result. After a subpar season that year, I had an opportunity to play in the Chicago Cubs' Instructional League to work on my skills. I was much older than the other prospects who were in this program, since most players were just starting out. Gamboa saw quickly that I looked like someone who had been beaten down, defensive, sensitive to criticism, yet the scouting report also showed my first-round skills. He understood why the stats underrepresented the potential once he heard about my emotional history in my minor league development, but he did not accept that a good way to move forward was to stay bottled up out of concern of making a mistake. From my perspective, making a mistake in Triple-A was often Armageddon, so I concluded it was better not to take any risks. This was a problem for me, a player whose main strengths revolved around speed and the need to use it as a weapon.

He soon took me under his wing that fall by helping me find my confidence from his blanket of positive energy and aggressive thinking. It centered around what I could do, not what I had not done. Then in time, I wanted to play winter ball to apply his teachings, so I started asking him about the prospect of my playing abroad to hone my new-found focus. Little did I know that he was a manager in Puerto Rico and had the power to bring me down there as part of his team, but he needed to see that I was ready because, as he later told me, "I am there to win, not to develop."

Eventually, I made a couple of transformational plays in that instructional league that convinced him I could help him win. This began not only my MVP, All-Star, and championship run in Puerto Rico, but became, undeniably, the key turning point for my major league playing success.

Gamboa had this kind of impact in part because he had his own language. He spoke as if he was almost hovering over the mundane, earthly world of doubt and negativity. He exuded a self-actualizing power that resonated, and he combined this influence with leadership skills that allowed his pupils to embody the message. There was never hesitation in anything he did. He spoke with conviction, he decided with certainty, and should it not work out the way he hoped, he believed it was meant to go that way, there was no second-guessing, just lessons.

It could be best described by the phrase he said that stuck with me: "Fellas, we did not lose tonight, we just ran out of innings."

And this is Tom Gamboa—life is a game to be enjoyed and "failure is not an option." There was no reason to conclude that you failed unless you did not try, or did not have faith in self and in what is bigger than self. I imagine that if a baseball game had infinite innings, everyone would eventually win, so in effect, we all just run out of innings, and Gamby knew this better than anyone.

Of course he still had expectations. Play hard and give an honest effort, to respect the game and one's teammates. He did not post slogans on a wall in the corner of a dingy locker room, he exemplified it. Here he was, managing in Mayaguez, Puerto Rico, with a largely Spanish-as-a-first-language team, where he led without an iota of pause. He would drop in Spanish as needed, and even if it was not fluent, he spoke like he was delivering the presidential address.

And it worked, championship after championship.

He was also your best and most loyal cheerleader once he saw that you were ready to fulfill your mission. He could tell stories about what you did in a game that even you wondered, "Is he talking about me?" The poetry, the story-telling was second to none. It was almost as if he were a born motivational speaker. Speaking of which, when years later, he was viciously attacked on the field by drunk fans in Chicago while coaching first base, he turned into a spokesman for a company that specialized in personal safety. Gamboa did not turn lemons into just lemonade, he made lemon pie, lemon juice, and used the rind to heal burns.

Personally, I feel a debt of gratitude for the opportunity to get to know Tom Gamboa. That introduction led to an enduring friendship that began with my finding self in a way that was pleasantly unexpected. His humility did not allow him to take credit for making me the player that I became, because he always expressed that he was just providing the voice and platform for the true player to come out. But I know that he picked up the pieces of my career with love and care, with honesty and faith. As he once said to me, "From your Triple-A experience with your manager, you had a built-in excuse to explain why you did not make it to the major leagues. People would have understood if your bubble gum card ended after Triple-A, but that would have been your loss. Do not let anyone take you away from your destiny."

Time has an amazing way to reveal or reset all. After that impassioned season in winter ball, I went to spring training with the Cubs and thrived. Then I was sent back down to Triple-A and into the arms of the same manager who gave me all those headaches. But this time, I was ready and focused. I met with the general manager, Ed Lynch, to make sure he would support me more than I was supported the season before. At the time, he was not happy with my asserting myself about staff issues, but nearly 20 years later, Ed Lynch stopped me at a restaurant and expressed that he was impressed with how I was respectful in how I made my case that day in 1996. That meant a lot towards understanding that lessons from Gamby are enduring.

I was excited when I heard Tom would be writing this book. He is truly one of the most interesting men in the world. He walked caminos in Spain, he has retired and un-retired more times than Brett Favre, because of his amazing passion for the game we both love. He has Native American heritage. He acted in a blockbuster movie with aplomb and professional skill as if he acted his entire life. Forces of nature need to be documented, and Tom is surely a force of nature.

So I hope you enjoy the journey of the life and lessons from my good friend, mentor, father figure, and baseball genius, Tom Gamboa. I am sure we all will learn more from reading this book, and knowing him, it will probably change your life for the better.

And you will be smiling all the way.

Outfielder Doug Glanville played for the Phillies, Cubs and Rangers. He was an analyst for ESPN, and is the author of The Game from Where I Stand.

Introduction

My baseball friends and I always thought that if someone kept a journal of what goes on, it would be a great book. Dirk Hayhurst, a former minor league player of mine with the Padres, wrote a book on a season of minor league life in baseball which gave further credit to the idea that I should do this.

I think that most kids dream of being a policeman, a fireman, a doctor, a lawyer or an athlete. In my case, when I look back at my childhood, I just played. I had no ideas or thoughts about the future until my stepdad, Jack Gamboa, taught me how to play baseball and I played my first Little League game. The excitement of the ball hitting the bat was helped by the fact that I was born with excellent hand-eye coordination. On every team I was on, I was the toughest to strike out. Being able to hit the ball, and being part of a team, and everything that goes with that, the friendship, the camaraderie, rowing the boat in the same direction, everything that went with it was so exhilarating to me, that I told my parents at the dinner table that I would be doing this my whole life.

Now I can look back and see how fortunate I was when I look at my own kids and my friends' kids, sometimes being in their 20s and still not knowing what they want to do. I thought I was the norm and then realized how exceptional that was.

Unfortunately, although I was a star in high school and college, my skills weren't good enough to make it to the big leagues. But I hope that my book encourages people to find a way, whatever their passion is, to find a way to make a living within that. Some of my friends are teaching golf pros, so although weren't good enough to go on tour they organize tournaments at the club, by selling golf apparel in the pro shop, giving lessons, they found a way to make a living in their passion.

I found my real gift in being able to take a team of 25 guys and get them all to leave their egos at the door, because I didn't ask or hope by chance, but I demanded that everyone was going to fit into the mold of the club. I won with high school teams, at all levels of the minors and in the Puerto Rican winter league. I have the good fortune of wrapping up my career by getting my first experience in international ball as the bench coach for Team Israel in the World Baseball Classic.

I think the reader will find that baseball is certainly a life of work, many hours of work on the field, and behind the scenes in the clubhouses, hotel rooms and restaurants, building self-esteem of players and overcoming whatever personal hurdles they may have. There's certainly a lot of sacrifice, particularly in time spent away from home and family due to the length of the season. Hopefully the reader will enjoy the humorous episodes that occurred along the way.

Baseball is a world of its own, unlike the real world. There is no race, religion or creed. Anyone and everybody is subject to being picked on in a humorous, good-natured way within the walls of the clubhouse. All managers, coaches and players see each other as family and look past where they're from or the color of their skin. All that stuff in the real world that is, unfortunately, out there does not exist.

A Childhood in Baseball

I didn't follow baseball until my mom married my stepdad, Jack Gamboa, when I was nine. My stepdad was a big Cubs fan, and my uncle was a huge White Sox fan because they were from Chicago. When I was nine, the White Sox came in to play the Angels at the old Wrigley Field in Los Angeles, and we went to a doubleheader. Nowadays that might seem like a drag to a lot of people, but I thought it was really fun having peanuts, a hot dog and a Coke while watching baseball.

My stepdad taught me to play and signed me up for Little League when I was ten. I was on a team called the Gallenkamps, which was the name of a local shoe store where I grew up in Southern California. Our uniform was green and white.

After my first game, I came home, ate dinner in my uniform and told my parents, "I'll be doing this my whole life."

My stepdad laughed and said, "You might not be good enough."

I said, "It won't make any difference. I'll play till I can't play anymore and then I'll be a coach." As the years went by, I realized how lucky I was compared to most people that I discovered my passion when I was ten. From that point on, my whole life was centered around baseball. My parents bought a cabin in Lake Arrowhead in San Bernardino, and when I was 12 they took up skiing. One year they brought me up. Everybody had skis, boots and the appropriate cold weather clothing, but mine never saw the snow. I had an opportunity to start playing on a winter ball team when I was 13, so I asked my parents if I had to go, and they said I didn't have to go if I didn't want to. So I got to stay home by myself at 13 because I was playing baseball even in the winter. I never partook in skiing although I heard it was a lot of fun.

When I saw "Stand By Me," it reminded me of my own childhood. We were middle-class and I lived in an apartment on a cul-de-sac. I was lucky that from age ten through high school, there were a lot of boys around my age that lived on Rye Street. A group of guys that lived in houses on the south side of the boulevard were on Mary Ellen Street. During summer vacations, we would walk to the park every day and would play games between the Rye Street Rejects and the Mary Ellen Jammers. We had the Frear brothers, Bob and Jimmy, who are still close friends of mine. Bob was the oldest so he was the captain and organizer. There were the Murkey brothers, Rick and the twins, Dennis and Mike. There was Gene Lamke, Rick Sagerman, Eugene Parker and myself. If anybody couldn't make it, I snuck in Rick Magnante. Rick lived on the rich side of town but was a sometime Rye Street Reject.

The Jammers had two people of note. Jeff Temkin, their pitcher, became the ring announcer in *Rocky II* and *Rocky III* and was the ring announcer for a Muhammad Ali–Ken Norton bout. Kim Weiskopf, their left-handed power hitter, became a writer on *Three's Company, The Jeffersons* and *Good Times.*

When the Dodgers came to Los Angeles in 1958, I was ten years old. I had my little pink transistor radio and listened to every game while I did my homework. Vin Scully was able to paint a picture so vivid you actually felt like you were at the game.

The Dodgers weren't good in 1958. We never got to see the real Duke Snider when he came out here. He had a beautiful swing and still played center field and still hit some home runs, but he was a Hall of Famer because of his Brooklyn days.

Before Dodger Stadium was built in Chavez Ravine, they had to play in the Los Angeles Coliseum, which was a football stadium. To center and right it was legit, but it wasn't even 260 down the left field line. It was so short by major league standards that they erected a high net that went out from left to left-center.

Wally Moon was the Dodgers' left fielder and had basically been a singles and doubles hitter his whole career, but he developed an inside-out swing to be able to loft balls over that screen. He became a predominant home run hitter, and the *LA Times* always called them "moon shots." He developed the perfect swing for the park they were playing in. You didn't have to hit it far but you had to hit it high to get it over that net.

It was really exciting when the Dodgers turned it around and won the World Series in 1959. That was the year Larry Sherry excelled out of the bullpen. That was an era before relief pitchers got their due. It's automatic nowadays. But Sherry was so spectacular in that particular Series which he got a lot of recognition for.

Years before Mike Wallace was on *60 Minutes*, he did a lot of sports stuff before his main career focused on news. In the 1960s, the Dodgers had an up-and-coming prospect who had done really good all the way through the farm system, and Wallace did a profile on him. It was a black and white show called *Biography of a Rookie*, and it was on a guy named Willie Davis. When I saw that, I instantly became a Willie Davis fan. Whatever team I was on as a kid, I tried to get number three because that was his number. He played center field like I did. And we were both left-handed.

Davis had a pretty good career with the Dodgers. He had a 31-game hitting streak and made a couple of All-Star teams. Unfortunately, drugs ruined his career and he passed away before he should have, but he was my favorite Dodger.

My favorite player overall was Billy Williams. Because my dad was from Chicago and was a huge Ernie Banks fan, we would go see the Cubs when they came to Dodger Stadium. Banks was great and obviously headed to the Hall of Fame, but I loved Williams' pure, effortless stroke and the fact that he was left-handed like me. He was nicknamed "Sweet-Swinging Billy Williams." It was a thrill when, decades later, Billy and I were locker mates and seatmates on the plane when I was coaching third for the Cubs and he was the hitting instructor.

Another memorable moment was when my mom and I went to visit her brother and uncle in Boston during the summer of 1962. We went to see a Red Sox game and Floyd Robinson, a White Sox outfielder, tied the major league record with six hits in a nine-inning game.

That was an era when the Dodgers were based on pitching and speed. They had Sandy Koufax, Don Drysdale, Claude Osteen, and Johnny Podres. For speed, Maury Wills stole 104 bases in 1962. A few years later, the Dodgers became the first team in history to have an all-switch-hitting infield, with Wes Parker, Jim Lefebvre, Maury Wills and Jim Gilliam.

Koufax became a national figure in 1963 when they swept the Yankees in four straight. Koufax set the tone in the first game by striking out 15. The Yankees were this powerhouse, they were the Yankees. In the '50s, it seemed like the two teams would always meet in the World Series, and the Yankees won all but once against Brooklyn. The Dodgers were always the second banana, but in 1963 they put it all together and just completely dominated.

I went to Notre Dame High School in Sherman Oaks, in the San Fernando Valley. All the priests and brothers knew I was a huge baseball fan. The brothers of Holy Cross ran Notre Dame High School. They had season tickets right behind home plate, and if they weren't using one, they gave it to me. I didn't drive until I was 18, so I would take an hour-long bus ride from Sherman Oaks to Chavez Ravine.

There are hills all around Los Angeles, and Chavez Ravine was built right in the middle of the hills. The bus didn't go right to Dodger Stadium. You got dropped off at the bottom of a hill and then walked up a big hill and then down into this big bowl to get into where Chavez Ravine was.

I got to go to my first World Series in 1965. My parents bought tickets and I got to miss a day of school when the Dodgers played Minnesota. I still have the program. That was the year the Series started on Yom Kippur, and Koufax wasn't going to pitch on that day. Drysdale started Game One and Koufax didn't pitch until Game Two.

Koufax won Game Five and then started Game Seven. It was a tough decision for manager Walt Alston because it was Drysdale's day, but he bypassed him and went with Koufax on two days' rest. Koufax pitched a complete-game, three-hit shutout and struck out ten.

Having had great seasons in 1965, Koufax and Drysdale pulled a tandem holdout. That was the first time that happened in baseball, where the two of them used their leverage as a team to hold out against owner Walter O'Malley for higher salaries. They didn't report to spring training in March 1966, and Drysdale, who lived near my high school, needed a place to work out. He asked my coach if he could have a left- and a right-handed hitter to throw batting practice to every other day.

So as a high school senior I got to face Don Drysdale. He was a sidearm pitcher and being a left-handed batter, the pitches came into me. He threw hard but I felt proud of myself. It was a boost of confidence that as a high school senior I hit his fastball. We had the benefit of knowing what he was going to throw, which makes it a whole different ballgame than not knowing what he's throwing.

He wasn't there to help us. He was there to get himself in shape. They knew at some point he was going to sign. Drysdale wasn't pitching in terms of simulated games or trying to get us out.

He was known for throwing a spitball, which he called a sinker. When he threw that, my bat came up with air. When he threw that so-called sinker, even though I knew it was coming, it was nice just to make contact. Being in high school, I hadn't seen anything like that.

After one of the workouts we were in the dugout. Don asked, "Tommy, do you know what the single best pitch in baseball is?"

I said, "Yeah, it's that so-called sinker you throw."

He said, "No. The best pitch in baseball is the second knockdown

In my youth, before a Babe Ruth League game. I knew even at 10 years old that I wanted to be in baseball for the rest of my life.

pitch. That's so the hitter knows that the first one wasn't a fucking accident."

For anybody that followed baseball in the 1960s, Drysdale and Bob Gibson were noted for not letting you have the inside of the plate. Hitters weren't comfortable facing them because they were not only ultra-competitive, they didn't think anything of hitting a guy if they thought it would give them an edge.

Koufax was exactly the opposite. Koufax was such a gentleman and was never known to throw at anybody. He went from having horrible control to having impeccable control. Hitters were more comfortable in the box against Koufax than they were against Drysdale.

I had two major disappointments as a Dodgers fan growing up. The first was in 1962. The Dodgers and Giants had tied for the National League pennant. This was pre-playoffs, just eight teams in each league, and the teams with the best records played in the World Series. This was a three-game playoff, and the teams split the first two games. In Game 3, the Dodgers led 4–2 going into the ninth inning and I was jumping up and down, watching the game by myself. That game was in black and white. It was just so different than it is today. More people were glued to the TV sets in storefront windows and their transistor radios because you didn't have the media you have today. The Dodgers were three outs away from the pennant when all hell broke loose. Against Ed Roebuck and Stan Williams, the Giants scored four runs in the top of the ninth to win, 6–4. I was crushed.

The other one was in 1966, when the Dodgers won the pennant and played the Baltimore Orioles in the World Series. It turned out that Baltimore had four great pitchers, but at the time they were young and nobody on the West Coast had ever heard of these guys. Being a Dodgers fan, I thought the Series should be over in five games, if not four. The Orioles swept four straight and held the Dodgers to two runs in the Series. Baltimore had Jim Palmer, Dave McNally, and Wally Bunker. It was a combination of them pitching great games and the Dodgers going cold.

In one of the games, Willie Davis set a World Series record by making three errors in one inning. In fairness, there were two plays where he was battling the sun. The balls got lost in the sun and he got handcuffed by them, it's not like he just flat-out dropped them. After the second one, panic set in and he picked it up and overthrew everybody, and the ball went into the dugout. Later in the Series, one of the Orioles had a sure home run and Davis made a phenomenal catch by leaping over the fence with his arm reaching way back and snatched it. He was a gifted athlete.

Those errors wouldn't have happened now because all the World Series games are at night. Back then all the World Series games were in the daytime. People would take off from work. In school, the teacher would give you an in-class assignment and turn the radio up at the teacher's desk so you got to listen to it. There was no such thing as anybody missing a World Series game.

My mom tried to bribe me to go to my senior prom. She told me that I'd always regret it if I didn't go to my prom. She was going to pay whatever it cost to go to the prom and give me 50 bucks. But I had tickets from the brothers to sit in the first row behind home plate at the Dodgers game. It was a no-brainer. I'm not going to go to a *dance* when I can go see the Dodgers play. I never regretted it.

I was a baseball fanatic.

Everybody has their team, but I think I was fortunate to be a teenager in the '60s in LA when you look at the people that played. Getting to see Koufax and Drysdale win Cy Young Awards. Koufax threw four no-hitters, including a perfect game that I was in the front row for. Wills stealing 100 bases. Tommy Davis winning the batting title and driving in 153 runs in one year. Big Frank Howard who had a lot of strikeouts but also hit prodigious home runs. The all-switch-hitting infield. They were a force. There was something exciting happening all the time.

I played in the Babe Ruth League, which was ages 13–15, and was a two-time All-Star. When I was 16, I was asked to play on an Angels rookie team in the winter. So I was playing on weekends on a team with guys in the Angels organization who were on low-level minor league teams. I was way over my head but it was a great way to improve. I played American Legion ball, which was from ages 16–18.

At Notre Dame High School, I was on the JV team in tenth grade and the varsity team in 11th and 12th, and was an All-league player in both of those years. At that time my closest friend was Rick Magnante, who was heading to Santa Clara University while I was heading toward the University of San Diego. UC Santa Barbara was upgrading their program and at the last minute offered us scholarships. We were elated that we got to go to the same college and room together.

I was a Gaucho for four years and a two-time All-conference player. During all four summers, I played on an Orioles rookie team. My big thrill on the club came in my final year, which was after my junior year of college. I had been an All-Star in the California Collegiate League, and we were introduced on the field before a game at Dodger Stadium.

During my time in college, I met my wife. All the baseball players were in the Lambda Chi Alpha fraternity, and the football players were SAEs. It seemed like most of the guys in our fraternity were dating girls that were ether Pi Chis or Thetas.

I had a one-track mind in college. I made extra money every weekend being the bartender for our fraternity party, because everyone knew I would never have a date. They could save money on a bartender because they automatically knew I would do it. I liked making money and listening to the music, but I didn't date at all. I was 100 percent focused on baseball.

In my junior year we were having an oldies party, meaning early '60s music which is what I really liked. When I expressed interest to go, my fraternity brothers were knocking themselves out to get me a date because it was a big thing. We had 50 guys living in a big fraternity house. When I saw "Animal House" it brought back memories of my fraternity days. One of the guys fixed me up with a blind date named Sandi Snyder, and that was it for me. We ended up married within 13 months.

What was disappointing was that even though I was the MVP on my college team, I did not get drafted after my senior year. I ended up playing baseball in Canada, in Stratford, Ontario. Halfway through my first season, the manager got fired, and being one of the few Americans on the team, they asked me to be a player-manager. I guess it was destiny. During my senior year in college when we played against teams like USC and UCLA, against guys that were going to be first-round draft picks, I could see that my skills were good but not good enough to play at the big league level. Then you have to readjust. My focus was going to be to get into coaching, but I had no idea how fortunate I was going to be to start it so soon.

As player-manager, it was strange to be playing center field and call timeout to come in and make a pitching change, but I had signs to people in the bullpen just like I had if I was a base runner to give to the third base coach. I enjoyed it so much that when I went back for my second year, I moved from center field to first base so I would be able to have more of a leadership quality and control of the team. It was easier to make the pitching moves.

I was a two-time All-Star and we made the playoffs both years. Not only was I managing the baseball team, but the city of Stratford asked me if I would run a day baseball camp at the ballpark for kids. So I got my first experience not only coaching guys my age, but teaching and coaching kids. And the local paper, *The Stratford Beacon*, asked me to write a column. Baseball was still in its infancy in Canada. I played there in 1970 and 1971, and the Expos had only started playing in 1969. Hockey was the big

In the field during a practice game. I was a left-hander, just like my favorite player, Dodgers standout Willie Davis.

thing in Canada. I wrote this column and they liked it so much that they asked me to keep doing it. I wrote about a dozen articles on tips about baseball.

The Canadian experience, especially for a young guy, was great. I came to play and ended up managing and running a camp. Mike Gillespie, from USC, and Dave Gorrie, my coach at UC Santa Barbara, are both in the College Coaches Hall of Fame, and I had a baseball camp with each of them that lasted about 16 years. My beginnings of how to organize and how to teach kids started in Canada.

I had gotten married right out of college, and my wife was already pregnant during my first season in Canada. I had a degree but didn't have a job once baseball season ended. To teach in a public school, you had to have a teaching credential, and I didn't have the luxury of going to college for another year, so I sent out a bunch of resumes to private schools, knowing that all you had to have was a degree. The week before I left for Canada, St. John Bosco and Santa Clara both offered me a job teaching U.S. history, which was my major, and the opportunity to coach varsity baseball. Santa

Clara was like a 2-A level school, and St. John Bosco was the top level, 4-A.

The first year teaching, I taught only U.S. history but a week before my second year started, one of the Spanish teachers quit. People that taught in a Catholic school back in the '70s were going to night school to get a teaching credential to make the jump into the public school system because they paid way better. The principal, Father Carmen, was scrambling to figure out what to do to fill the spot. They went through the resumes of everybody on the faculty, and because I took four years of Spanish in high school, by process of elimination I was hand-picked to teach ninth grade Spanish.

Of course I had forgotten most of what I learned. I was reading the roll sheet on the first day and I'm reading off names like Aguilar, Lopez, Rodriguez and Hidalgo. I was laughing inside, thinking "Oh my God, some of these kids are going to know more Spanish than I do and I'm supposed to be the one teaching it."

It turned out to be a plus in my career because teaching Spanish for two years brought the recall back to the forefront of what I learned in high school. Little did I know that I was going to spend 44 years in professional baseball, and with the plethora of Latin players coming into the game, and myself spending nine winters in Puerto Rico and one in Mexico, speaking Spanish has been a huge plus for me. I've had a good rapport with the Latin players.

During the winter, I was teaching in Los Angeles and coaching baseball at St. John Bosco. I was going to night school to get my Masters, with the intent to be a college baseball coach, when the Orioles came calling and asked me to be a full-time scout.

My first child, Brett, was born in September 1971. Stratford is about three hours north of Detroit, and we drove cross-country to California with her already at her due date. There was a joke between Sandi and me that each morning when we got up and started to drive, we should hope to make it to the next major city. We were in our early 20s, so we were young and stupid. There were stretches from Wyoming to Utah where there's just nothing. Brett could have been born on the highway somewhere. Fortunately, she didn't go into labor until we made it to California.

Kristin was born in April 1974, right at the end of the Bosco baseball season, and I had already taken the job with the Orioles which would start in June. Jamie was born in February 1976, in Concord. The twins, Becky and Shannon, were born in March 1978 when we were living in Valencia and I was with the scouting bureau.

Scouting

I was asked to play on an Orioles team out of high school and each of my college summers, which consisted of guys that they were interested in. The manager of that team, Ray Poitevint, ended up becoming a top scout for the Orioles. After being trained and working under Ray, the Orioles hired me as a full-time scout in 1974.

The scouting director was a young, aggressive, ex-military guy named Dave Ritterpusch. Dave hired three people that became baseball lifers, so I guess he saw something in us. He hired Joe McIlvane, who later became the general manager of the Padres and Mets. He hired Bob Engle, a long-time international scouting director with the Blue Jays and Mariners. And he hired me.

I started in scouting, which is kind of the backbone of baseball because that's where it starts. But with my personality, I just felt like I belonged on the field.

When I scouted in the '70s and early '80s, scouts would be seen at a ballgame with a little black book and a stopwatch. Nowadays they're carrying radar guns, laptops and iPhones so they can take videos. It's gone way high-tech.

For a position player, a scout is trained to look for five tools: the ability to run, throw, field, hit, and hit for power. Then the sixth thing you grade is an intangible, the makeup of a player. That's everything you see about him that doesn't show up on the field. His competitiveness, sportsmanship, determination, and perseverance. His character. Is he the type of guy that's going to pout because he went 0-for-4, or is he the type of guy that goes all-out all the time, whether he's hot or cold?

That's what you're looking for. There's not a scout who doesn't want to see a player when he's struggling so that he can get a feel for his makeup and to see how well he handles adversity. Even at the highest level, the best hitters are going to fail seven times out of ten. When you're talking about playing 140 games in the minor leagues or 162 in the big leagues, you'd better have a guy that has the personality that can stay on an even keel and handle that.

I was fortunate enough to manage Ken Caminiti in Puerto Rico after his Triple-A season. Without question he had one of the best makeups I was ever fortunate enough to manage. Because of the way he was raised and the way he played the game, if you came to the ballpark late and watched him ground out, you would have no way of knowing whether he was four-for-five or oh-for-five. Ken only knew one way to play the game: all-out, all the time. If he didn't do it with the bat, he'd make a diving play or break up a double play to extend an inning. He did so many things to win games in so many different ways.

On the other side of the coin is Billy Beane, who is now a successful general manager with Oakland. In the prospect scene in the film "Moneyball," you can see that he regretted signing as a number one draft choice out of high school with the Mets. I happened to scout him when he was at Mount Carmel High School in the San Diego area. He was a very gifted all-around athlete in both baseball and football. He was an intelligent 4.0 student, a multi-sport guy, and had a full scholarship to Stanford. I think they portrayed it well in the movie that he wishes that he had finished off his college career first and matured more as an individual before he underwent his baseball career. Although he made it to the big leagues with the Mets and Twins, he'd be the first to tell you that statistically and because of the number of years played, he did not become the big league player that he was projected to be. A big part of that was mental.

Billy was unbelievably competitive, as he is as a GM, and had a lot of good qualities. The one that eluded him was the ability to handle failure and stay on an even keel. Late in his career, I had Billy in Triple-A with the Toledo Mud Hens. Billy would get so emotional. If he got a good pitch to hit and popped up with the bases loaded, he just couldn't deal with the failure of how he could've missed that pitch when it was right in his hot zone. Sometimes one at-bat would carry over to the next. He would put so much pressure on himself to try to make up for it in the next at-bat because he failed in the previous one. All the other qualities were pluses, as were his tools. It takes a strong mental character to be able to make it in baseball because it's inevitable that you're going to face adversity, no matter how good you are. Slumps are unfortunately a part of the game.

Scouts grade on a scale of two to eight, with two being poor, five being average, and eight being outstanding. The scouts are trained to give their grades comparing prospects to major league players. That's the tough part. When a scout goes to watch a high school kid, you're grading him as to how he would compare against a big leaguer, so you give him a present grade which obviously in most cases is not going to be very good. But then you give him a future grade based on your projection of what that player is going to be like by the time he's a 23-year-old man with continued development as opposed to a 17- or 18-year-old-kid you're watching in high school. The more tools that a youngster has, the higher he's going to be drafted in June.

The most notarized player at the high school level in all my years of scouting was Darryl Strawberry. The Mets took him as the first pick in the draft. Darryl went to Crenshaw High School in Los Angeles and was an unbelievably gifted athlete. He was 6'6", weighed 190 pounds and could run like a deer, just an effortless stride. He had a plus throwing arm and had great arm action from the outfield. It looked like he could catch a ball bare-handed, as if he didn't need a glove. It didn't take a scout to see the ability to run, throw, and field. And with his bat, the only guy I could think of who had a swing like Strawberry was Ken Griffey, Jr., who came later. It was just that beautiful, classic, left-handed swing with great bat speed and very little effort to generate it. If you're fortunate enough as a scout to see a guy that you can project as a five-tool player, you're basically telling the organization that this guy is going to be a superstar. There aren't many five-tool guys in the big leagues at any given time. Darryl went on to have a stellar career. Unfortunately, drug problems came about, but he was certainly a gifted athlete and still had a hell of a career.

There's actually a formula for how you would grade a player using the two to eight scale, and the final grade is Overall Future Potential from a 20–80. Using Strawberry as an example, he was a six runner, a seven arm, a six outfielder, at least a six hitter with eight power. So that's a 33, and divide that by the five tools and you have a 66. Then the scout had leeway of plus or minus ten points based on his mental attitude or makeup. The people in our organization thought the makeup was a plus. There were no signs of drugs. It would've been easy to give him another four points, and now you're talking about a 70. With a 70, you're talking about some greats. Roberto Clemente at that stage would've been around a 65, and he's in the Hall of Fame. Somebody like Willie Mays would've been an 80. In his prime, he had eights across the board. That's why he's arguably the best all-around player ever.

Scouts judge pitchers on the same two to eight scale. You would grade his fastball, curveball and changeup from two to eight. If it's sixes across the board, he'd have a 60. Fifty is an average big league player, which is a pretty goddamn good ballplayer. Anything above 50 is certainly a guy that's going to get drafted fairly high. Before radar guns, you had to use your eye and the hitters' bats to see how well they reacted or didn't react to the pitcher's fastball to gauge what he was throwing. Now you can actually put a number on it. If a high school kid is throwing 94, it doesn't take a genius to know he's going to be taken fairly high in the draft.

There was a left-handed pitcher from Mercer Island, Washington, named Mike Lentz. There was certainly a lot of interest in him at the time. I went to scout him, and it was the finest pitching performance that I ever saw with my own eyes. I mean, there's Sandy Koufax's perfect game and Kerry Wood striking out 20 Astros, but I have to go with Lentz if we go strictly by numbers.

Mike Lentz threw a perfect game and struck out 19 of the 21 hitters that he faced. For the first three innings, every pitch that he threw was a strike. It was comical because the umpire was like a robot. Nine pitches, nine strikes. Nobody fouled one off. He threw his first ball in the fourth inning. In the fourth or fifth, somebody fouled one off, which drew some applause from the parents on the other team. There was a bunt for an out and a groundout. That was it. The other 19 outs were via the strikeout.

With the draft nearing, Poitevint told me I was going to have to take another trip to Washington. I assumed another pitcher had popped up late. When I asked who they wanted me to see, I was told that Lentz might be a first-round pick. I told them I wasn't going back. I saw him strikeout 19 of 21 batters. I couldn't possibly see him pitch any better. Nothing against Lentz, but scouting is very subjective, and I felt that if he was a first-round pick, then at least there will be someone better for us to take. I couldn't project his size. He was about 5'10" and 175 pounds. There have been pitchers of that size who have been successful, but you're looking for the ideal pitchers' body, especially when you're looking at the first couple of rounds. Someone who is 6'3" or 6'4", with broad shoulders and long arms. Guys who are built like Doc Gooden or Bob Welch or Don Drysdale. I certainly could've been wrong on Mike Lentz, but as it turned out he was a number one pick of the Padres and the second overall pick. He did well in rookie ball but had an arm injury when he got to High-A, and never got to the big leagues.

Some parents get caught up strictly on the results. The results are not necessarily what the scouts are looking for, because they are just looking for raw tools. Sometimes people would tell me that their son hit .420 in high school but someone else hit .280 and was drafted in the third round. They're caught up in the numbers rather than the actual skills and the projection.

One of the interesting things for me as a young scout was the progression of a scout. You're given an area, and then as you pile up experience you get promoted. In my case, I became a West Coast supervisor. Los Angeles has always been a hotbed because of the weather, the population and the number of teams that play year-round. Then I started covering all the states in the Northwest. Being a scout is like being a tax accountant. Everything for a tax accountant is based around April 15. In scouting, you have the whole year to see players and evaluate them, but panic can start setting in during May, because the draft is usually the first Monday in June. Sometimes a player would pop up late or a pitcher who had been hurt is now healthy, and you're trying to see these guys to be able to compare them before the draft.

One year, I saw three players in the three different states in the same day. When I was scouting in the Northwest, I found a big, strong, physical outfielder named Mark Higgins, who was a tools guy. Mark was about 6'3", 205 pounds, and could run a 6.6 60. That's plus speed, especially for a big man, and he had raw power. He looked like he would be a decent outfielder. Their season was over so I worked him out at Central Valley High School in Spokane, Washington, at nine in the morning with his coach. Then I caught a flight out of Spokane to Portland, Oregon, and saw an afternoon All-Star Game of the best players in the state. One was a big right-handed pitcher, Jay Ballard, who went on to have a career in the big leagues with the Phillies. After getting to see him pitch his one or two innings, I caught a flight from Portland to Los Angeles and saw a night game in the city of Commerce. At the time, this was where USC played home games, and I watched them take on Arizona State. Even some of the scouts couldn't believe that I had already worked out a player in Washington and seen an All-Star game in Oregon, and now was at a night game in California.

Even as an area scout I traveled all around to different parts in a day. The Red Sox had a part-time scout named Milt Axe, who had to be in his 70s, and we were watching a night game in South San Francisco together one year during Easter week. With so many games that week, the dozens of scouts don't know who was going to pitch what game. Somebody asked if anybody knew when the pitcher up in Napa would pitch. I said that I had seen him pitch that morning and he wouldn't pitch again until Friday. Somebody asked about another pitcher in the East Bay in Walnut Creek, and I said that I went to his team's game that afternoon and that his coach said he would pitch tomorrow. And now here I was at a night game in South San Francisco. Napa is about 35 miles north of San Francisco. Walnut Creek is an hour east of it. Milt Axe thought about the driving and said, "My God, Tom, you've been to all those places just today?" I said yes. In front of a group of scouts he said, "Well I'll tell you one thing. If you don't make it in this business as a scout, you'll certainly make it as a Greyhound bus driver."

When I started with the Baltimore Orioles, they gave me Northern California. My wife and I moved to Concord, which is east of Oakland. When my boss, Ray Poitevint, became the Western State Supervisor for the Major League Scouting Bureau, he wanted me to come with him to the bureau to scout Southern California. He was my mentor and I was his protégé, so I went with him and got the opportunity to go back to Southern California.

Scouting was a very individualized profession because you were supposed to gather information, and sometimes get it from other scouts, but at the same time you weren't supposed to give up any information on players you had interest in. But you cultivate friendships. It's a part of life. Rich Schlenker was a scout with the Padres who was a few years older than me but had a lot more experience. We both lived in Concord, we went to the same church and we both had a passion for golf. Although you're supposed to go to games by yourself, there was one year during Easter week where Schlenker's car was in the shop, and he asked if I could give him a ride. I had a 1971, dark green Ford Pinto because it sold brand new for $1,995. My car was already legendary because I had accumulated 160,000 miles on it. I went to see a game over in Stockton with Schlenker, and then we took Highway 99 south down to Fresno. A couple of days before this, I had backed into a post which had put a little dent in the bumper but also hit the muffler. The exhaust fumes were coming up through the back seat of the car, so I told Schlenker that we had to keep all the windows down and couldn't use the air conditioning. We drove close to 400 miles, and it was cold coming back with the windows down. I cannot remember if or when I had ever replaced the tires on my car. When Schlenker got out of the car, he thanked me for the ride and said, "I don't think I've ever rode 400 miles in a car on square tires before. I'll ask my wife if we have a humidifier so I can try to pump the exhaust fumes out of my lungs while I sleep tonight."

That story spread among the scouts. Bob Bishop was a scout for the Mets and was a very meticulous guy about everything. And he would change the oil on his car after every 1,000 miles. As we were leaving a game, he said, "I'm calling bullshit on your car. Everybody changes their oil at the recommended times, don't they?" I didn't know you were ever supposed to change it. I obviously knew you put gas in the car, but I didn't know about the oil. Bishop had me unlock my hood latch and took an old cloth out of the trunk of his car to check my oil, and when he pulled the oil dipstick out there was nothing liquid on it. It was just sludge. I said, "Oh my God, does that mean I should add a quart?" Bishop goes, "I wouldn't do that. Your car is used to running on this sludge. I wouldn't do anything to upset it."

Three Smiths

I had three interesting scouting experiences with three different players named Smith. One became a good big league player, one never made it to the majors, and the other made it to the Hall of Fame.

When I became a scout, you got very little training. Basically you were given a stopwatch, a little black book and were told to go get 'em. It's like being an apprentice. You just learned on the job by watching players. The first guy I came up with was a right-handed pitcher in 1974.

I found a pitcher at a senior Babe Ruth League tournament that I really liked. I thought he had major league ability, had plus control, and had a makeup that was off the charts. In terms of his competiveness, his will to win, and the support of his teammates, you could see in one game that this guy was a gamer. I wanted to sign him but my boss tried to talk me out of it. Ray Poitevint said, "Tom, this guy has been through three drafts and nobody ever thought enough of him to draft him anywhere, so why in God's name would you want to sign him?" (In those days there were two drafts. There was a January draft strictly for junior college players and then a June draft for high school, junior college, and college players who had finished their junior year.)

I said, "Ray, I have the courage of my convictions. I thought this guy can pitch in the big leagues. And you hired me." Ray said that sometimes you have to learn from mistakes and gave the pitcher $2,000.

Fortunately for me, Bryn Smith wasn't really interested in school. He went to Hancock Junior College in Santa Maria, California, and took the two grand and went to spring training with the Orioles. He pitched well enough that he bypassed the rookie league and went right to the Florida State League. And then Smith pitched so well in the minors that the Orioles traded him to the Expos for Don Stanhouse and Gary Roenicke, two players that helped Baltimore get to the 1979 World Series.

As a young scout, I was bummed out that Bryn got traded because I took it as though the Orioles had given up on him. He had won ten games in High-A ball. With more experience, I later found out that he had done so well that he helped us get players who helped the Orioles win a pennant. And Bryn Smith went to an up-and-coming Expos team, and went 18–5 one year. He later went to the Cardinals and hung around so long that he was even on the expansion Colorado Rockies in 1993.

I'm glad to say that even though a lot of mistakes are made in scouting, it was satisfying that my first signing was a home run. Bryn was a 13-year major leaguer. He made a lot of money for himself. There was a banquet a few years ago in Santa Maria, where Bryn was born and raised and still lives. He saw me in the audience and gave me a shout-out. He said, "I don't know if I ever would've had a career but for somebody here who, although it wasn't a lot of money, thought enough of me to take a chance to give me an opportunity in pro ball." That was gratifying.

At the time my territory was from Fresno to the Oregon border. I moved to Concord in 1974, about an hour and 15 minutes from Sacramento. Around the same time I signed Bryn, I was on my way home to the Bay Area when I saw some lights off the freeway. Ray always believed in being ahead of the next guy. The only way to be a good scout is to see games. When a scout watches a game and then goes home to eat dinner, the guy that sees two games is going to be a step ahead of him. When I saw the lights on in Vallejo, I thought it was an adult softball league. But since I wasn't in a rush, I got off the freeway and worked my way to what turned out to be a city league field where high school kids were playing.

There was a kid playing left field on one of the teams you couldn't help but notice because he ran so fast that it was unbelievable. Bobby Glen Smith was 5'10" and weighed 175 pounds. At the plate he had a real short, quick swing. It was the perfect type of stroke for a guy that could really run. I saw him line a base hit to left and thought my watch was wrong when I got him in four seconds flat making a turn at first base. Not running through the bag, but making a turn. This guy could fly. In his next at-bat, he hit a ground ball to short and made it bang-bang at first. I got him at 3.75 down the line, which is unheard of. The only guy I ever clocked faster from home to first than Bobby Glen Smith was Mickey Rivers. Oakland had a few pitchers work on a combined no-hitter on the last day of the 1975 season against the Angels, and Rivers made the last out on a ground ball to short in which he went from home to first in 3.7 flat.

From a scouting standpoint, Smith was a horrible outfielder and could not throw. From a two to eight scale, his arm was a one. It didn't even make two. It was that bad. The type of swing he had was a non-power swing, a slash-and-run type stroke. I had a great friend that was birddogging for me named Jerry Weinstein, who was the coach at Sacramento City College. Jerry was thrilled to get Bobby Glen in his program. He got him a place to live, and Bobby Glen was going to be his leadoff man. Jerry was a terrific college coach, and he's now been in pro ball for a long time. I knew Jerry would want to work and develop him because the kid wasn't really ready to go into pro ball. But I knew that in terms of speed and contact ability, this was a guy that I wanted to sign.

Jerry's program was so good that scouts would come out and watch his team play in the winter. As it got close to the winter draft, Jerry told me that the Dodgers had interest in Bobby Glen and were watching his workouts and games. I felt like I had found this guy and put all this time in, and now I'm only going to have one chance of getting this kid in the draft. My boss told me I'd better go ahead and sign Bobby Glen. I felt bad for Jerry because this was potentially going to be the best player on his team. I told him that the Orioles were afraid they weren't going to get him. On Christmas Eve, just before the close period, we signed him.

Bobby went to spring training but wasn't ready to make the team because of his defensive liabilities. He stayed in extended spring and went to Bluefield, West Virginia, which was the Orioles' long-time rookie league team. He had a chance to be the first player since Tony Oliva to hit .400 in the minors. He had his only slump in August and finished at .365. If he didn't hit the ball right at an infielder, it was going to be a base hit. He went to the Florida State League and won a batting title, and then he went to Double-A and won another batting title. Somewhere along the way, he was released by the Orioles. His defensive shortcomings were flagrant.

By that time I was in Milwaukee, and Ray signed him. Bobby Glen won another batting title in the Texas League and that got him on a big league roster. But his only experience in the big leagues was in spring training. He went to Triple-A in the Pacific Coast League, and I believe he won another batting title. Because of his defensive shortcomings he didn't get called up, despite his success with the bat. His aptitude for defense, learning to bunt, and learning to steal didn't progress like a normal big-leaguer would in those areas. I don't know if it was stubbornness or lack of aptitude.

Because of his success with the bat, Bobby Glen was immature and arrogant. He was sporting mutton chops and was acting like a big leaguer who wasn't in the big leagues. He was released and played in the Mexican League, where the talent is the equivalent of Triple-A. Lots of ex-big leaguers go to play there. Bobby Glen won another batting title. He won five or six overall, but never got an at-bat in the big leagues.

When I was with the Major League Scouting Bureau, my territory included San Luis Obispo, so I got to see a youngster named Ozzie Smith who had been drafted by Detroit the year before but didn't sign with the Tigers. I knew just from watching him take ground balls in infield practice that I could never see somebody so athletic and catch a ground ball so easily if I scouted for 50 years. He had such quick, live feet and soft hands with unbelievable, cat-like quickness and reaction. It was hard to watch the hitters take batting practice because you couldn't take your eyes off him taking ground balls and throwing across the diamond. He was like an artist.

Believe it or not, I had one scout question how I could turn that guy in to be drafted because at 150 pounds he wouldn't have the strength or stamina to get through the season, and the pitchers would knock the bat out of his hands. I don't know that anyone was sure of what he was going to hit. I told the scout that all I knew was that at the very worst, Ozzie would be a defensive specialist in the late innings to protect a lead. If everything went wrong, I at least thought he could be a utility player. He could run and field, and had an okay arm at the time. You knew he could play shortstop because his feet were so good. As a kid, he threw the ball against a wall over and over again and tested himself by getting closer and closer to the wall to quicken his reflexes and reactions. When he became a big league player, his arm strength got way better. My hat is off to him and the instructor who helped him with the bat along the way, because nobody could foresee what he would do offensively in the big leagues.

The rest is history and he's now in the Hall of Fame. Ozzie is known as a Cardinal, but people forget that the Padres drafted him and he came up with San Diego. For years, a play he made with the Padres was shown on "This Week In Baseball." Jeff Burroughs hit a rocket up the middle and Ozzie dove to his left. In the middle of his dive, the ball took a bad hop. With his glove outstretched, Ozzie reached up with his bare hand, speared the ball, finished his dive, got to his feet and threw Burroughs out. It gives you chills.

The Major League Scouting Bureau was a way for teams to cut down on expenses, because they didn't need as many of their own scouts when they utilized this service. Part of their motto was to leave no stone unturned. You were supposed to try to see literally every single high school, junior college, and college in your territory, and more than once if they had a player that warranted being seen.

MAJOR LEAGUE SCOUTING BUREAU

FREE AGENT REPORT

Overall future potential 49 Report No. 2

PLAYER Smith (Last name) Osburn (First name) Earl (Middle name) Position SS

Current Address [redacted] San Luis Obispo (City) Ca. (State) [redacted] (Zip Code)

Telephone [redacted] (Area Code) Date of Birth 12-26-54 Ht. 510 Wt. 150 Bats S Throws R

Permanent address (If different from above) [redacted]

Team Name Cal Poly SLO City San Luis Obispo State Ca.

Scout T. Gamboa Date 5-20-77 Race B Games 6 Innings 32

RATING KEY	NON-PITCHERS		Pres.	Fut.	PITCHERS		Pres.	Fut.	USE WORD DESCRIPTION
8–Outstanding	Hitting Ability	*	3	4	Fast Ball	*			Habits Good
7–Very Good	Power	*	2	2	Curve	*			Dedication Good
6–Above Average	Running Speed	*	5	5	Control				Agility Exel
5–Average	Base Running		6	7	Change of Pace				Aptitude Good
4–Below Average	Arm Strength	*	4	4	Slider	*			Phys. Maturity Fair
3–Well Below Average	Arm Accuracy		4	5	Knuckle Ball				Emot. Maturity Good
2 Poor	Fielding	*	6	7	Other	*			Married No
	Range		7	7	Poise				
Use One Grade	Baseball Instinct		7	7	Baseball Instinct				Date eligible 6-77
Grade On Major	Aggressiveness		6	6	Aggressiveness				
League Standards	Pull / Str. Away / Opp. Field				Arm Action				Phase Regular
Not Amateur	X (Str. Away)				Delivery				

Physical Description (Injuries, Glasses, etc.) GRADUATION 6-77

Slight, wiry build. Small boned. Built similar to Bert Campaneris, but not as strong.

Home phone: (213) 581[redacted]

Abilities

Exceptionally quick hands and feet. Exel. body control. Soft, sure hands. Cat-like inf. actions, range, and release are pluses. Runs 4.2 from left side. Instincts and quickness to steal bases. Makes contact.

Weaknesses

Arm strength is BA. Circles and winds up on ball in the hole. No pwr. Loops bat as LHH and hits too many balls in air.

Summation and Signability [redacted] Will He Sign ____ Will Sign For ____

Raised OFP #5 pts. due to exceptional defensive skills and base stealing ability. Arm is borderline but will have to play his way off of SS. Drafted #146 by Detroit 6-76.

My scouting report for Ozzie Smith. Even then it was clear that the kid they would come to call the Wiz had exceptional defensive skills.

When the bureau came into existence and teams were firing 75 percent of their scouts to save money, I inherited the Northwest. Going into my second year, I was responsible not only for Northern California, but several Northwestern states, Utah, Wyoming, Montana, and Nevada. When the draft is over, it's like April 16 for a tax accountant. Now you've got nothing but time and no pressure. I got in my car and, not having been to any of those states, drove to several of them.

There was no such thing as travel teams back then. The big things were American Legion ball and the Senior Babe Ruth League. I drove through Oregon and a lot of towns in Washington. No matter where I went in the Northwest, I kept hearing these legendary stories about a third baseman in Yakima, Washington, who sounded like the second coming of Babe Ruth. I remember telling other scouts that by the time I get to Yakima, it wasn't going to be possible for this kid, Jamie Allen, to live up to the stories.

I finally get to Yakima and saw Allen, who was going into his senior year in high school. They had an American Legion team that went to the World Series for Legion ball, and played in an old pro park with wooden fences. In the first at-bat I saw, Jamie hit a ball off the fence in dead center for a triple. Wow. The second time up, he hit a ball that looked like a Tiger Woods 3-wood that went out of the park to left-center. This guy had actually lived up to everything I had heard about him. I knew at that moment he'd be at the top of my list. When compared to a big leaguer, he had a chance to be in the mold of Harmon Killabrew. He was 5'11", and when you saw the genetics you knew you were looking at a body where weight would be a factor, and the injury factor goes up. His dad weighed about 260 pounds. If you're long and lean, the percentages are more with you. But this guy had great power and terrific athletic ability. He could make all the plays at third base and could pitch and close out games.

The Orioles had Jimmy Russo, who was a legendary scout. Jimmy flew out all the way from Baltimore to watch him and called me from an airport. I had seen six or seven games, but a cross-checker only gets one look. Jimmy, who I had on a pedestal, agreed that this was a major league bat. Jamie was taken in the first round by the Twins but he went to Arizona State and played in the College World Series a couple of times. He was drafted out of Arizona State but because of the weight and injuries, he never did fulfill what everybody thought he was going to do. He played a little for the Mariners one year. But he was a high school legend.

I also had a great learning experience in Utah as a young scout. Because of the weather in Utah, I never went to watch high school games there. You could cover the state strictly through American Legion ball, which was huge in Utah. There was a state tournament in Salt Lake City each summer, and if you came out to Salt Lake City for a week, you could see all the players in the state and have it covered for the year. There were only four or five scouts at this tournament. It's an awkward place to go in the summer. It's not exactly a hotbed for baseball.

I saw a left-handed pitcher with a terrific curveball, big hands, and long fingers. He was a high school junior from St. George, and I thought I had this guy hidden away for the next year. The next time I went to the ballpark to see him, there must have been 75 scouts. I didn't realize the extent of computers and info sharing even in the mid–'70s. At first there were a few guys, and each of us thought he'd be good, and now everybody's watching. The pitcher was longtime major leaguer Bruce Hurst, who was a number one pick of the Red Sox. He came out of Dixie, a little town, and the scouting bureau had given knowledge to everyone about this guy. That was an eye-opening experience for me.

Some of my friends ask me why I finally got out of scouting and went into player development. Part of the reason that I did not like scouting was that it was too negative for me. A lot of what you did in scouting was process of elimination. You'd go to see two high schools play, you'd watch them take infield, you'd watch three innings of the game and realize there wasn't anybody there that could play in terms of pro standards. All you had done was eliminated two teams in your territory, but you hadn't done anything productive. Sometimes you could go for days on end just seeing schools which didn't have any players of interest.

On the other hand, it was great when you would see somebody that got you excited. In the case of what I called "coverage," you wouldn't go to see a specific player, but rather the schools in your territory. This was back when there was a January draft. The June draft was the big one, with high school, junior college, four-year college juniors or 21-year-olds. The January draft was just junior college and for players who had dropped out from four-year schools, either because of grades or because they didn't like school and wanted to get drafted. There were no comparisons in the draft because the talent pool was so big in June and so small in January. The January one was about kids who had been passed over six months earlier. The January draft didn't have the financial equivalent of the June draft.

One year in the late '70s, I saw a 6', 150-pound pitcher at Santa Barbara City College who was very slender, had a nice delivery, nice arm action, and I loved his ability to compete. I turned him in as a marginal big league prospect. I had some people call me up and say that he was too frail and that he didn't throw hard enough to be a pro. There's something that needs to be understood about scouting. Oftentimes, scouts will try to kill two birds with one stone. If there are two games in proximity in an area, a scout would see a position player and a pitcher. There would be times where I would go to be sure I watched the position player take infield and get a couple of at-bats, and then I would drive a few miles to watch the pitcher work for three or four innings.

This brings us to Jesse Orosco. As a 150-pound freshman, if you saw him pitch in the first inning you would see a number of decent pitches. But if you had gone to another game first and then went to watch Orosco pitch in the middle innings, he would be topping out at 80 MPH. He just didn't have the stamina.

When you work for the bureau, your first job is to evaluate the talent. Once you turn the guy in as a prospect, your second job is to go into the home and actually get to know the player and his family, to find out if they're interested in signing. You don't want to give a team the wrong info and tell them to draft a player if the player is going to Arizona State or Stanford.

Orosco's parents lived in a trailer park, and you could tell from the moment you walked in the door that they were a real wholesome family. As is often the case with Latinos and people of Mexican descent, they were very family oriented. I immediately embraced the family and liked everything about them. I found that Jesse's only interest was in trying to get into pro ball. That made his ability to sign real easy, when you can tell teams that this is a guy who wants to play.

There was a longtime scout, Jesse Flores, who prided himself on scouting pitchers. Flores saw my report, made the drive up to Santa Barbara, saw him and liked him. He drafted Orosco and signed him to the Minnesota Twins. Orosco pitched for the rookie team in the Appalachian League. He did something right because the Mets people saw him and traded for him. The Twins certainly got him at a bargain basement price by drafting him in January, and the Mets get credit for recognizing his ability and developing him into the longtime big leaguer that he was.

Although I turned him in, I would never take credit for projecting him to be the kind of pitcher that he became. He got bigger. I had him as a small-frame guy but just loved his delivery and competitiveness. I thought he'd have a real good left-handed breaking ball and control, and that he'd throw hard enough to get to the big leagues. I had no idea that he was going to become a closer and record the final out of the 1986 World Series for the Mets. (Hurst started that game for Boston.) He pitched in more than 1,000 games over four decades.

The only thing I didn't like about the bureau was that I didn't have a team to root for. The big plus of being a scout with the bureau, when I look back on it now, was that every time I turned in a report, all the scouting directors would see it instead of just Dave Ritterpusch in Baltimore. I was a college educated guy and fairly smart. Baseball had been my whole life. I didn't realize at the time that I was exposing my abilities to all of the teams in the league. When they sent their people out to see a player, they would either be concurring with my opinion or going against it. It helped to get your name more widespread in the industry if you could qualify a player and write a decent report.

I left the bureau because Ray was asked to be the Player Development and Scouting Director of the Milwaukee Brewers. Once again he wanted me to follow in his footsteps, and that's when I became a scout for the Brewers, along with being a roving hitting instructor in the minor leagues.

Misses

Every scout has misses along the way. Scouting is like hitting in that you're lucky if you're three-for-ten on guys that you draft getting to the majors.

A friend of mine, Wayne Morgan, drafted Willie McGee out of high school. He was 6 feet, 150 pounds, ran like a deer and played center field with an okay arm. I just didn't think he was going to hit. I didn't see enough contact, but my friend signed him and gave him some money. Willie went on to become the MVP of the National League and was on some pennant-winning teams in St. Louis. Willie and Vince Coleman stole so many bases for the Cardinals and wreaked havoc on defenses. And he went from being a right-handed hitter in high school to a stellar career as a switch-hitter. The last game of his career was on the last day of the 1999 season with the Cardinals, which happened to be against the Cubs, where I was coaching third base.

Another one of my huge misses was Rickey Henderson, from Oakland Tech High School. A lot of people missed him, not just me. I saw him play at Bushrod Park in the heart of Oakland. Rickey was compact and stocky. He could run like a deer, but he had no arm in the outfield. He couldn't throw. And I could not project power. He did make contact, but I'm the first to admit that I missed on a guy who is in the Hall of Fame and holds the record for stolen bases. A lot of us missed that one. Most guys will say that they had him on their list and that they just didn't get him. I'm honest enough to say that I just flat-out missed on that one.

I did have Tony Gwynn, but in hindsight I didn't have him high enough. Tony was drafted in the third round by the Padres, so his Hall of Fame career shows that every team passed on him twice. He shouldn't have been available in the third round with the career he had. When I joined San Diego as the field coordinator in 1991, I looked at my old report on him. This was during an era where he won eight batting titles. In college he could flat-out hit and you couldn't strike him out. He was a star basketball guard at San Diego State, and his hand-eye coordination was terrific. He had a bazooka from right field, and he could run. Because Tony got so heavy over his career, a lot of people forget that when he was first in the big leagues he was stealing 40 and 50 bases. The running, throwing and fielding were there, and the bat was there. What Tony got knocked for, by me and a lot of scouts, was that you weren't projecting him to hit for power, and he didn't play center, like Paul Blair did in Baltimore. If a center fielder can turn doubles into outs, you could overlook hitting and power as long as he was making some contribution. So I had Gwynn in, but not high enough.

I also didn't have interest in Mark McGwire, but that's because he wasn't a position player yet. The scouting bureau turned in McGwire as a pitcher out of Damien High School in La Verne, California. He was a big, strong guy with the prototype body you're looking for in a pitcher. He had velocity, so it was easy to project his arm strength. I saw a typical, rolling high school breaking ball that was not projectable for me, and his fastball didn't have any movement. Knowing that he had a ride to USC and that it would take a lot of money to offset it, I didn't have any interest. He was a big, strong guy, about 6'5". I didn't care for him as a pitcher but then he went to USC and, as a freshman, pitched, played first base and was a designated hitter. Sophomore year they just made him the first baseman. He was such a good athlete that the A's made him a third baseman after using their first pick on him.

I can vouch for the pre-steroid McGwire because I scouted him in high school, saw him in college, and managed against his team when I was at Stockton. And he helped the A's win three straight pennants. In the minors, you coach third base in addition to managing. In our division, we would play each other about 20 times, and we met in the playoffs. With Mark playing third and me coaching third, we would talk in between innings during warm-ups. I would joke about how I didn't care for him as a pitcher but he sure found his niche as a hitter. He was a great teammate, intelligent, personable, and really cared about the game. Mark was a managers' kind of player. He didn't come into pro ball like some number ones do, the prima donna, "I'm God's Gift" to baseball attitude. It was obvious that he was well-raised, and I had an immediate respect for the guy.

We were very competitive. They won the first half of the season and we finished second. Then we won the second half of the season in extra innings on the last day to get into the post-season. We were fortunate enough to take three of four from them in the playoffs. Then our paths didn't cross again until I was with the Cubs and he was a big-time star with the Cardinals.

Base Running Blunder

Fresno State used to get a lot of schools to come in and play in an Easter Tournament during spring break. In 1982, the final game was between Terry Pendleton's Fresno State team and Wally Joyner and BYU. Pendleton was a center fielder at the time, before becoming an All-Star third baseman in the big leagues. There were about 60 scouts at this one.

Fresno State led, 9–2, heading into the ninth but BYU was making this unbelievable comeback and cut the lead to 9–7 with the bases loaded and one out. A guy hit a bomb to center field, and Pendleton turned his back to home plate and was racing towards the fence.

The runner at third did the right thing and tagged up. The runner at first base did the right thing. His job, if a ball may or may not be caught, is to go as far as he can off the base, consistent with his ability to get back to it if the ball should be caught. In this case, the runner went all the way to second, knowing that if Pendleton made a basket catch, he would have time to go back and retrace the 90 feet.

The runner at second base was totally confused as to what to do. With his lead and his secondary lead with the pitch, when the ball was hit he naturally broke toward third. But then in looking back and seeing Pendleton racing toward the fence, he actually thought that the ball might be caught. And since he was the tying run, he started sprinting back to second base so he could tag and go to third if the ball was caught.

The ball short-hopped the fence and came right into Pendleton's lap. The runner from third easily scored to make it 9–8. But the runner at second who was on his way back to second now rerouted himself, coming toward third, with the runner on first right behind him, and the poor third base coach had no choice but to send both because they were right next to each other. Pendleton started a perfect relay, and the catcher dove to the inside part of the plate to tag the first guy and, from his knees, turned around and dove toward the outside part of the plate and tagged the second runner.

The umpire called, "You're out! You're out!" All of us scouts were wondering: how does the guy on second base not score on a 400-foot double to center field?

To this day, that is the number one base running mistake that I see, and have seen, in all levels of baseball, including the big leagues. When I was coaching in extended spring training, as I worked on this book, I had all of my players standing at second base and asked them what their responsibilities were with none out. They all knew to tag up so they could get to third with one out. Not one player knew what the answer was with one out. That's why I make it a point to tell the BYU story each year to whatever team I'm with and to cover it in base running. With one out, the runner has to be absolutely positive that he can score if the ball is not caught, and tagging up is not any part of the equation.

The Best Pitchers

The two best pitchers I ever saw as a scout went on to have major league careers that didn't match the projections and expectations. One was Tim Leary, who reminded me a lot of Don Drysdale. In my report, I mentioned that he didn't throw from as low as Drysdale, but was a three-quarters guy whose ball bore in on right-handed hitters, and he'd break a lot of bats. And he had a nasty slider going away. He could get you inside and outside. Leary pitched at UCLA and had an ideal body for a pitcher from a scouting standpoint. He was broad-shouldered, had height, good leverage, and had long, loose arms. He had plus velocity, with plus, plus movement. Leary had a natural ability not to throw a ball straight, which is a plus when you're a pitcher because it makes him that much harder to hit. He had a nasty slider, command, and feel. He had the best pure stuff of any pitcher I scouted.

During the years that I scouted, there was no doubt in my mind that he was the best and the highest projected guy that I'd ever come across, and Leary was drafted accordingly. He did help the Dodgers win the World Series in 1988 with 17 wins and an ERA under three. But for a lot of his career, it seemed like he kind of treaded water as a .500-type guy. He made his debut with the Mets and hurt his elbow in his first game, which kept him out for a long time. Maybe the injury was the reason.

We all make mistakes, but his stuff was electrifying. He still had a

13-year career. Anybody who pitches in the big leagues is a success in my eyes, but he was so overpowering in college that I think all the teams projected an exceptional career for him in the big leagues. To that level, it didn't happen.

After Leary, the guy with the second-best stuff was Mike Harkey from Cal-State Fullerton. He was a big, strong, right-handed pitcher in the mold of Ferguson Jenkins. He was 6'5", 225 pounds, and had dominant stuff. He could throw 95, had a breaking ball, and command of his pitches. He was drafted early in the first round. Everyone that scouted him had high expectations of major league dominance. I loved the guy. Once again, it didn't happen. He had some injuries, including one where he hurt himself doing cartwheels in the outfield. He still pitched for eight years in the majors. As much as I saw him pitch, he always seemed to come up on the losing end, whether the score was 1–0, 2–1 or 3–2. I don't mean that as a knock on him, because he always pitched great. But I never came away from a game seeing him win, which I thought was odd. Generally when I saw the best pitchers, they'd come out on the winning end.

It was nice when I'd see a guy who can't miss who actually turns out to have a great pro career. For me, it was Gary Sheffield as a senior in high school in Tampa. I went to watch Sheffield with Bill Lajoie, the Tigers GM, and his wife. You didn't have to be a genius to see that you were looking at a guy who should be an impact player in the majors. He swung the bat like it was made out of balsa wood. He had such quickness, good hand-eye coordination and athletic ability. He played shortstop although it looked like he might get too big and have to move to third base. He was already built like a man. With the aluminum bats, you had the feeling someone would get hurt. Sheffield drove the ball out of the park in high school like it was a Little League field. The opposing third baseman, who couldn't have weighed 140 pounds, was at third with his hands on knees, and in Sheffield's last at-bat he turned on a ball and hit a rocket line drive that went past the third baseman's head hardly before his hands were off his knees. Thank God the ball wasn't hit at this kid or he could've been killed. An aluminum bat in the hands of someone like Sheffield was a weapon.

He had his last at-bat, but just as we were getting ready to leave, Sheffield came in to pitch the last inning. We knew we had no interest in his pitching, but it was impressive to see him throwing 93. In the draft, Gary was taken early but not number one overall. In our draft room, I was wondering how he wasn't being taken. Usually there are a half-dozen guys that you're comfortable with as your first-round pick, but that year he was by himself. The rest is history. He went through the minors like it was nothing and hit more than 500 home runs in the majors.

I was a cross-checker for a couple of years. I still have friends who are doing it, and I tip my hat to them. There was sort of a pyramid system to scouting. Scouts who worked for the Major League Scouting Bureau, which is being done away with, would find players, and then teams would send their own scouts to qualify the player. For example, if there were ten good shortstops in Southern California, I'd go around to evaluate the ten, and then I'd put them in order. It was like playing stickball as a kid when you'd put your hand on the bat and whoever got the knob would get to pick first. Then all the players on the playground would go in order. We knew who was good and who the worst player was. A pro draft is really no more than that, only it's more magnified.

So the area scout would see all ten and then teams had a supervisor. Then the Western State Supervisor would not only see my ten, but he'd go to Northern California, Oregon, and Washington and see the best ten shortstops in those areas. In a bigger spectrum, he was able to say who the five best shortstops on the West Coast were. Above him was the national cross-checker. From February to May, the national cross-checker would be flying around the United States seeing the top 200 players in the nation, and comparing the best of the West, East, and Midwest. Then he'd be able to say that he found the next Ken Griffey, Jr., or the next Sandy Koufax and put them in a national order.

The fun thing is you're seeing the top 200 players in the country. Every time you go to a game, you're seeing someone who can play, unlike an area scout. You almost know before you even go to the game that you're going to like the player to some degree and that it's just a matter of where he's going to fit in the total scheme of things. And it's thrilling when you get to see a guy that you know is going to be a star.

The downside of being a cross-checker, for me, is that they put you on a plane almost each and every day for those four months. It's a lot of wear and tear on your body. There were a lot of rushes to the airport, pre–9/11. They didn't have the screening, but you're still flying into a city that you've never been to before, renting a car, carrying all your luggage, and asking the rent-a-car people for directions to whatever high school or college you were going to because there was no GPS or Internet yet. It was work.

When I saw Shawon Dunston, I flew from Los Angeles to New York City, fought traffic, and was getting directions as I tried to find the Parade Grounds. I got through Harlem and then I saw 40 other scouts there to watch him. Watching Dunston play was like a watching a man play with a bunch of kids. As a senior in high school, his athletic ability was just incredible. He had very live, wiry strength. He was 6'1", 175 pounds, had cat-like quickness and great hands. Shawon had an unbelievable cannon for a throwing arm but was erratic, which followed him to the big leagues. When they were Cubs teammates, Mark Grace would tease Dunston for making him famous for his ability to scoop balls out of the dirt. They were like brothers. They had such an incredible relationship.

Tool-wise, Shawon was electrifying to watch. His fielding technique was crude. Being from inner-city New York, he needed some coaching, but the raw skills were exceptional and he was a very aggressive player. He singled, tripled and homered when I saw him. The Cubs took him as the number one overall pick.

After seeing Dunston, I had to fight the traffic getting back to the airport because I had a flight the same night. I flew to Austin, Texas, to see an eventual MLB player, Spike Owen, at the University of Texas, only to wake up and see it was pouring rain. The game was called off. That's frustrating. When you're an area scout and it rains in your territory, you can usually get in your car and drive somewhere to see a game. But when you're a cross-checker and you're in Austin, and it's pouring rain, not only have you lost a day but there's extra frustration in knowing that I'd have to fly back to see this guy.

That's the perfect example of a problem as a cross-checker. You'd organize a schedule and then the rain would completely throw it out of whack. Meanwhile, you only have a certain amount of days to see all of these guys before the draft. I felt it was very demanding physically and mentally. There was constant traffic and trips to airports. Some of my friends have done this for 30 years, and I don't know how they do it. I did it for two years and was worn out. Plus, when you're an area scout, you're home more often. You might be gone for a week during an Easter tournament, but you have more of a home base. You can have a family life, and you can go out and play golf in the morning on a lot of days. High school games started at 3:15 because of classes. During the week, kids couldn't take batting practice before a game, so as long as you were at the park at 2:30, you had the morning free. As a cross-checker, I was under the gun with all the traveling.

Brewers Years

In 1978, Ray Poitevint became the farm director and the scouting director for the Milwaukee Brewers. He wanted me to come with him but I was under contract to the scouting bureau. The way that Ray got me out of my contract was by trading a scout, Dick Bogarde, for me. Ray claimed that was the first time there had ever been a trade of scouts. I don't know if that's true or not. The scouting bureau needed a cross-checker, and I was just an area scout at the time.

I became a scouting supervisor in the minor leagues and a hitting instructor for the Milwaukee Brewers. I would work with the hitters in spring training, then I would scout until the June draft. I would spend the summer roving our farm teams, working with the hitters. As soon as I became the hitting guy for them in the Instructional League, I got to work with not one, but two five-tool players. One was a switch-hitting center-fielder named Kevin Bass. The other was a right fielder from Nicaragua named David Green.

Kevin went on to have a lengthy and very successful big league career, mainly with the Astros and then the Giants at the tail end of his career. In 2011, I was going to manage the Angels' Class-A team in Lake Elsinore, California. Inland Empire was the name of the team. On the first day of spring training, I'm throwing batting practice to a group of players, and this one guy had such a familiar face but he was 19 or 20 years old. It's my first day, I don't know anybody there. After I finished throwing and was picking up baseballs, this youngster says, "Hey, Mr. Gamboa, my dad said to say hi to you."

I looked at his face and said, "Oh my God, you must be Kevin Bass's son."

He smiled and said, "Yes. I'm Justin."

I said, "Justin, you just ruined my whole day." He got a big frown on his face and I said, "It's not you. It's just the fact that I feel like I'm 100 all of a sudden. Just the fact that I'm managing the son of a former player I had back in 1979." We all experience how fast life goes by because in my mind, it seems like just a few years ago that I was watching Kevin play and work in the cage. His career had come and gone, and now he has a son playing pro ball. When Kevin and his wife came to watch their son play, it was a chance to renew a friendship and talk about old times.

David Green became a star for a short time with the Cardinals. It was fun working with guys with that kind of talent that you knew were going to play in the big leagues. David was a youngster who didn't speak any English, and his skill level was such that in his first year in the states, he bypassed rookie league and Low-A, and we put him in the California League, which was way over his head. His running, throwing and fielding skills were up to the league. But with the bat, the pitchers just overmatched him.

The fact that I was bilingual really helped me to converse with David. He was a big, strong guy with quick reflexes and great bat speed who could hit anybody's fastball. But like a lot of youngsters, he was very heavy on his front foot when he took his stride, so he was very susceptible to off-speed pitches and breaking balls. He couldn't hit the ball to the opposite field because everything was committed to pull. One day I told David that taking a stride into a pitch should be much like, "No rompen los huevos," which in Spanish means, "Don't break the eggs."

I was trying to get him to understand that the stride he took should be much shorter and much softer so that he could keep his weight back. David laughed at my saying, but it stuck in his mind. Our paths crossed a few years later and when he saw me he smiled and said, "No rompen los huevos." It became a key for him to learn how to wait. He learned what I called the three-stage process of hitting a breaking ball the other way. Wait longer, lean into it with your front shoulder, and don't lift it but drive it to the opposite field. Wait, lean, and drive, along with not breaking the eggs in your stride.

David and I worked on drills, and in the second half of the California League, he really caught up to the level of competition. He had a very quick rise to the big leagues. We knew he was a hell of a prospect, and he was involved in a trade with the Cardinals in which Milwaukee got Rollie Fingers, Ted Simmons and Pete Vuckovich, three guys who helped the Brewers win the AL pennant in 1982. It's not like we gave David away. We knew he would be a good player, but we needed pitching.

Unfortunately, David never reached the level that his skills should have got to. He had a drinking problem that cut his career short, but he played several more years in Mexico.

My first signing as a scout with the Brewers was an outfielder named Doug Loman. Doug was from Bakersfield Junior College and had never been drafted, but I loved his determination and competitiveness. He was just like a bulldog. Doug was a 5'11", 185-pound right fielder who could hit, and we took him in the second round of the January draft. Then I managed him in the Instructional League and worked with him as a hitter while I was roving in the minor leagues. Doug had a very short career. He could throw and he could put the bat on the baseball, but he probably didn't have enough home run power. If you're a corner outfielder in the big leagues, you'd better be hitting a ton of home runs or stealing a lot of bases. He played for two years with the Brewers, and I think that anybody that makes it to the big leagues is a huge success story because not many people can say they got there.

When Robin Yount first signed, he played in the New York-Penn League in Newark. That winter, I had so many minor league players with the Orioles who lived in Southern California, that the Orioles had a winter team in SoCal that I managed. We played against the junior colleges and four-year schools, but we didn't have a shortstop. Robin, being from Woodland Hills, somehow got the okay to play on our team, and so I had to manage him in the winter after his rookie year. That was fun. You're watching a guy and there was no doubt that he was going to be a real outstanding big league player. Nobody knew that he was going to be a Hall of Famer. At 19, Robin could run, throw, field and hit. At 6'1", 170 pounds, I don't think anybody projected him to be a power guy. I certainly didn't. He was a bullet line drive type of hitter. There wasn't a lot of loft to the swing.

He became the starting shortstop for the Brewers the next spring training. It's quite a jump to go from the NYPL to the big leagues. And he hit .255 as a 19-year-old.

As a scouting supervisor in 1980, I went to cross-check Dion James, an outfielder. Our Northern California scout, Harry Smith, had put James in as a potential first-round pick. Dion's season was over but I had never seen, to that point in my scouting career, such a fluid, effortless swing. Almost a sweet-swinging Billy Williams swing from the left side, but with no loft, only bullet line drives to all fields. I only got to see him take batting practice but was able to back Harry up that this guy should be our first-round pick. We picked late in the first round but I said in a meeting, "This is one guy that if I had to give the money out of my own bank account I wouldn't hesitate because I'm that sure that this youngster will play in the big leagues." And I didn't even get to see him play in a game.

I was fortunate enough to manage Dion as well. Our rookie league manager in Butte, Montana, was a college coach, Kenny Richardson. College started in August, and for a couple of years that we had Kenny, I would go into Butte and leave my role as the roving hitting coach. And since I knew all the players, I would take over as manager of the team.

Dion hit .300 in every minor league city he went to, was the everyday center fielder for the Brewers at 21 and hit .295. He was disappointed because he had never hit below .300 in his life. I said, "Hey, this is the big leagues. There's no higher league than this. For a rookie you did fine."

Unfortunately, Dion had his problems with drugs and, like David Green, never fulfilled his potential. He got derailed. At one point, coming off the drugs, Dion was signed by Atlanta and was fifth in the National League in hitting. But the off-the-field problems kind of haunted him. He finished his career with the Yankees and got pulled over for a violation and they found stuff in the car. The Yankees released him.

I was with the Cubs at the time, and Dion called me to see if he could get a place. As much as I wanted to, I couldn't go to bat for him because there had just been too many off-the-field problems, which was a shame because this guy could really hit.

A guy that stands out from that 1980 team is Randy Ready. Randy was a middle infielder who could really hit. And he could really drive a breaking ball to the other field with authority, which you don't see a lot. He was kind of chunky, short legs, long torso. During the short time I had with that club, I told Poitevint, "I don't know where this kid is going to play but I have no doubt his bat will get him to the major leagues." He became a great, double-switch role player mainly with San Diego and Philadelphia. He could play second, third, left and a little first.

There are certain people you just click with. Sometimes two hitting coaches can be saying the same thing, but it's about how it relates to the player. That's why I'm always looking for analogies. Like not breaking the eggs for David Green. That really hit home with him. There was Bill Schroeder, a catcher in Butte. Bill was a strong, right-handed hitting catcher and had big-time power. But he had a lot of contact issues, a lot of swings and misses. We developed such a rapport that it became a standard joke that when I would come into town for five days, I'd bring him out early and we'd work on things. I remember when Tony Muser was managing the Stockton team and Muser was throwing him batting practice.

I was making suggestions to Bill around the cage, and that night his approach to the ball was better.

I've always believed that a good hitting approach is like a chain of dominoes. If your stride into the ball is such that your lead side is closed, and your hands and weight are back, you're in a good position to hit. The rest of it is like knocking down one domino and the rest of the chain falls down. I would almost think that the way Bill took that breaking ball for a ball, if something is in the zone he's going to crush it. Inevitably he'd hit a home run. I can't remember watching a series without him hitting a home run. He went on to catch in the big leagues with Milwaukee and had a long career as the Brewers' announcer.

Dale Sveum had gone to Pinole Valley High School in the Bay area, just north of Oakland. Dale was a switch-hitting shortstop and a terrific athlete. He could play football, baseball, basketball, and golf. Dale was actually one of the few five-star quarterbacks in the country. He was heading for Arizona State until the Brewers took him with their first pick. He had done real poorly in the minors, and Arizona State came back because of it. Being a young guy, Dale had a change of heart and thought he had made a mistake.

When I got word that he was going to quit, I felt like that money had come out of my own pocket. He was the first guy I had ever given over $100,000 to, which in 1981 was a ton of money. Being a young guy, I was worried that I would be fired for making a bad decision. The Brewers had me on the first plane to the Bay Area to talk to his parents. Dale, his dad and I played a round of golf, and we had lunch. His dad was a terrific person and an ethical person, like I would be in the same situation.

His dad looked at Dale and said, "Dale, you took the money from the Brewers in good faith and I don't think that that's long enough to fulfill the commitment that these people think you can play in the big leagues. I think you have to trust their judgment and honor the contract."

The next year we advanced him to Stockton, where he was only a little over an hour away from his home, his parents and his girlfriend. Dale is actually one of the few guys I know who is married to the same girl that he was with in high school. He and Darlene have been together since they were 15 or 16. Being the athlete that he was, he started to catch up. He became the everyday shortstop for the Brewers. He made his debut in 1986 and then in 1987 he hit 25 homers and drove in 95 runs, mainly hitting in the nine-spot. Shortly after that, he was involved in a really bad collision on a little Texas Leaguer with Sveum going out and Darryl Hamilton coming in. Dale broke his leg in two places and missed the rest of the season. To Dale's credit, he played through the 1999 season as a utility player. The sad thing is he never became the player he could've become because of the injury. He ultimately managed the Cubs and is now credited as being one of the finest hitting instructors. He was on the Royals staff that won the 2015 World Series.

Another guy who had potential of being a great baseball player was John Elway, who I scouted in Granada Hills, which wasn't even 15 miles from where I lived. We knew Elway was gifted at football and had a full scholarship to Stanford, but he was also an outstanding baseball player. He was a right fielder, and it goes without saying that he had a tremendous arm. He had power and a beautiful left-handed swing, and I don't think there's a team that wouldn't have had him on its draft board except everybody backed off because they knew football was his number one priority. The Yankees drafted him because George Steinbrenner always got what he wanted. Elway was drafted ahead of Tony Gwynn. Steinbrenner let Elway play football but wanted him to play baseball during the summer in the hopes that they would win him over. Elway played one year for Oneonta in the New York-Penn League.

In 1981 and 1982, Ray used me as a national cross-checker, plus I'd still be the hitting guy. But at the end of the '82 season, my wife divorced me and, having five kids, I knew I wanted to be in development full-time. I knew that the taste that I had in managing in Butte those two years, and for one week in Triple-A, I knew that was what I wanted to do. I hadn't done it previously because I was trying to keep my family together.

I had been with the organization for five seasons and didn't want to see somebody get fired just so I could selfishly do what I wanted to do, so I gave the Brewers my notice that I was going to look for a job somewhere else. I didn't want to leave, but I knew I wanted to go into development. At the end of 1982 they decided to make a managerial change, and they told me that they didn't want me to go but they didn't want to lose my scouting experience either. They asked if I would like to scout in 1983 and then manage the rookie team the whole summer. Plus the team was moving from Butte to Paintsville, Kentucky. I felt like I was having my cake and eating it too.

My goal was to play in the big leagues and it didn't happen, but once I got into managing, I found out very early in my career that my gift was being able to get 25 players, regardless of their race, religion, creed, or ethnicity, and bring them together for the common good and to play together as a team. Whether it was early in my career at Milwaukee or later with Detroit, or in my capacity as a field coordinator working with both staff and players, and certainly in my tenure in Puerto Rico, it was a consistent ability to be able to relate to players and to inspire and get them to play together as one and leave their egos at the door. We all have our gifts, and I guess that was mine.

When I was running the major and minor league camps, I was so focused on setting up the whole day, that one day during my first year I was going to the copy machine to make schedules for the whole staff and we had a pitching coach named Oscar Acosta who said hello to me and I didn't acknowledge it. Unbeknownst to me, Tony Muser, who had been with the Cubs for years, and Oscar were dressing in the clubhouse, and Oscar made a comment about how my shit must be too good to acknowledge a Mexican-American pitching coach who was in the minors. Oscar had faced a lot of prejudice, so I see where that came from. Muser thought he was joking and asked if he was out of his mind. Oscar told him what happened, and Tony's response was, "Oscar, I've known this guy for over 20 years. Gamboa's a guy that treats everybody from the custodian and janitor of the locker room to the president of the team the same. He just is what you see. There's no pretense. His mind must have just been preoccupied with what he has going on during the day, I guarantee that he didn't even hear or see you." Over a beer, I felt horrible as the story was relayed to me that night. The next day I was in a tower watching workouts, and I had Oscar come up and I apologized to him for my omission. I invited Oscar to dinner with the rest of the coaches that night, and that cemented a bond between Oscar, God rest his soul, and myself to the extent that I asked him to be my pitching coach one year when Guy Hansen couldn't go down there. Oscar became the major league pitching coach for the Cubs and was later killed in a tragic car accident in the Dominican Republic while in the Yankees system.

I believe that a team is like a wagon rolling downhill. To pick up some speed and get some momentum, everything has to function. I looked at the manager, coaches and players as being like a wagon wheel, with every player and coach being one of the spokes, and as the manager I was no more important than anybody else and nobody's boss, but I was the hub of the wheel that had to keep the spokes greased so that we could function. I believed in the four P's: being passionate, being positive, being patient and being persistent.

When the team made the managerial change, it made it easy for me to stay. Then I was the benefactor of probably the best overall draft that the Brewers had had up to that time. I had a talented starting rotation in Paintsville. Dan Plesac, our first-round pick out of North Carolina State, went on to have a long career as a reliever and is now on the MLB Network. Mike Birkbeck, a right-hander with a terrific curveball, was another high draft pick who went on to pitch in the big leagues with the Brewers and Mets. Our third starter was Jeff Reece, a left-hander with a terrific curveball. I don't know why he didn't make it to the big leagues. He was a stylish lefty with enough velocity and a curveball. He did have some arm issues.

The fourth starter was Mark Ciardi, a small, compact right-hander. He was a great competitor with a borderline fastball but with a good slider that he could throw in any count. When the Brewers started 13–0 in 1987, Ciardi got one of those wins. He was a short-term big leaguer and then went on to become a Hollywood producer. His claim to fame is some of the sports movies that Disney has done. He did "Miracle," about the 1980 U.S. hockey team. He did the Secretariat movie. And he did "The Rookie," which was about Jim Morris, who happened to be the fifth starter in Paintsville.

When I saw *The Rookie*, then Morris really made sense to me, because Jimmy was a fish out of water when he came into pro ball. He was a first-round pick in the January draft. When he came into pro ball, his velocity was very marginal. He had the makings of a good breaking ball, but he had no command of his stuff. His walk ratio was off the chart, and he had zero confidence. As I found out in the movie, the lack of relationship between him and his dad is what I think caused him to be so introverted. He was the type of guy who had his head down, and it was hard for him to look you in the eye. And he always saw the glass as half-empty rather than half-full.

LaVel Freeman hit third in Paintsville and when he got to Double-A, he had one year in which he nearly hit .400 in the Texas League. Our cleanup hitter was our second-round choice, Glenn Braggs. He was a five-tool player and won the Triple Crown that season. He was built like a Greek God. Glenn was an unbelievable physical specimen. The bulk of his time in the majors came with the Reds. He was a terrific person as well.

I was fortunate to start my managing career with a crew like that. We went 47–25 that year. The Pulaski Braves didn't have as much talent as us, but they were a pesky group. Buddy Bailey was a young manager like me, and he did a great job with his club. We had a seven-game lead with a month to go, but with 13 games left our lead was down to three. There were eight teams in the league, with no divisions. You just played it right through.

I had a clubhouse meeting because I was sensing a lot of tension on my team. A lot of guys were getting tight. I thought I had to get guys to see this the way I was seeing it and turn this around. I said,

> I'm glad that Pulaski is winning all these games because in your first year in pro ball, or even for me as a manager, if we'd have won this thing by 10 games it wouldn't have meant as much. Winning is winning but this is going to the last week, maybe even the last day. There are six other teams that are just playing out the schedule. To think that for these last 13 games, every inning pitched, every at-bat, every play you make on defense is going to have some outcome on the bearing of the season, this is going to be fun. And what I want you guys to think is that someday when you get to the big leagues and you're in a pennant race in September and the games are on TV, you're going to be able to draw back from this as one of the experiences to know that you can not only play in a pennant race but that you can thrive in it. This is what makes it fun. We have the best talent and we're going to win but you don't need me to tell you that we've all been getting a little uptight. Just relax, trust your skills and relish this because in two short weeks you're all going to go home to your families and it's going to be over, so enjoy the moment.

Jimmy Morris was the only undependable starter on the club. He finished the season with an ERA over five. His control was just so lacking that I knew the bullpen was going to get a workout. As Pulaski closed on us in the last month, our farm director, Bruce Manno, told me that if I wanted to take Morris out of the rotation, I had the okay to do that. As much as I wanted to win, I told Bruce that I had been trying to build Jimmy's confidence all year and if I pulled him now, it would send him spiraling. Jimmy pitched the second-to-last game of the season while we were hanging on to a one-game lead. But he had come far enough and he pitched five innings and got the win. I pulled him so he could keep his confidence high.

Little did I know that Pulaski was going to win their last 13 in a row. We won 11 of our last 13 to win the pennant by one game. Pulaski went 26–5 in the last month.

Our last game was at Elizabethton, and it was Plesac's turn to pitch. Dan came to my room and told me, "I've never played on a winning team in my whole life. Not in Little League, not in high school and not in college. But I always dreamed of getting a chance to pitch the big game. To think that my first year in pro ball, my number is up. It's going to happen tomorrow. There's no way that I'm not winning that game tomorrow."

Pulaski played a day game and won. So we were either going to win or be co-champions. Plesac pitched his ass off into the eighth inning and we won, 3–1. When he ran out of gas, we had a college closer, Jeff Gilbert, come in. He wasn't a prospect but at that level if a pitcher can throw a curveball for a strike, he's going to get them out. Gilbert was a dominant closer at that level and got the last five outs. I was happy for all the players and I was thrilled for Plesac. It was a big thrill to come out on top.

Plesac had never played for a winning team, and our team was so dominant that there was a point in that season, also at Elizabethton, when Plesac started while he was off to a hot start that year. We were winning that game, 5–0, in the fifth and Dan was three outs away from qualifying for the win. When Plesac was warming up, he was warming up as if it was a Sunday softball game. I don't know what Plesac and our catcher, John Beuerlein, were talking about, but Plesac had a smile on his face when he was throwing one of his warm-up pitches.

I thought to myself that he was losing his focus. Winning is coming too easy for him and complacency is setting in. This game can bite you in the ass in a heartbeat if you're not focused. And sure enough, there were a couple of walks and a base hit to load the bases. Plesac usually dominated lefties, but Rafael Codinach hit a grand slam and now all of a sudden it was 5–4 with two outs in the fifth. I had somebody warming up before the inning began because I didn't like how Plesac was going through the motions. I came out of the dugout, and Plesac threw his hands up as though I had forgotten that I had already made a trip to the mound, and this would be to take him out. I came out, took the ball from him, and then we scored ten runs the next inning and won in a rout.

He missed out on a sure win. Plesac finished 9–1, so this cost him what should've been a double-digit-win season. And he cost himself that win. He had stuff but he didn't really know what competing was, not to the level that I expect. Plesac was so upset after that game that I brought him into my office. I didn't air him out because I had already sent the message. I said,

> Dan, I want to tell you a story. Because I grew up in Los Angeles as a die-hard Dodger fan, I listened to every game on my transistor radio while I did my homework. I'm going to tell you about two great Dodgers pitchers who had a difference between them. There's Sandy Koufax, who once threw a three-hit shutout and won 10–0. On the postgame show, Vin Scully asked him how he was able to maintain his focus and pitch that quality of a game with the score being so one-sided. Sandy said that he didn't have control over whether his team was scoring runs or not but all he knew was if he mentally relaxed once, it would be easier to do a second time, and four days later he might be in a one-run game where he might not have that luxury. That's my definition of a total professional. If Don Sutton, who I have the utmost respect for, had a 10–0 lead, it would usually finish 10–3 or 10–4. When he talked about his game he would admit that once it got to 10–0 he would basically throw four-seam fastballs down the middle that ended up in the seats. Dan, you've got great stuff. There's a reason you were our number one pick, but today's game should show you that the moment you turn that light switch off and start resting on your

laurels, this game can bite you in the ass. I hate to take the win away from you but I think there's a lesson to be learned here.

Five days later, we're playing at home against the Bristol Tigers. Mike Pazik, our pitching rover, was in town. I was working with some guys, and Plesac came in with his North Carolina State sweatsuit. As he walked by me at the cage, I said, "Dan, how's it going?"

For the only time that I can remember a player disrespecting me, Plesac, in a soft tone, said, "Fuck you." He just kept walking. I wasn't mad at all. I took it as "I'm focused and this is my fucking game." I turned to Mike and said, "Well, I don't think you're going to get to see anyone in the bullpen today because we know he's focused."

Plesac threw a masterpiece against the Tigers. He gave up two or three hits in seven innings and struck out 13. I think that learning experience went a long way in toughening him up. Dan was the class clown on the bus. He could imitate anybody and was quick with a sarcastic line. I think he learned that once he walked across the white lines, it was time for the laughter to end. And he had a reputation for being a bulldog closer when he got to the big leagues with Milwaukee. I thought he could be a 200 inning per year starter and a 20-game winner, but by the time he got to Triple-A, the need was for a closer. I give credit to whoever decided to put him in the bullpen.

After winning in 1983 in Paintsville, I managed in Beloit, the Low-A team, in 1984. A lot of the players were the same. Guys like Plesac, Braggs and Freeman. I had Chris Bosio, who was struggling with Beloit although you couldn't question his stuff. Because of the ability level on that team, a lot of the key guys bypassed Beloit and went right to Stockton.

Beloit was in Wisconsin, about 80 miles from Milwaukee. At that time, I didn't have a pitching or hitting coach. It was just me and 25 players, and then the roving instructors would come in. Nowadays, teams fly after spring training, but back then the Brewers had us bus from Phoenix to Beloit. That came out to about 40 hours on the bus over three days.

Being as competitive as I was and as organized as I was, I didn't want any excuses for why we weren't organized. On the first day we bussed from Phoenix to El Paso, Texas, and stayed at a Motel 6. When we got off the bus, I told everybody that they had 30 minutes to get into their rooms, unwind, and change into their shorts and sneakers because we were going to meet in the parking lot.

I had the hotel manager call rooms to move cars that were in the parking lot. I wanted to keep the arms in shape, so we warmed up, took ground balls and played pepper in the parking lot of a Motel 6. I led the

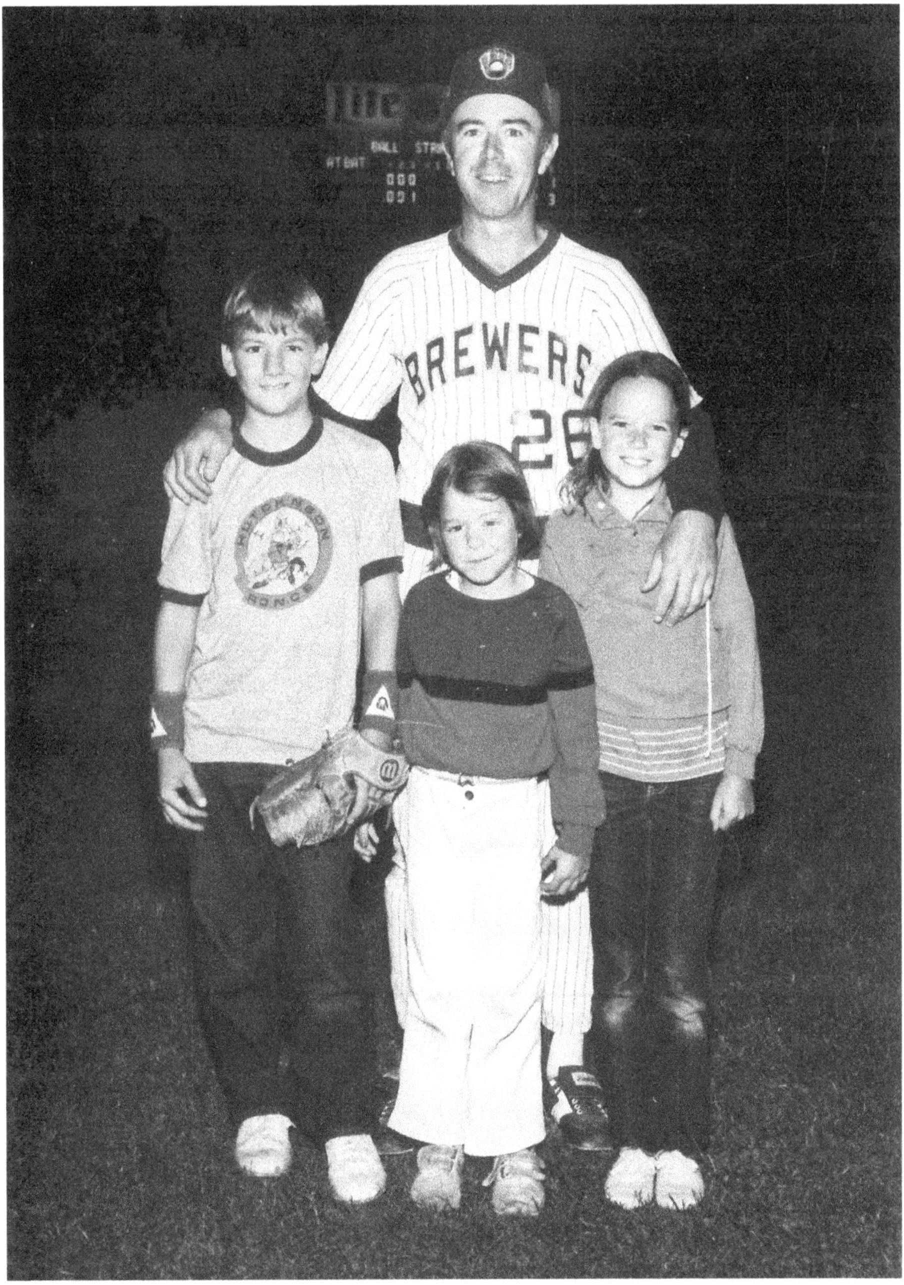

With Brett, Jamie and Kristin in Beloit, 1984. My Beloit club made it to the playoffs behind an excellent pitching staff that included Dan Plesac, Chris Bosio and Jim Morris.

guys in a jog from the off-ramp that we were at to the next off-ramp, which was a mile away. I didn't want guys to stiffen up on the bus ride or lose the edge from all the work we had done in spring training. That sent a message right away to the guys about how seriously I was taking my job and their development.

When we got to Beloit, the field was covered with snow. We didn't have a clubhouse, but there was an ice rink adjacent to the ballpark, so we used the clubhouse in the ice rink for the season. We had to walk 100 yards from the clubhouse in the ice rink to get to our ballpark. I had the city guy melt the ice in the ice rink so that we would be able to work out indoors in the ice rink. I had a machine that would shoot wiffleballs that we used for batting practice in this ice rink. Then I had the trainer go to the local sporting goods store and buy three dozen badminton birdies. If you had one guy throw them like darts and the batter took a baseball swing and hit the rubber part dead-center, you could drive it 30 or 40 feet. But if you just caught the feathers, the thing would foul tip right at your feet. I had the guys pair up and take batting practice with badminton birdies just to work on their hand-eye coordination and keep their swings sharp.

In spring training, our roving catching instructor, Andy Etchebarren, told me that it was good I won my first year because this was going to be a long year. He said that the pitching looked good but that we wouldn't be able to score any runs. In spite of all my efforts, we started 16–24. I guess we weren't a cold weather team. It was damn cold in April and early May. We took our lumps.

I went to dinner with the Beloit ownership. The team had started in 1982, and they didn't really know how pro ball worked. They asked me why Stockton, the other A team, got all the good players while we got the leftovers. I explained that there was a hierarchy like in a high school. The goal was to get people to Milwaukee as soon as possible but without rushing them. The high drafts should be able to skip a rookie league. I told the owners not to give up on the team yet because I thought there was a lot of talent there.

The game revolves around pitching and defense. I knew we had good speed at Beloit. After starting 16–24, we won 70 of our next 99. At one point we went 41–9.

Brian Finley, our leadoff hitter, stole 66 bases. We had Eddie Irvine, a veteran guy from Arizona State. Eddie was 27 and had played at the Triple-A level. They didn't want to release him because he was a good insurance policy in case somebody at the Double or Triple-A level got hurt. Larry Jackson did well for us hitting third.

The cleanup hitter was Joey Meyer, a big guy from Hawaii. He was 6'3", 275 pounds. Joey won the Triple Crown by hitting .320 with 30 homers and 102 RBI. And Braggs had won the Triple Crown for me the year before. Who has two Triple Crown winners in his first two years as manager? And for Joey to win it, there were no infield hits. He was built like Steve Balboni. People tried to get him out inside because they thought they could get the ball in on his hands, but if they made a mistake out over the plate and he got his arms extended, there wasn't a park he couldn't hit it out of, including Yellowstone. They have a seat painted a different color at Mile High Stadium to mark where he hit a home run with the Denver Zephyrs, the Brewers' Triple-A club. It went 582 feet. When I managed Toledo, we went there for a game and I saw the seat and found it hard to believe that somebody really hit a ball there. I had heard about it in baseball lore, but when I was at home plate before the game it looked like somebody hit a Titleist Two to reach that distance.

We had a big, right-hand hitting third baseman named Kerry Everett hitting behind Meyer. Once that team got it together, and believed in itself, we were like a runaway train. Winning leads to an attitude where you just never say die. You just assume that as long as you have an out left, something good can happen.

There was a game against Duffy Dyer's Kenosha Twins team during our 41–9 run. We had already won the first two games with come-from-behind wins. In the third game, we were being no-hit into the ninth inning and trailed, 2–0. While warming up for the ninth inning, the Kenosha pitcher stepped in the hole our pitcher had made with his stride foot. Somehow he missed his spot, twisted his ankle, and had to come out of the game. As soon as the reliever came in from the bullpen, I had a premonition that it was going to happen again. Boom, the no-hitter was gone. A walk and a hit later, the shutout was gone. Then suddenly there was a walk-off double and we won the game, 3–2. As I was leaving the dugout amidst all the pandemonium, I saw Duffy take a bat to the bat rack and dismantle it like a logger chopping wood. The next day, our general manager came to me and asked what he should do about the bat rack. I said, "Good God, whatever you do, don't send them a bill for it. Just have the grounds crew make another one." I could relate to how Duffy felt. When you're caught up with a team that's on a streak, the good team is sensing that things are going to happen, and the other side is wondering how they're going to get beat today.

The Quad Cities Cubs had struggled all season. Losing teams have losing confidence. You find ways to lose. We beat them like a drum. We had a three-game series and won the first two. In the third game we were (again) being no-hit into the ninth inning and trailing, 5–0. Hector Freytes, the Cubs' third baseman, looked at me, smiled and said, "We've given you guys a good game today. I know somehow, someway, your team is going to win but we've given you a good one."

We broke up the no-hitter and the shutout. We cut the lead to 5–3, and they were rushing to get their closer ready. LaVel Freeman had struggled in the California League, was sent down and became my three-hitter. I was giving him a day off but with two on and two out, I sent him up as a pinch-hitter. He hit a ball halfway up the light tower in right-center. As Freeman was circling the bases, Freytes put his glove up to his mouth and said to me, "I told you. I knew it was going to happen. I just didn't know how."

We stole one. You're going to win one-third of your games and lose one-third of your games. It's the other third that make the difference. Down 5–0, as a manager, you start rationalizing. Okay, we've had a good road trip and the goal is to win two of every three. Then the rally starts, your adrenaline picks up and you realize you still have a chance.

We didn't know who would close in 1984. Jeff Gilbert was a good stabilizer, a good guy for a rookie league team, but he was released. We had Dave Stapleton, a little left-hander from Grand Canyon College, a four-year school where he would later coach. And he had developed a screwball. He didn't throw it a lot. It was my fault. As a manager and a scout, it's like bigger guys have to prove that they can't play and smaller guys have to prove that they can. A guy with velocity has to prove that he can't pitch, and a guy with no velocity has to prove that he can. For the first few weeks, it was bullpen by committee. Dave Stapleton was the 12th man on a 12-man staff. He was small and threw about 83 mph. Because of a rainout, we had a doubleheader in Peoria and I needed innings. Sometimes you sacrifice a battle to win the war. You don't want to overextend your pitching. Stapleton threw a few innings against Joe Maddon's Peoria team. And for the few innings Dave pitched, nobody was making good contact against him. From the dugout, I was wondering how they were missing these pitches. I didn't give his screwball and his ability to pitch enough credit. He was throwing enough screwballs that when he came inside with a fastball it looked 90, even though it was 83.

That won me over, and nobody else was rising to the front, so we made him the closer and he had a hell of a season. He was a huge cog in us winning. When we got to Stockton, Stapleton lost the closer role to Jeff Parrett, who was on the fast track to the majors. About a month into the season, Dave and his wife, Patty, came to see me. Dave told me he wanted to quit baseball and become a chimney sweep. I asked him if he was out of his mind.

Dave said, "No. I have a chance to get into this business. I just don't think I'm going anywhere in baseball." He added that he was small and didn't throw hard, all the things I would've said the year before until I saw him pitch.

I said, "Dave, you've got the rest of your life to get into some kind of business. If I didn't think you could pitch in the big leagues, I'd be the first one to tell you to get on with the rest of your life. In my heart, I know that you have a pitch. I didn't believe in you until I saw it. You made a believer out of me and you're going to make a believer out of other people. You really need to stick this out and see this through."

He pitched middle relief and set-up in the 1985 season. In the big leagues, Dave Stapleton pitched, and won, a game at Yankee Stadium. He wasn't in the big leagues for very long but I was thrilled for him and Patty that he stuck it out. He won in the big leagues, and nobody can take that away from him. Stapleton became a successful coach at his old high school and is now in the Angels organization.

Jeff Parrett was our ninth-round pick out of Kentucky and looked like the Marlboro Man. He was 6'3", 205, dark hair, just a great-looking guy who should've been a male model. Jeff was a real nice guy but wasn't confident. Jeff was a sixth starter in Paintsville and could pitch out of the bullpen while making the occasional spot start. It was the same thing when we got to Beloit, except that Parrett was one of these guys that, when the game was on the line, he just tightened up so bad. Tony Muser used to call it the "sphincter factor." It's easy to pitch in a 10–0 game, but when it's 1–1 or 2–1, it's a whole different animal. The game is still the game but the situation is what causes certain people to tense up and put pressure on themselves.

Mike Pazik happened to be at a game where Parrett came in from the bullpen in a close game and pitched horribly. We were on the bus back to Beloit, and there was some talk about releasing Parrett. There was a discussion between Bruce, Mike and me. Fortunately we didn't release him. When we got back home, there was a game against Madison, and Parrett surrendered a three-run homer to Terry Steinbach which broke the game open. I remember thinking that it just wasn't going to happen for this poor guy. Right after that home run, it was like Parrett finally got upset with himself, all the competitiveness came out and he didn't hold anything back. He just started blowing people away.

We happened to come back and rather than make a pitching change, Mike wanted to keep Parrett in because he was on a roll and it was time, as Mike said, for Jeff to grow a pair of testicles. And Jeff dominated. After this game, there was a call to see if we were going to let Parrett go. Mike and I said that he was finally over the hump. He had finally pitched in a game that counted with the pressure on, rose to the occasion and showed better stuff than we had seen before. It shows how close a guy can be to seeing his dream end without even being aware of it.

The next year in Stockton, Jeff was the closer. And in a role where he only had to get three outs, all of his stuff got a full grade better because there was no holding back. He had a brilliant year in the California League. Jeff was a factor in us winning, and our pitching was so good that there were discussions about the 39th and 40th spots on the roster concerning Ciardi, Dan Murphy and Parrett. They had room for two of the three. The Brewers called up Ciardi and Murphy. In the December pro draft, the Expos took Parrett. When a guy is taken in that draft, he has to be kept on the team. So Parrett went right from the California League to big leagues with the Expos. After a couple of years in Montreal, he was traded to the Cardinals and had an extensive career.

The Beloit team won the division handily after our long hot streak. The problem with that was that we were playing meaningless games during the last few weeks of the season and we ended up being flat for the playoffs. We were better than the Springfield Cardinals, but they outplayed us. There's something to be said for being driven right to the wire and then carrying that momentum into the playoffs.

Then for 1985, I, like most of my team, was promoted to Stockton. I knew when we left spring training that we had a good team. We battled a Modesto A's team that had Mark McGwire and Walt Weiss. Modesto was right down the highway from us and was our rival. Modesto won the first half by one game. We didn't win but we developed because the next day, the farm director promoted almost a third of our team to El Paso, the Double-A team.

Although I was disappointed that we didn't win, I rationalized that the minor leagues are about development. I received eight replacements, including Billy Bates, a high-drafted second baseman from the University of Texas. I had some players sent up from Beloit, including Jimmy Morris.

Before I knew it, we started off the second half 5–15 and were in last place. I was no fun to be around. I was beside myself, wondering how a group of guys who had done nothing but win were now in last place. Not only were we losing, but I thought we were accepting that we were a last-place team.

The greatest lesson I learned in my baseball career was from a non-baseball person. I was so frustrated at all the time and effort that I was putting in to these 25 guys and wondering how we could be in last place. After a loss one night, I was having some beers in my office well past midnight. We had a first-year trainer, Todd Franz, who didn't really know anything about baseball. In the minors, the trainer is everything. He's the trainer, clubhouse guy, and traveling secretary.

Todd was doing the laundry, came in the office and said, "This is my first year doing this but I know that through the first half, to a man, these guys would run through a wall for you. But now, the tide is turning and when you're not around I hear some of the guys in their little cliques saying bad things about how sarcastic you are, and how you're so down on them, and they just don't get it."

I was basically like, "Screw these guys. I'm working my ass off, we're in last place and nobody seems to care except me. Yet, it's their careers, not mine."

Todd said, "The difference is you're still expecting them to win and there's not a guy in that locker room that thinks that they can win. That's why they don't understand why you're so hard on them."

I asked what he meant by that, because the guys in that locker room had done nothing but win in Paintsville and Beloit, and we had just gone to the last day of the first half in Stockton.

He said, "But eight of the best guys on this team aren't here anymore." Only then did a light go off in my head. I realized that I still had expectations to win, but the 25 guys on the team had an excuse to lose because the better guys weren't here. I learned not to assume that the team sees things the same way that you do, because perception becomes reality.

The next day, I called off batting practice and we had a team meeting. I told them about my talk with Todd, and I went around the room pointing fingers at some of the guys on the team and said,

> I know all we've ever done is win. And I know that eight guys have moved on. That's what the game is about. Some of you that were long relievers are now getting a chance to start. And a utility infielder, now it's your chance to start. The movement of guys is giving some of you an opportunity to show the organization that you're a better player than they thought. It took a first-year trainer to point out to me that I'm the only one in this room that's still expecting us to win with the talent that we've got here, but everybody else is content to be in last place just because the best players have moved on. I'm going to promise you guys one thing. If every guy in this room gives me the effort that I'm giving you and we don't want to finish less than

> first, I'll bite my tongue and be like I've always been, Mr. Positive, supportive and pat you on the back. But I know that there's still way more talent on this team than you guys think. I'm telling you right now, if you don't give me a winning effort, win, lose, or draw, then I will make this a miserable two months for everybody in this room. Just bond together and play as a team. We're obviously not going to score as many runs, so we'll have to hit-and-run more and steal more bases and let's see what can happen.

We had speed and we executed. The first three guys in my lineup, Brian Finley, Matthew Sferrazza, and LaVel Freeman, were three of the top guys in stolen bases in the league. Sferrazza had 57, Finley had 54, and Freeman had 38. After my Knute Rockne speech, we lost 1–0 to Salinas. But we finished that half 32–12 and went from last to tying for first on the last day of the half. We played Redwood, the Angels' affiliate, in the last series of the year. With the game tied in the tenth inning, Finley was at third with one out and I had the contact play on. His jump from third was so good that on a comebacker to the pitcher, he was safe at the plate. Finley was safe because the ball was hit to the glove side of the left-handed pitcher, and the time it took the pitcher to make the transfer and throw was too long. By the time the catcher tagged Finley's helmet, Finley was already across the plate. We worked on baserunning every day, and that was an unbelievable example of how little things can become huge things. We never teach a guy to go in head-first because with the catcher's gear the chances for injury are great, but Finley won it with a head-first dive.

The Beloit team had been flat in the playoffs, but this team entered with a lot of momentum. We beat the Modesto A's in a best-of-five series. The final series was against the Fresno Giants, managed by Wendell Kim, a longtime third base coach in the big leagues. Will Clark was on that Fresno team. We went all five but lost the decisive Game Five at home. We gave everything we had, but Fresno outplayed us in that series.

One of my batboys in Stockton was Ed Sprague, Jr., who went on to have a heck of a career at Stanford, was the third baseman on the first USA team to win a Gold Medal in the Olympics, and was the third baseman on the Blue Jays' World Series title teams in 1992 and 1993. His dad owned the Stockton team. Ed Sr., belonged to three different country clubs, so we would play golf in the morning, and then I'd have lunch and go to the ballpark. What a summer, basically combining golf and baseball on a daily basis. And back then, I had the energy to do it all day long.

We had Tim Crews on our Stockton team. Tim and his wife, Lori, were very nice. Some of the guys on the team were married. Our park in Stockton was on the grounds of a city park, and after the Sunday 1:00

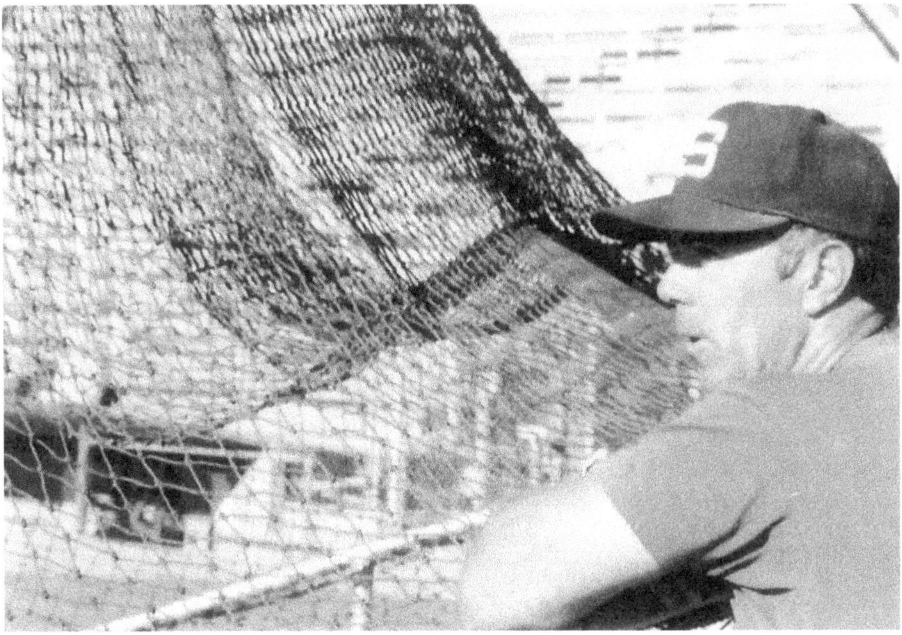

At the batting cage during my Stockton days, 1985. This is one of my favorite pictures, from a season that saw us win our division by five and a half games. Future big leaguers Jeff Parrett and Tim Crews were two of the notable names on the roster.

games, there would be potluck picnic dinners, which Tim and Lori were big leaders of. Tim pitched really well for us. That was his second year in the California League, and he had some temperamental immaturity problems when things didn't go right earlier in his career. I think married life, being older, and repeating the league made a difference, and he grew up mentally and as a leader. He took his control, which was already pretty good, to another level. It was just a couple of short years after that he was in the big leagues with the Dodgers, and then was traded to the Indians. In spring training 1993, while I was with the Padres, I was coming down for breakfast and heard some of the coaches talking about a tragic boating accident. I almost dropped my tray when they told me that Crews and Steve Olin were killed. It's bad no matter who it is, but I was shocked that it was one of my former players. His life was cut way too short.

At the end of the 1985 season, the Double-A job was open, and they went outside the organization and hired somebody else. I'm the most loyal person that anybody can ever hire. I'm also huge on principle, and I think that loyalty is supposed to be a two-way street. I figured with what I brought to the table as a scout, roving hitting instructor, national cross-checking, and leading three pennant winners, I deserved the Double-A job.

I would have gladly gone back to Stockton for three or four years if I had to wait my turn, but it was different because the job was open. Their answer was that they promoted me every year, and this was the first time that they didn't, but it was one time too many. I quit on the spot without having another job lined up. I hated leaving the Brewers because I knew everybody, I was at home, and my loyalty was there. But that's how big the principle was to me.

Jimmy Russo, the superscout, had taken a liking to me when I was breaking in during the 1970s. We had a drink in his room one night, and he promised me two things. He said, "You'll think I'm an idiot but you'll see I was right when you're my age." One topic was that no matter how good I thought I was, I would be fired during my career, which turned out to be true. The other thing dealt with family life.

Baseball had been in my life ever since I was ten. I had a passion for the game, almost too much so, because when I got married my priorities were way out of line and baseball came ahead of family. I learned the hard way, and I preach to younger people that family should always be number one because they're going to be with you throughout your lifetime.

Jimmy said, "I know you're married and have a couple of kids. I hope you got a great wife that loves and supports your baseball career because if she doesn't, you'll end up getting divorced." This was in 1974, and I had been married for a few years to the girl of my dreams. I asked him why he would say something like that. He described how, if I was any good at this, which he thought I was, all the time I would be spending away from home, or if I got into development, how much time that would take up. Jimmy said, "The more and more you're away from home, there's more and more of the wife being the mother and the father."

In the summer of 1982, the marriage fell apart and she divorced me. I knew I wasn't going to switch careers. I had seen a lot of baseball marriages fall apart because you're either home too much in the winter or away too much during the season. The only positive thing about being divorced was that there was nothing to keep me from going 100 percent into development and managing. My wife was vehemently opposed to the managing part. As a roving instructor, I always had a home base.

I never took the plunge a second time, but it made me a much better dad. From that point on, my life centered on my baseball career and my five kids, with no other distractions.

A few years after the divorce, I, like a lot of single guys managing in the minor leagues, met a gal and started dating her on the few off days you get in baseball. I dated her through the season, but I made it a point to tell her that she should feel free to date other guys because I was just there for the baseball season.

I wasn't looking for a full relationship. I was coming out of the divorce with five kids, and being Catholic and thinking I would be married for life, my philosophy was that if I couldn't make it work with the woman I had five kids with, then it certainly wasn't going to work with somebody else.

I told this woman, and other women I've dated, that I'm the perfect guy to date when she's between relationships because I love movies, I love going out to dinner, I love treating a woman well, the way she should be treated, but emotionally I was unavailable for the long run. I dated her for a year, and in the winter I took her to San Francisco. We ordered wine at some nice Italian restaurant, and she made a comment that she had known both of her husbands for a shorter time that she had known me. I told her that this was not a good subject for us to get on.

She closed her menu and said, "You know what, maybe this is a good time to talk about this."

I said, "If you're going to push this, it's going to ruin the weekend, because one thing about me, like with my players, I always tell it like it is. I pride myself on being honest and not sugarcoating anything. If you push this subject, I'm going to treat you like a player that's on my team but he's not starting and he's coming into the office to ask what his role is, and I'm not going to sugarcoat it."

She said, "Well, maybe I need to hear it because I have a lot of time invested in this."

I said,

> To put it in baseball terms, you're in the starting lineup, for what it's worth. I'm a one woman guy. I'm not dating anybody else or seeing anybody else when I'm on the road. But when I make out my lineup, and I'm not even proud of this, but leading off would have to be my baseball career. That's why I'm divorced in the first place, my priorities were out of whack. In the second spot of the lineup would be my five kids because once my wife divorced me, it made my kids more prominent and more important in my life. I was a guy that took family for granted, but being divorced really thrust them into the spotlight. Batting third in my lineup are my friends. I have the same friends as I did when I was nine. I've just added more and more along the way. My high school friends, my college friends, my pro baseball friends, my country club friends. I have an ever-expanding circle.
>
> I think I take after my mom, being an extrovert. Even when I was happily married, coming off a road trip it was rare for us to go to dinner and for it to be just my wife

and I. One of her criticisms was that although she liked our friends, there were always one or two couples that would go out with us. Even then it was a criticism that I was a friends kind of guy.

Batting cleanup is golf. When we get to five and six, now it becomes almost a toss-up, like a platoon situation. You've been to enough baseball games to know what platooning is.

She said, "Yeah, I've heard some of the wives at the games talk about it, where you have two left fielders and one bats left-handed and one bats right-handed."

I said, "Yeah, exactly. They'll play depending on the pitcher we're facing. The five and six spot is a toss-up between you and fishing. If I haven't been fishing for awhile with the players and they're planning a fishing trip on an off day, I'm with them. But if I haven't seen you for awhile, then you would be five and fishing would be six."

And she actually looked at me and said, "So you're telling me no matter what I do or how our relationship grows, that I don't have any chance to move up in this so-called lineup."

I said, "The first four are just etched in stone. I'm being blatantly honest."

With the time taken up by the games, then instructional league, winter ball, you're never around. A lot of women get to the point where they wonder what the point of being married is when we're apart so much, and they move on. When my wife divorced me, it was the biggest failure of my life. You're talking about a family of seven. I was never a believer in counseling, number one because we weren't making that much money and I didn't think it was affordable. And two, I thought that people should work out their own problems. With life experience, I've since realized there's a place for that.

Not for the right reason, but to try to win her back, I went to a counselor. I met with the counselor for about an hour and a half, and as I was leaving, the guy said, "I don't mean to undermine or diminish the importance of the marriage, but you're a smart guy and I'm used to dealing with people that really have trouble figuring things out. I don't think you need to come back here. But I'm going to tell you one thing about yourself that's kind of ironic. It's very fitting that you happen to be in professional baseball."

I asked what he meant. He said, "The one thing that's crystal clear in this hour and a half is that you are 100 percent a black and white guy, like baseball. Everything with you is win or lose, out or safe, black or white, ball or strike. You don't see any gray areas."

I said, "Well no, I guess I really don't."

He said, "Well, that scares me. I know without asking that when you were a kid, you never stole a candy bar from a store."

I said, "Good God, no. I didn't."

He said, "That's what scares me. Because you're the type of person that could really go ballistic on somebody that stole something from you if you were to catch him in the act, because that's just so foreign to your way of thinking. Most people have stolen something when they were a kid, so as an adult they're able to see the gray areas or cut some slack. So it's funny that you're in a game of absolutes."

That has been part of my temperament. When it goes, it goes all the way.

I'm an only child, and I think when you're an only child you can't help but be narcissistic because everything's about you. Ironically, I ended up as a divorced parent with five kids. Years later, I had my granddaughter Mackenzie, who was four, at my dream house in Palm Springs that I had just bought. I had just bought all the bedding and comforters and everything. And son of a gun if Mackenzie didn't wake up in the morning and take some Hershey bars out of the kitchen while everybody else was in bed. With it being warm, the chocolate melted in her hands and the chocolate was all over the brand new white comforter for the guest room.

My reaction was to have a mini-snap because I had just bought it the day before, and now it's all stained with chocolate. Kristin immediately stripped the bedding and the comforter and put everything in the washing machine. She was crying and said that they would head back after spending the weekend. I was confused because they had just gotten here the night before.

She didn't say it to hurt me, but just telling the truth, Kristin said, "My kids love you and she's only four, it's not like she did it on purpose. I don't want my kids to be afraid of you like we were." And I'm telling you that just stopped me in my tracks. I said, "What does that mean?"

When she calmed down, she said, "Dad, you were the most fun dad we could have ever had and we loved you to death, but we were also afraid of you." I never realized that. I asked her how so. She said, "Your temper wasn't just reserved for umpires. If somebody did something stupid, like this smearing the chocolate, you would just lash out. And to you it was just normal, but to us we were afraid."

I guess I had never looked in the mirror to be aware of that. I thought, "Wow. That's not the type of dad or grandfather that I want to be." At that time, my daughter was 30 and my kids had been raised, and it was what it was. I knew then that I had an opportunity to mend my ways and be a better grandparent than I was as a parent in regards to my temper or understanding that kids will be kids. And I think that's a life lesson that some people never learn.

Some people are so set in their ways, but the feedback that I get from my kids is that I'm way different, in a better way, now than when they were being raised. I'd like to think that old dogs can learn new tricks. That was certainly a valuable life lesson and one that I've never forgotten.

Tigers Years

After splitting from the Brewers, the first phone call I made was to Bill Lajoie, the general manager of the Detroit Tigers. He knew of me because he liked my reports from the scouting bureau. At the time, he was one of the most respected GMs in the game. He was a true, old-fashioned baseball guy. The Tigers had just lost their scouting director, so his interest in me was for my scouting experience rather than my managing.

I turned him down at first because he wanted to hire me on the spot. He called me the next day and said, "Look, you're going to work for the Detroit Tigers. I don't know what kind of manager you are, but I do know what kind of scout you are." Bill told me I could do the scouting on the West Coast and manage the rookie league team in Bristol, and that if I was sincere about managing, I would eventually be managing the Double-A or Triple-A team.

I looked at it as a step backwards for a year in terms of my managing career, but he was going to raise my salary $10,000. Back in the 1980s, you were lucky if you got a $1,500 raise. And $2,000 was huge in those days. To get a $10,000 raise in that era made me feel that he really wanted me to come over there.

For one year, he was going to go without a scouting director. He wanted just three supervisors (East, West and Midwest), and he wanted the three guys working together to make a draft list. I worked with two great guys. One was Bill Schudlich, a longtime Tigers scout, the Midwest supervisor and ultimately the head of the three of us, because somebody had to make the decision. The East Coast guy was Jax Robertson. The three of us got along really well.

I was managing the rookie league team in Bristol in the Appalachian League, where I had started my career with the Brewers. As soon as the season ended, the Tigers created a new position, the field coordinator, who would be in charge of all the minor leagues. On the pecking order, it was going to be above managing Double-A and Triple-A. They wanted me to take that, and that job detailed a nice raise as well. At the time, the only organization with that position was the San Francisco Giants. Jimmy Lefebvre was doing that, so I gave him a call. Jimmy told me that this position would soon be the most important that an organization would have outside of the front office.

The job would be tantamount to being superintendent of a school in the educational system. If an organization had six farm teams and six three-man coaching staffs, you're the one that's hiring those 18 positions and supervising them. The field coordinator is the one who dictates what's going to be taught, how it's going to be taught, and what the atmosphere and discipline will be. Basically, everything that happens between the white lines.

In 1987, Joe McDonald, the Director of Player Development, and I thought that coming out of spring training, we had a very good team in Glens Falls, New York, our Double-A team in the Eastern League. For whatever reason, the thought was that they were underachieving, and my boss fired Tom Burgess, a longtime baseball veteran. They wanted me to take over the team but didn't want me to give up my field coordinating duties. I managed the club for a week or two and then Paul Felix, a player-coach on the team, took over. It was a very interesting team because we did have quite a bit of talent.

There were a number of guys who got prominent executive positions. One was Steve Philips, a left-handed-hitting second baseman, who went on to become General Manager of the Mets. Donny Rowland, a right-handed-hitting second baseman, became the scouting director for the Angels. He had some prominent draft picks in his era, and he took a lot of guys that helped Anaheim win the World Series in 2002.

The most famous player on the 1987 Glens Falls team was John Smoltz, who struggled at the time. Smoltz went 4–10 with a 5.68 ERA that season. I had only been managing the team for a couple of days when I got a phone call from Lajoie saying that we had just made a trade. Smoltz was sent to Atlanta for Doyle Alexander. The Tigers were fighting to win the AL East. Alexander went 9–0 down the stretch and helped Detroit win the division. And Smoltz went on to have a Hall of Fame career.

Smoltz had electric stuff. In a *Baseball America* poll of managers, Smoltz was voted as having the best fastball and best slider in the league and was the best pitching prospect, but in terms of results he was far from the finished product. The Tigers knew what they were giving up. He was our best pitching prospect, but that's what it took to get a pitcher of Doyle's caliber. There was a decision to give up the long run for the short run. Not that anybody thought he'd be a Hall of Famer, but we all thought he'd be a very good number one or number two starter.

At Glens Falls, the raw essentials were there. He had an ideal pitchers' body, and he was young, driven, and competitive. And of course he had major league stuff. What he didn't have was command of his pitches. Not only was his walk ratio high for a starting pitcher, but a high walk ratio indicates that he's going to be behind in the count. Smoltz's pitch per inning numbers were higher than they should've been, as was his ERA, because of the lack of command of his pitches. Along with that, his confidence was not good.

When I was in the big leagues with the Cubs, I asked Smoltz what had transpired, just for my own info. He told me that when he went to the Instructional League with Atlanta, they knew what they were getting stuff-wise, but the Braves were one of the first teams to utilize a mental skills coach, which every team uses now. They had John work with a sports psychologist. All of those sports psychologists are programmed to retrain an athlete's mind to see that the glass is half-full rather than half-empty, to visualize success and throwing the ball where you want it, rather than "Oh Gosh, I'm probably going to walk this guy again."

John told me that the mental outlook and the training that he got helped him immensely. It was very soon after the trade that he made it to the big leagues with Atlanta. With us, he hadn't been successful in Double-A, let alone getting to Triple-A. The rest is history. He won over 200 games as a starter, and after having a series of operations he came back as a dominant closer and had over 150 saves. John had a brilliant career and was a great guy. In the Instructional League, we would play golf on off-days, and the coaches would play behind Smoltz and his buddy Kevin Ritz. Ritz was on the 1987 Glens Falls team and later pitched for the expansion Rockies in 1993. Smoltz was a hell of a golfer too.

Another interesting player on that team, and one of my favorites because of a relationship that we had on and off the field, was Chris Hoiles. Chris had a quiet confidence about him. He was mature. He was kind of a born leader, and it helped to have somebody of his stature and temperament on that club. And he performed very well.

After managing him for a season, I took him to the Instructional League after I became the field coordinator, and I knew in my mind that we would push him to get closer to the big leagues because he was a college guy. Chris basically skipped all of A-ball. He went from rookie league to Double-A. When I would go into Glens Falls as the field coordinator, oftentimes after a day game we would jump in a canoe and go fishing for smallmouth bass before dark. Chris knew some people who lived on a lake outside of town, and they would let us use their canoe. We had a bond away from the ballpark, whether it was fishing or golfing.

There was a meeting with all the managers, coaches and rovers discussing players, and I was surprised that out of 20 people in the room, I was the only one that felt that Chris Hoiles was a major-league prospect.

Bill Lajoie, whom I have the utmost respect for, said, "Tom, you're too close to him. You've managed him in the rookie league and the Double-A level. You've had him in two instructional leagues and I know you guys fish and play golf together. You're looking at him like a parent looking at a son."

I said,

> All of that is true, but I disagree because I scouted for ten years. I'm the first to admit that his arm is not what you're looking for in an everyday catcher in the big leagues. If we play a team that's a running club, he might have to DH or play first base. But he's an intelligent guy that calls a good game and gives a good target. Although he's going to have his strikeouts here and there, this guy has big league power, and if he gets one hit in a game it always comes with a guy at second base to drive in a run. He's a run producer. I honestly see this guy hitting fifth in our lineup in the big leagues, hitting above .270, hitting 20 home runs and driving in 90.

I played Chris a lot at first base in Bristol because our first round pick, Phil Clark, was a catcher. Phil made it to the big leagues, as did our second round pick, Milton Cuyler. During the 1989 season, Bill Lajoie called me before the deadline and said, "We just made a trade. I don't want you saying anything negative if you're asked about this." I asked who we gave up, and he told me that Chris Hoiles had been traded. I was crushed.

You're wrong a lot in this business, and if 19 people disagree with me, then they disagree with me, but I had the courage of my convictions to know what I believed, based on my experience and Hoiles' makeup, to know what I felt he could do. We traded Chris to the Orioles for an aging Fred Lynn. Fred was a great player but was 37 years old at the time. Hoiles did well in the Orioles organization and went to the majors. In 1993, Chris hit 29 homers. He became viable for them for almost a decade. I felt vindicated and very happy for Chris because we were kind of tied at the hip. My prediction panned out. I just wish that those years had been with Detroit rather than Baltimore.

We had Doug Strange, a switch-hitting third baseman. What kept him from being more than a utility player was the fact that he didn't hit for enough power for a third baseman. He had doubles power. He was a great fielding third baseman with a bazooka for an arm. My first game as a manager was against Mark Grace's Vermont Cubs. Strange hit a homer in the bottom of the eighth and we won, 3–2. Strange later became assistant to the general manager in Pittsburgh.

Jeff Jones was on the Glens Falls team and was later the pitching coach on the Toledo Triple-A team I managed in 1990. Jones had a long career as the Tigers' Triple-A pitching coach and the major league bullpen coach, and now is the major league pitching coach.

We went on a nice run. A team that had underachieved ended up playing to its potential. Tom Burgess had been like a grandfather figure. I was young and aggressive. Tom was a terrific baseball guy and a good friend. I know the whole team was shocked when he was let go. The team started to play better after the transition.

As the field coordinator, I went to see Fayetteville play the final four games of the season against the Gastonia Rangers, a team that finished 58–82. I second-guessed myself for going when I saw Gastonia's record. I watched the games and was unbelievably impressed with Wilson Alvarez, a left-handed pitcher for the Rangers who went on to throw a no-hitter in the big leagues and have a successful career. They had Terry Mathews, a right-hander with a real good arm. I was also watching Juan Gonzalez in right field and Sammy Sosa in center, and seeing just the athleticism and the physical tools they possessed. There were other young guys like catcher Bill Haselman, Dean Palmer at third and Rey Sanchez in the middle of the infield. Ten players from that team went to the majors. My experience has been that on a normal minor league roster of 25 players, you'll generally see three off any given team that end up playing in the big leagues. But to have ten off a team with such a horrible record just goes to show you how player development goes, and from early to late you never know what you're going to turn up with.

While I was field coordinator, the 1988 Toledo team had Billy Beane and Bill Bean on the team. We referred to them as Big and Little. Billy Beane, the Oakland GM, was 6'4", 215 pounds, and Bill Bean, MLB's first Ambassador for Inclusion, was 6', 175 pounds. Beane was right-handed and Bean was left-handed. Beane played right field and Bean played center. It was funny having both of them.

In 1990, the Toledo manager was a good friend of mine, John Wockenfuss, an ex-Tiger and a guy who taught me how to bass fish. I still have a ten-and-a-half-pound large-mouth bass mounted on my wall at home.

I caught it the first time that John took me to fish in one of phosphate pits in Lakeland. He told me that I basically made a hole-in-one in bass fishing and that I would never catch one that big again.

He was a famous ex-Tigers catcher and first baseman who was known for his unorthodox batting stance. John came back into baseball, and we groomed him as a manager. He did a good job for us but for whatever reason at the Triple-A level, Joe McDonald called me less than a full month into the season. He told me that he knew John and I were good friends, but he was not calling to ask my input, he had made the decision to let Wockenfuss go. He didn't tell me why, I guess out of respect for my friendship with him. He wanted me to take over the Triple-A team.

We had Phil Clark and Milt Cuyler from my Bristol days. We had Scott Aldred, a former Michigan product and a number one pick. Aldred at the Triple-A level was like Smoltz at the Double-A level. Scott was 6–15 with an ERA just under five, but was third in the league in strikeouts. The stuff was there, you knew he would pitch in the big leagues, but the command wasn't there yet. The strikeouts reflected what kind of stuff he had, but the won-lost record and the walks showed why he was still in Triple-A.

Travis Fryman, our first-round pick from 1987, was the shortstop on Toledo. Now that I'm much older and have spent most of my life in minor league development, I find it very strange that Fryman had played every inning of every game that he had ever played at shortstop, but when he went to the majors, he played third base. In 1990, Alan Trammell was an All-Star shortstop, so when Travis was in the big leagues he played his entire career at third base. Looking back on my time as the Triple-A manager, it's very strange that nobody called me and told me to start playing Fryman at third base in some games. Granted, they're both on the left side of the diamond, but third base is so much more of a reaction position. It's tough enough to break into the big leagues, let alone doing it at a position you never played before.

At the All-Star break, I took Travis and Steve Searcy, and their girlfriends, to dinner. Searcy was a left-hander with a nasty slider. I was congratulating them because they were both going to the big leagues. It's always a thrill when you tell a youngster for the first time that he's going to the show. Searcy, for whatever reason, was one of those 4-A players. He could do real well in the minors, but it just didn't happen at the big league level, and I'm perplexed as to why.

Another guy from that I team that I have fond memories of is Scott Livingstone, our third baseman. He was a left-handed hitter who was a high draft pick out of Texas A&M. He was 6'1", 180 pounds. He hit a lot of home runs with an aluminum bat but when he switched to a wooden bat, he really struggled, in part because of an uppercut swing that had a lot of holes in it. He was a dead pull hitter.

When you get high school or college kids out of the draft, you give them an opportunity to show what they did to get themselves drafted. I think it's a huge mistake to jump in and make changes right away because if the player does not do well, then he has an alibi for failure. There's more than one way to skin a cat. There have been a lot of successful people in the big leagues with different batting stances. When you have a player who is trying to get acclimated to pro ball, you're looking for a chance for the player to be himself. And you're showing confidence in the scout in your organization who signed this guy and gave him some money.

Livingstone and I developed a very good bond. The good thing about working with a struggling player is that you've got a more receptive student when he has failed and is looking for help. Even coming out of college, Scott was immature. He was a helmet thrower. You try to keep an even keel but because of his competitiveness and frustration level, his attitude would impact proceeding at-bats. The power was non-existent although, to his credit, he played a good third base.

When the season ended, we took him to Instructional League, and Scott was more than eager to listen and make some adjustments. The adjustment to pro ball was much more difficult than he thought it would be. If they see you're a pull hitter, they're going to pitch you in and let you pull it foul. Then they'll pitch you away and get you out when you roll over and keep grounding the ball to the first or second baseman. The left side of the diamond was completely foreign to him. We did some short batting practice drills in the cage where my goal was to get Scott to wait on the ball longer, lean into it with his right shoulder, and drive it to the opposite field.

We would spend countless reps trying to get him to hit the ball the other way with backspin. To his credit, not only did he have a good instructional league, he found a way to neutralize the pitchers who were trying to get him out. The Tigers felt that he actually became too opposite-field-conscious, but he did make it to the majors as a backup to Fryman to third. He hit .310, but what kept him from being an everyday player was that he was a third baseman who hit for average and had a good on-base percentage but he didn't have power. I did feel proud that through his trust factor in me, the drills, and what I had to say, he became a better hitter.

Torey Lovullo was a second baseman on the team. He could hit anybody's fastball and had limited range. God didn't give him any speed. If Torey hit the ball on the ground, it was going to be a double play. He gave max effort all the time and went on to have a lengthy and successful coaching career. He took over the Red Sox as interim manager in 2015 when John Farrell left because of a health issue. A couple of teams wanted to interview him, but the Red Sox wouldn't give them permission. He has since become the manager of the Diamondbacks and led the team to the 2017 playoffs.

Steve Lombardozzi, one of the heroes for the Twins in the 1987 World Series, was playing for Toledo. He loved baseball and was at the end of his career. He has a son in the big leagues now. Steve was a charismatic guy who played hard. He had been there and done it and wanted to get back. He was content playing Triple-A, but knew that if somebody got hurt in the big leagues he might go up for two weeks. That didn't happen, and he never made it back. However, Steve was a great guy and a consummate number two hitter. He knew how the game should be played.

Another World Series champion we had was John Shelby, a member of the 1983 Orioles and 1988 Dodgers. What an unbelievably class guy he was. I can't say enough good things about him. When I think of John, the first word that comes into my mind is "professionalism." Professionalism in every way, on and off the field. He was totally businesslike and totally about the team. John was called up and played with the Tigers. He's gone on to have a long coaching career.

Sparky Anderson, the Tigers manager at the time, always favored veterans. He was tough on youngsters. Where a lot of managers would gradually break a guy in, Sparky was more about letting them sink or swim, which may not be a bad idea. I always tried to pick a spot, when a young pitcher came up, to put him in a multiple-run-lead game so that his confidence won't be dealt a blow. His performance can't really impact the outcome of the game, but let him get his feet wet and get his jitters out of the way.

When I came to the Tigers' organization, I knew Doug Baker, a scrappy second baseman from southern California. He had gone to Valley College and Arizona State. A journeyman type of guy, Doug came up through the Tigers' farm system and ended up in the majors. Sparky put him in a game and wanted Doug to get a sac bunt down, but Baker couldn't execute. Doug was sent back to the minors the next day. Sparky's message was, "with your skill set getting a sac bunt down is something you have to do." The big leagues is not a "try" league. It's a "can do" league. All the trying is done in the minors, and when you come to the majors, you get it done or else we find someone else who can.

With the Detroit organization in the late 1980s, I worked with up-and-comers like John Smoltz and Travis Fryman as well as veterans John Shelby, Steve Lombardozzi and Jody Davis.

That idea struck me as harsh when I first heard it, but as a development guy I have to say that Sparky's right. And I used that message over the years to the players. The minor leagues can be a real drudgery because it's the same thing every day, just in a different city. It's 140 games. The batting practice is done the same way: two sac bunts, visualizing a hit-and-run, a man on second and getting him over, a ground ball to score a run with the infield back, then with the infield in you look for a ball that you can elevate and drive to the outfield, and sometimes a squeeze, and then you take your seven swings. And that can get very monotonous. Sometimes players may just go through the motions, getting the execution stuff out of the way so they can take their swings. We have to remind them that although they may not get a bunt situation or a hit-and-run situation for a week, you have an opportunity to practice it each and every day in batting practice, and you had best find a way to maintain your mental focus and get it done.

I try to impress on these guys that it's a different beast in the majors. While managing the Brooklyn Cyclones, I told Michael Conforto, "At Brooklyn, at Binghamton, at St. Lucie, you're going to be hitting third. But when you get to New York, shocker, you might be hitting sixth or seventh. That makes it a whole different ballgame. If the Mets are in a scoreless tie in the fifth inning and they have a runner or two on, you might be asked to bunt, which may not happen in the minor leagues." Even if they think your speech doesn't relate to them, it will take them time to get acclimated. Conforto should be in the middle of the lineup for 10–15 years.

Later in the 1990 season, we acquired Jody Davis, who had been on the 1984 Cubs' playoff team. Jody loved hunting and fishing. He was in the twilight of his career and wanted to get back to the big leagues, but he also wanted to retire and was smart enough to know that the demands of the catching position had taken its toll. That season was the last for Jody in pro baseball.

Our left fielder was Shawn Hare, a gifted player. He was a middle-round draft pick and could put the bat on the ball, always hit the ball where it was pitched. He didn't have enough speed or power to be the everyday guy, but had enough of both to make the majors.

There was also a pitcher named Shawn Holman. I've often wondered over the years why he didn't have a longer career or more success in the big leagues. He had something you can't teach. He was a right-handed pitcher with a slightly better than average fastball but with unbelievable movement to it. He could throw a power sinker that had so much life to it that it was tough for him to harness it in the strike zone. He'd have outings where you'd bring him out of the bullpen and the hitters would have no chance, and then there would be times where he'd be victimized by his own command. Stuff-wise, Holman was comparable to Jason Grimsley, who I had in Kansas City. Both of them had real flush movement on their power sinkers. The difference was that Grimsley got a lot of time in the big leagues and Holman had just a little.

Rich Rowland was like a lumberjack. Rich was from some part of Northern California where baseball isn't big but cutting down trees is. He almost escaped the draft. I give credit to the scout who signed him. Rich was strong like an ox and had one asset: raw strength. He had incredible determination, took what the coaches gave him and learned to become a fairly decent catcher. He had the arm strength so he quickened his release. Rich became a catcher and designated hitter for the Red Sox. Rich deserves a lot of credit for getting to the majors with his limited baseball background. He would've been successful in any business that he had gone into because of his personality and his work ethic.

LaVel Freeman, one of my favorite guys from my Brewers days, played for me in Toledo. He was at the end of his career and we needed help in the outfield, so the Tigers acquired him. I was glad to be reunited with him, but by 1990 he was older and wasn't as hungry as he was before. His skill set was a shell of what it was in Paintsville and Beloit.

The Mud Hens finished 58–86. To that point in my career, I had never had a team that hadn't won, let alone finish under .500, and it was a struggle. If I could go back and do anything over, it would be that season. The first two and a half months were like all the other teams I had. It was totally positive and true to my philosophy of positive, patient, and persistent. Over the last six weeks, never having experienced not winning as a manager, my frustration level and ego got involved. I took the losses more and more personally, and I wasn't a fun guy to be around.

Later on, when I worked with Jim Riggleman on the Cubs and we were losing in 1999, Jim stayed as strong as the Rock of Gibraltar. Players could depend on that same guy all the time, which I greatly admired. I didn't handle losing in Toledo well at all. The last month and a half was not fun for me or the guys on the team, because I wasn't a fun guy to be around. My psychology was well, I'm in a bad mood and that will make them play better because nobody likes to lose.

I was fired after the season. With the shortcomings and my attitude, I deserved to be fired. That's the only time in my career that I deserved it. It turned out to be a plus.

The team was making changes. Former Michigan football coach Bo Schembechler was the President of the Tigers. The Tigers' owner, Tom Monaghan, was a Michigan graduate, idolized Bo and brought him in. Unfortunately, Bo didn't know anything about baseball. One day that year, Bo spent time with me, and I was talking about development and the classes of minor league baseball while we watched a rookie ball game. One of our young outfielders overthrew the cutoff man and the batter/runner took second base.

Bo looked at me and asked, "So what happens when a guy makes a mistake like that?"

I said, "Well, when this inning ends and the team comes off the field, you'll see one of the coaches go up and address the guy and tell him if he misses the cutoff guy, he should miss low to freeze the batter/runner and keep the double play in order."

Bo said, "That's it? All they're going to do is talk to him?"

I said, "Well, yeah."

Bo said, "Well, this sport has a lot of changing to do. In my business, one of the coaches should walk up to that young man and bust a clipboard over his head to get his attention. That way, we'll be sure that it won't happen again."

I knew right there and then that this wasn't going to work. In the era of Bo and Woody Hayes, it was about being tougher with kids and more demanding. Society and sports have changed since then. But when he made that statement, whether it was in jest or in reality, I realized that this Hall of Fame football coach didn't know anything about baseball. He was out of his element, which I would be if someone put me in charge of a football team.

Puerto Rico

Some of the clips of our team winning the final game of the Puerto Rican championship are on YouTube, and I watched some videos before working on this. It's pretty amazing. It's like watching a European soccer match with the capacity crowds. At the one I just watched, from 1998, our fans were literally on the field while the game was still being played. They were in foul territory, but you could see that the police officers just couldn't hold them back. They came crawling out of the stands with two outs to go because we were winning, 11–3.

You can get a feel for the unbelievable passion and intensity of Puerto Rican fans. My pitching coach, Guy Hansen, and I kept getting closer to the plate because we wanted to get out in front of the fans so we could watch the game.

During the 1988 season, while I was the field coordinator with the Tigers, one of our coaches was Juan Lopez. Juan had played for me years earlier when I was with the Brewers. Lopez was a good-fielding infielder who had played many, many years in Puerto Rico, and had been a coach in Mayaguez. Mayaguez had won more championships than any other team in league history and had won the year before under Jim Riggleman. Riggleman was made farm director of the St. Louis Cardinals, which was a year-round job.

Luis Gomez was looking for a manager, and Lopez recommended me, telling them I was bilingual, that I had managed everywhere from rookie league to Double-A, had been a field coordinator, really knew the game, and handled players well.

The major league All-Star Game was in Cincinnati in July 1988, and Luis asked me if I would fly in and interview for the job. Our interview, which extended through lunch, became intense. I think he could feel my passion, and his passion is off the charts. He had owned the club for ten years at that point and was a very successful businessman who was unbelievably passionate about baseball and very thorough. He not only had plans for his team, but he had contingency plans in the event that someone got hurt. He had a backup list of Americans he would call to fill in on his roster.

I was impressed, and I was shocked that by the end of the lunch he asked me, if he cancelled the rest of his interviews, whether I was prepared to sign a contract right then and there to manage the club, which I did. My only reservation was that my son was going into his senior year of high school, while my daughters were younger and living with their mom. But having aspirations to manage in the big leagues, I figured it was too good an opportunity to turn down. I would enhance my career and make some more money.

I went down in October 1988, and Gomez had put together a team which was my first opportunity to manage a club of major leaguers. Most of the guys on the team had already been in the big leagues. Three of the guys that hadn't made it yet were Ken Caminiti, our third baseman, Steve Finley, our center fielder, and Jeff Brantley, a relief pitcher.

We lost on Opening Night in Arecibo, and then we set a record winning streak with 14 wins in a row. As I mentioned in the scouting section, Caminiti had one of the best makeups of any player I had the opportunity to manage. He was a promising prospect for the Astros at that time. When we tied the streak, we were in Ponce, and the game ended with us hanging on by one run in the ninth, and they had the tying and winning runs on second and third with two outs. Somebody hit a laser down the third base line and Caminiti dove, back-handed it, got up and threw a rocket across the diamond for the game-ending out. He had a bazooka. I almost had tears in my eyes, it was so exciting to watch a guy just totally lay out. He was all about team, all about winning at any cost.

That included when it meant breaking up a double play. There was a game that year where Caminiti took out a guy on a double play (he would've been out under the new slide rule) that would've ended the game, but instead gave us one more out. Ricky Jordan, who was a big, power-hitting first baseman with the Phillies, came up and hit one out. In a team meeting, I praised Caminiti and team baseball because what he did never showed up in the box score, but that's the type of unsung thing that wins games. When you get everyone caught up in the team aspect of the game, it makes everybody better.

When we broke the streak, it was a big TV game. Puerto Rico used to have a game of the week on Sunday afternoon. We were on the verge of breaking the record, and Caminiti showed up and was vomiting in the clubhouse. The trainer told me that he wanted to send Ken home, and I agreed. Ken was in my office and practically dry-heaving but said, "We have a chance to break the record today and I want to be a part of it."

I said, "No. I'd rather lose a battle and win the war. I'd rather have you miss one day than have this thing drag on." In Puerto Rico, Mondays were off days, so he'd have two days to rest up.

We sent him home, and little did I know he was watching the game on TV. Ken was newly married, and he and his wife lived in the same building that I did. We fell behind but made a nice comeback. I came in from coaching third in the late innings, and the trainer said, "Caminiti wanted to tell me to tell you he's feeling better and he drove back here to the park and he's getting dressed if you need him."

It's winter ball. This is where Americans further their careers and experience the Caribbean with their girlfriends or wives. But here's a guy that's sick and already been sent home, now coming back to the ballpark to see if there's any way to help his teammates, and lo and behold if we didn't rally in the eighth inning. With a runner on third and one out, I pinch-hit him, and he drove one to the track in center field to drive in the winning run, and then he went in defensively at third base and started a game-ending double play.

He was a four-tool player. He had okay speed but everything else was a plus. He could hit, he had power, he was a switch-hitter, he was a terrific fielder, and he had a bazooka for an arm. At the time, working for the Tigers, we needed a third baseman, and I was raving to our people in Detroit about his abilities. I think Houston knew what they had because they didn't consider trading him. Eventually he was in a multi-player trade with the Padres, went on to win the NL MVP Award in 1996, and helped the Padres get to the World Series in 1998.

Ken wasn't the only pro in Puerto Rico. We had three major league catchers. We had Chris Hoiles, who, like Caminiti, wasn't in the big leagues yet but became a pro. I brought him down from Detroit. Kirt Manwaring, who was already catching in the big leagues with the Giants, was in Mayaguez. And we had Tom Pagnozzi, who was the everyday catcher for the Cardinals. Ricky Jordan was at first base. Al Newman, a utility infielder with the Twins, was our second baseman and captain. Luis Rivera, who had already played in the majors with Montreal and Boston, was our shortstop. In left field we had John Cangelosi, Thomas Howard and Kenny Gerhart, all of whom played in the big leagues. Steve Finley, a future teammate of Caminiti's on the 1998 Padres, was in center. He was still in the Orioles system and hadn't been to the big leagues yet, but he went on to have an outstanding big league career with over 300 homers and 300 stolen bases. Ronnie Jones, already with the Phillies, was our right fielder. Luis Quiñones was our utility infielder and a utility infielder with the Reds. We had a major leaguer at every position except Caminiti and Finley. And they both surfaced in the big leagues in 1989.

Future All-Star pitcher and announcer Jeff Brantley was on the team. Brantley was a teammate of Will Clark and Rafael Palmeiro at Mississippi State during their college days. Brantley was drafted and signed by the Giants and pitched against me in the California League. He was a starter in college and pro ball. He was one of those 5'11", 190-pound, strong, stout pitchers, but not your classic 6'4", 225.

Brantley was an unbelievable competitor. When I evaluate players as a manager, I ask myself if I want this guy playing for me or against me, and I did not like Brantley playing against me in a championship series with Fresno back in 1985. He was so tenacious and such a winner that you couldn't help but like him. But I think he got lost in the Giants' organization because he didn't have the classic pitcher's body. His career stagnated to the point where he was very frustrated.

Jeff was on Riggleman's title team as a starter, but when he came back for the winter of 1988–1989 we didn't have a closer. Luis Gomez, Mark Riggins, our pitching coach who held the same job in the Cardinals' system, and I felt that Brantley had the perfect makeup and stuff to be a closer. The only thing that was going to be a question was his resiliency.

I had discussions with him about how he had been a starter his whole life. I said, "Jeff, I liked you as a starter too, but it hasn't got you where you want to get to. Usually the quickest way to get to the big leagues is out of the bullpen." He not only gave it a shot, but was outstanding from day one. The resiliency was not an issue, and if anything, his velocity got better because he came in knowing he only had to get three or four outs. He had such a great winter for us and was instrumental in us winning a championship. At that time, Sparky's closers in Detroit were Aurelio Lopez and Willie Hernandez, pitchers who were well into their 30s. I was pushing for Brantley to get with the Tigers. Bill Lajoie sent Joe Klein, his top assistant and former GM of the Rangers, to scout Caminiti and Brantley. When Joe came down, he liked both guys.

Houston wasn't letting go of Caminiti, but Brantley wasn't going anywhere in the Giants' system, so we really thought we could get him. We made an attempt to trade for Brantley, and the surprising thing was that the Giants didn't even send anyone to Puerto Rico to watch Brantley, one of their own guys, pitch. But because of the success he was having statistically, which they saw, and because of our interest, they told Brantley and his agent that they were going to bring him into camp as a non-roster guy.

I remember Brantley being pissed one day at the ballpark because he thought he would have an opportunity in Detroit, and he knew I was pushing for the trade. He said, "Dammit, if they don't have any interest in me then why aren't they letting me go?"

I said, "Jeff, this is nothing but good for you. There's nothing for you to get upset about. You can be frustrated, but let's understand that the success you're having means they are going to bring you to camp, and you're going to get a chance to show what you're doing down here in a different role. And if they still don't recognize it and you're still not in their plans, we're still going to have interest in Detroit. So this is almost a no-lose situation for you."

Brantley not only went to camp and made the Giants club that year, but he made the All-Star team. I think it's a testament to winter ball in general, where guys can go down and improve or take their game to another level, or in his case go into a different role and improve his sharpness. Brantley always had the stuff. I think it got better because it became a sprint and not a marathon in that role. A couple of years later, Brantley was traded over to Cincinnati, where he spent the bulk of his career. He was a real bulldog, and he was very instrumental in the success we had.

At that time, it was a 60-game winter schedule, and the top four teams played an 18-game round-robin. Then it was a best-of-seven final, in which we played our perennial rival, San Juan. We won in five games.

The last highlight of that year was that Game Five was played in Mayaguez in front of a standing room only crowd. A left-handed-hitting first baseman/outfielder named Keith Hughes, who was a good Triple-A player who got some time with the Yankees, hit a grand slam off lefty Ed Olwine in the bottom of the ninth for a walk-off championship home run in my first year in winter league. That was going to be tough to match.

That catapulted us into the Caribbean World Series. For those who aren't aware, the major league seasons in Latin America occur during our winter months. That's Mexico, the Dominican Republic, Puerto Rico and Venezuela. At the end of each of those respective seasons, there's a Caribbean World Series in the first week of February, which pits those four winners in a very festive atmosphere. That year it was in Mazatlán, Mexico.

Our club played great down in Mazatlán, and in the final game we took a 2–0 lead into the ninth. Luis Aquino, a big league pitcher, pitched a masterpiece. And it's the only time I remember Caminiti making an error the whole year. He probably made others, but I don't remember it. He got a two-out ground ball in the ninth but almost had too much time to think and threw it over the first baseman's head. Phil Stevenson, a left-handed hitter in the Padres' organization who was an All-American at Wichita State, hit a two-run homer with two outs to tie the game. We had an opportunity to win it in 11 when Orlando Merced, who had a long career with the Pirates, came up with a runner at third and one out. He was a switch-hitter and was much better from the left side, but was hitting righty. He bunted through a squeeze, we missed our opportunity to score, and then Stevenson hit a three-run home run homer in the 13th to beat us, 5–2, and that's how our season ended.

It was a great experience and a great season right up until the last inning of the last game.

I didn't go back in 1989–1990 but I did go back in 1990–1991, and when I got there, a lot of Mayaguez's native players who had been playing in the big leagues were not playing any more. We were picked to finish last by the media. There was one article that said that after coming down my first year and winning a championship, I would get my comeuppance because now I didn't have the caliber of players I had before.

When we started to practice, I thought that we had the makings of a pretty good club even though there were no stars. We had traded Luis Rivera, who had been the shortstop when I was there. My owner, Ivan Mendez, told me that he was trying to put together a trade for a shortstop or to get an American shortstop. On the first day, I was hitting ground balls to a 19-year-old Puerto Rican shortstop named Wilfredo Cordero. After practice, I told the owner not to worry about getting a shortstop because I liked the one that we had.

I was always big on development although people in Puerto Rico weren't into that. They were into winning. But Cordero had such athletic ability. I often told the press down there that trying to sneak a fastball past Wil Cordero was like trying to sneak the sun past a rooster. There was no chance of that happening. He had a lightning-quick bat. Cordero played Double-A with the Expos, made the big leagues a year later and eventually became an All-Star. Unfortunately, later in his career he became one of the first guys to have publicized domestic violence problems, which really hurt his career with the Red Sox.

In 1990, we didn't have superstars but we had a good team of guys who played together as a group. I had a lot of core players from my first year. We had a saying in the clubhouse, "Nunca dice muere," which means

"Never Say Die." We adopted a philosophy that as long as we had an out left, we believed that we were always on the verge of a comeback. We won't lose. Sometimes we'll just run out of innings or outs. That's not to say it always happens, but when you get your team to buy into that type of attitude, it lends itself to improbable comebacks because you're always expecting it.

The game that stands out from that year came against San Juan, our rival. They scored nine runs in the first inning in a game at Mayaguez. We went through three pitchers in the top of the first. Our pitching coach was Dick Egan, who was a bullpen coach with the Texas Rangers. Dick stood in the dugout and challenged the team. He said, "I want to know if there's even one guy in this dugout who doesn't think we're still in this game." The character of our team was one to keep coming back, and Dick just wanted to echo that loud and clear. You don't want to be down 9–0, but if you are, it's better to be down in the first inning where you have nine innings to come back.

My first baseman was Rod Brewer, and I credit the owner for bringing him down. You're allowed a certain number of American imports to fill out your team, and we needed a first baseman. Ivan Mendez brought down this left-handed-hitting minor leaguer from the Cardinals. Rod was a journeyman kind of guy but a real student of the game, and I liked the way he played the game. I just didn't like the fact that his swing was too long. Brewer would come out early every day, and we would work on a drill to shorten his stroke. I'd have him hit a bat's length away from the cage so that if his swing was too long, he would hit the netted cage with it. I would throw short-pitch BP to him to shorten his swing. Rod told me that Dal Maxvill, the GM of the Cardinals, and Ted Simmons, the farm director, were coming down to Puerto Rico to watch some of their players, and they were at this particular game.

Rod had been working his butt off on shortening his stroke and was real gifted defensively. Rod hit a homer as we inched closer and closer. When I went out to coach third in the sixth inning, Carlos Baerga said, "What is it with your team? Against anybody else this game would've been over in the first inning. I just have this uncomfortable feeling that you guys keep coming back. This game isn't over."

I said, "Carlos, this game is far from over."

We were down by three runs in the bottom of the ninth, and son of a gun if Brewer didn't come up with the bases loaded and two outs. Now I'm real big on how hitters take pitches. I've always believed that a good swing is like a chain of dominoes. If you set them up the right way and knock one over, they all fall over. I've always preached that if they take a pitch that they don't like, their lead side, meaning their front shoulder, should be closed, with their hands back and their weight back. Those are three checkpoints for me. Lead side in, hands back, weight back.

Brewer took the first two pitches for balls and was in perfect hitting position. I told the runner at third, "If this guy throws him a strike, this ball is going to go out of here like a laser." Sure enough, Brewer hit one that looked like a three-wood leaving the ballpark to straightaway right field. That game reflected that team. We had a bunch of grinders and guys who were fighting their way to the big leagues and were determined to succeed.

Roberto Hernandez was a starter who went on to become a 40-save closer. Wil Cordero was in Double-A, but went on to become an All-Star. Brewer got a little time in the majors but was a solid Triple-A player. José Valentín went on to have a long career in the big leagues but was in Triple-A at the time. Pedro Muñoz was an outfielder with the Twins. It was a fun team to manage, and it was the only one of my clubs during my tenure in Puerto Rico where there was no pressure, because we had been picked to finish last.

We finished second, and the top four teams went to the playoffs. We ended up with the best record in the round-robin, which meant we got home-field in the finals. We played Santurce in the finals and lost, five games to three. We lost Game Eight in ten innings but I can't tell you how proud I was of that team. It was a team of non-stars but a real team in the true sense of the word.

Now I had managed in Puerto Rico twice, had won a championship and gotten to the finals. Although the owner wanted me and Dick Egan back, I had teenage kids in California. I wanted to spend time with them and go golfing. And Dick got married for a second time. I had no intentions of going back, and I didn't for several years.

But in 1993–1994, Mayaguez finished last for the only time in their illustrious history. Ivan Mendez called me in June, while I was working as field coordinator for the Padres, to come back and manage. I was flattered, I thanked him, but I had no intention. He called me in July, and I was flattered but I had no intention. When he called in August, the money was so good and for him to call me a third time, I realized how much he wanted me. My closest friend in baseball at the time was Guy Hansen, who was also my golf partner. Guy and I would take vacations to Hawaii at the end of the season. He was never able to go with me on my prior trips to Puerto Rico. He told me that if I went back down there, he would join me and we could play our golf in Puerto Rico.

I agreed to go in 1994–1995, and I noticed from day one that the baseball fans knew my name in every park that we went to. The people there are so passionate about baseball, and they know so much about it. Between the 1990–1991 season, when we surprised people and made it to the finals, and the style of play that we had, the Rocky Balboa knocked down but not out, I think the people on the island really liked our style of play.

Being the leader of it, I noticed I was being asked to sign baseballs, programs and ticket stubs in opposing ballparks for the first time. I told people that I considered Mayaguez and Puerto Rico to be my second home. Respect goes both ways. When people see that you like their country, and they saw that I was back for a third time, they thought of me not only as a baseball man but as someone who really liked the country.

As part of my contract, I would get a car and a place to stay. One year I told them I wanted to live in Rincón, about 20 minutes outside Mayaguez, which is a destination on the world surf tour. My daughter, Kristin, flew down by herself to see me one year, and I told her to order a pizza for us while I was in the shower. She called Domino's but they only delivered in Mayaguez. She said her name was Kristin Gamboa, and the owner asked if she was Tom Gamboa's daughter. She said yes, and the guy told her that they'd have the pizza in 30 minutes. He drove it to us himself.

You had notoriety in Puerto Rico if you were winning in baseball. In the old days, the priority list for Puerto Ricans would be their religion, family and baseball, and not necessarily in that order.

In San Juan, there's a huge mall across the street from the ballpark. One Christmas, I had all five of my kids down, and we were walking through the mall where there was a little kiosk with sports collectibles. One of my daughters saw my card in the window, and it was like, "Oh my God, dad, there's your card." Obviously, that would be good for anybody's ego until we walked into the store and saw that my card was selling for 25 cents. It was very humbling.

I knew the 1994–1995 team was one to be reckoned with before the first pitch was thrown. Guy Hansen had scouted for many years, and at that time he was the major league pitching coach with the Royals. We were allowed to pick eight or nine Americans, and I trusted Guy's judgment so he brought down some players from Kansas City. I was with the Padres, and I brought down Brian Johnson, a minor league catcher we had acquired from the Yankees and who went on to have some productive years with the Giants. I brought down Doug Brocail, a Triple-A pitcher in the Padres' system who later was involved in a big trade to Houston which brought back Ken Caminiti. Brocail went 10–1 for us in Puerto Rico, and that season was what got him on Houston's radar.

Guy brought down Chris Haney, a left-handed pitcher, who went 10–0. We had a dynamic 1–2 punch. Brian Johnson was calling the games and had a real productive year at the plate. Brian felt that year was instrumental in getting him over the hump and into the majors. Guy also brought down Sal Fasano, a catcher. Sal was a terrific receiver but was overmatched with the bat, and we ended up having to send him home. I also brought down Scott Champarino, a pitcher in the San Diego organization with high expectations and a high ceiling, but he ended up with arm troubles and never made it to the majors. He got into the sports agency business and worked for Scott Boras. I also took Ray McDavid, a left-handed-hitting center fielder with the Padres.

By this time, Wil Cordero had been an All-Star. Roberto Hernandez was an established pitcher. Pedro Muñoz was with the Oakland A's. José Valentín was an established big leaguer with the Brewers. Jose Hernandez was a utility player.

We won the regular season and the playoffs, and we ended up playing San Juan, with the winner of the best-of-nine going to the Caribbean World Series. We had home-field advantage, getting to play in Mayaguez in the odd-numbered games.

That season was the start of dream teams, and San Juan had the first. Trinidad Hubbard, a 4A player who was very good in Triple-A but spent minimal time in the majors, was the leadoff hitter. Roberto Alomar hit second. Carlos Baerga, who was in his prime, hit third. Carlos Delgado, in the year before he became well known, was the cleanup hitter. Edgar Martinez, probably the best DH in history, hit fifth. Juan Gonzalez, a future two-time MVP, hit sixth. Carmelo Martinez, who was at the end of his career but had been on the 1984 Padres, hit seventh. Rey Sanchez, a long-time big league shortstop, hit eighth. And Pedro Valdez, who played a bit in the majors, hit ninth. The team was loaded. Our Mayaguez team had two players you could call stars, Cordero and Hernandez.

Delgado was catching for San Juan. He was not known in America, but it was apparent to everyone there that he was going to be a huge impact player in the big leagues. He had a Barry Bonds–type of season. He was the MVP and led the league in homers and RBI.

As I work on this book, there was a recent series when the Cubs walked Bryce Harper 13 times in four games. I admire what Joe Maddon did because I would've done the same thing. I told our club at a team meeting that Delgado was going to be a non-factor because we just weren't going to pitch to him. I had the utmost respect for Edgar Martinez, who was hitting behind Delgado, but I was not going to let Delgado be a factor.

In the first inning of the first game, Alomar was on third with two outs and I called for Chris Haney to walk Delgado intentionally. Guy Hansen said, "Geez, Tom, it's only the first inning. This doesn't breed confidence in our pitcher."

I said, "Guy, I told you in the meeting that Delgado's going to be a non-factor." We walked Delgado intentionally in his first three at-bats, and we escaped the damage each time. Delgado and I had a great rapport, and when I walked past him to coach third in the seventh inning, he said, "I want to play, too." I said, "Carlos, you're going to be a non-factor."

We had a 4–3 lead in the ninth, and with two outs Carlos Baerga reached on a seeing-eye base hit, and Delgado came up again. My inclination was to walk him for a fourth time, but that would've put the tying run at second base, where they could tie the game on a single. And I had Roberto Hernandez, a 35–40-save closer in the majors, on the mound throwing 98.

We pitched to Delgado, and he turned a 98 MPH fastball around and hit it over both fences to dead center. It was at least a 450-foot homer that beat us, 5–4. So much for my strategy. I should've stuck with it all the way through.

Game Two was my favorite game that I was ever involved in. To my dying day, I'll tell people that we did not lose that game, we just ran out of innings. We started Brocail, who had his only off day of the whole year. When we came to the plate in the top of the seventh, we were down, 10–0, and had only one hit.

I had tremendous respect for Delgado, but Toronto was making a mistake because they were determined to make a catcher out of him. I knew Carlos would be an impact player, but I told friends of mine who worked for Toronto that they were going to have a guy capable of hitting 400 or 500 home runs and he'd get to the big leagues a lot faster when they made him a first baseman or DH. The responsibility of calling a game and throwing people out was retarding his progress, in my opinion. And I had a running team, so the only reason we won the regular season pennant over this dream team was that they couldn't score enough runs to offset the runs being scored when we played them. We abused Carlos as a catcher.

When I had the team in the dugout after the sixth inning, I said, "Guys, when we start hitting, and I hope it's pretty soon because we're running out of innings, let's not forget what got us here was the running game. Regardless of the signs, we're going to steal everything that's not nailed down and run ourselves back into this ballgame."

Alex Diaz led off with a base hit and he took second on the next pitch. They weren't holding us on because of the score. Armando Rios singled him in, and since he wasn't being held on, he took second on the next pitch. Cordero singled him in to make it 10–2.

Our team got the greatest compliment it could ever get. Roberto Alomar was the second baseman, and Carmelo Martinez was still not holding on Cordero at first. My first-base coach, Juan "Porky" Lopez, told me after the inning that Alomar told Martinez to hold Cordero on. Carmelo said that they were telling him from the dugout to play back. Alomar said, "I don't care what they're telling you, I'm telling you to hold him on. They're going to run themselves right back into this game."

The score was 10–2. I was flattered that our style of play had Alomar thinking about a possible comeback. Just to prove a point and to get into Delgado's head, I had Cordero steal second even though he was held on. Cordero came around to score to make it 10–3.

We ended up stealing eight bases in eight attempts over the last three innings. We scored three runs in the seventh, three in the eighth, and three in the ninth. They scored an insurance run late, but we had the bases loaded and two outs with a chance to win the game and Cordero up, but he flew out to left to end the game.

I was never as proud of any team I'd ever been associated with over the way we just kept coming back. When I had my meeting with the press and walked into the locker room, you'd have thought somebody died. Usually in Puerto Rico after the games, win or lose, the Latin music is on and players are at the spread, but it was stone silence.

I came in and said, "Hey guys, nobody died. If anything, we've got them right where we want them. We may be down two games to none, but let's remember it's a best-of-nine. And secondly, we were down 10–0 in the seventh. We did not lose this game tonight. We just ran out of innings. We needed one more out to turn this game around, so let's get that music on and let's have some fun."

We won not only Game Three but also Game Four at their place. A pivotal Game Five was played in Mayaguez in front of 14,000 fans in a 10,000-seat stadium, with people sitting in aisles, on top of the dugout and on top of the wall. Game Five was tied in the bottom of the 11th with the bases loaded and one out. Then came a wild base running play that involved four major leaguers. This isn't a development story where some minor league guys didn't know the rules. José Valentín was at third, Jose Hernandez was at second, and Alex Diaz, Ken Griffey, Jr.'s backup center fielder in Seattle, was at first base. The hitter was John Cangelosi, a little switch-hitting center fielder. He was known for his defense, base running and handling of the bat. John was known for fouling off pitches and taking a walk.

With a 1–0 count, I put on a suicide squeeze to end the game. A squeeze play with the bases loaded is not something that you see every day, but in my mind it was the ideal time for it. I had a great bunter at the plate, and with a 1–0 count we had the element of surprise due to the bases being loaded. I didn't think they would pitch out and risk going 2–0 when a walk would end the game.

The unfortunate thing for us was that we had the first base dugout. On the 1–0 pitch, Cangelosi dragged a bunt to the first base side of the mound and started jogging down to first base. All three runners were going because of the suicide squeeze. Valentín was sprinting towards home plate, and Cangelosi, in his eagerness to be acclaimed by his teammates, peeled off towards the first base dugout when he saw Valentín touch home plate. He didn't touch first base, which you would think he would do, being an experienced big league player.

Coaching third, I saw Valentín score and was pointing at the third base bag in front of me to make sure that Hernandez touched it, which he did, and then we sprinted across the field and joined in the celebration, as did 10,000 fans that had run on the field.

In the midst of all this celebrating, one of the umpires pulled me out from the mob and said, "Tom, we're gonna have chaos in this ballpark because we have an inning-ending double play."

I said, "What are you talking about?"

I knew that Cangelosi never made it to first, but the umpire told me that in all the pandemonium, Roberto Alomar picked up the bunt, went and stepped on second, and took one of the umpires with him and stepped on first. It was an unassisted double play. Having Alomar on the field was like having another coach. He had a sixth sense. Who would have the presence of mind to do that in that situation?

I asked the ump if he was absolutely positive that Alex Diaz didn't touch second base. The umpire said, "Tom, we would not make a call like this, believe us, if we were not absolutely positive." Alex had been so excited to join in the celebration that he got to within 15 feet of second base and then turned back to the celebration.

When they announced over the loudspeaker that the game was not over and was going to the 12th inning, the fans pelted the field with beer cans, bottles and oranges although the umpires did nothing wrong. They upheld the rule. Although my team completely lost its composure and focus, I had to get them to regroup. We had nobody to blame but ourselves. If just one of the two runners had touched the next base, the game would've been over.

From that point we used Jose Rosado, a lefty pitcher at the Single-A level in the Royals' system, who was 20 years old. At that time, a normal 20-year-old couldn't even handle pitching in the league, but Rosado had unbelievable composure. He went through the system very quickly, was in the majors in two years and became an All-Star as a starter. His career was cut short by a shoulder operation that he never recovered from. But he came in relief that night and gave us five scoreless innings until Delgado hit a ball over the light tower in the 17th to give them a 5–4 lead. Then we shocked them and scored twice in the bottom of the inning to win, 6–5.

Because the league had all the stars and Puerto Rico was hosting the Caribbean World Series, the league directors thought it would be a great time to coin the phrase "dream team" to represent the league. I was requested to go to the league president's office before Game Six because now that we were up 3–2, there was a fear from the league that we were actually going to win. It was no secret that they wanted San Juan to win because of all the recognizable names. I told them at the meeting that it was their league and that I didn't live in Puerto Rico, but their best hope was that San Juan would win.

They said they weren't pulling for anybody but wondered that if we won, if I would be agreeable to making it a dream team by taking on Pudge Rodriguez, Alomar, Delgado, and Juan Gonzalez. I told them that the reason my teams always did well with virtually no stars was because I was all about team. All for one and one for all. I would be hypocritical and would not be able to tell guys who helped us win the championship that they weren't going to the Caribbean Series. I saw why they wanted to do it, but it just went against what I'm all about. I was glad they asked my opinion and I told them that if we won, I would step aside and go back to California, and then return to Mayaguez the next year.

As it turned out, San Juan beat us in the final three games. They came into our park for Game Seven and won, 17–2, and hit eight home runs. Guy Hansen asked, "How did we ever beat this team?"

Game Eight in San Juan was rained out, and now the league was running out of time because the Caribbean World Series was supposed to

As manager of the Mayaguez Indios, 1988. My teams enjoyed a good bit of success in the Puerto Rican winter league.

start a day later. So Game Eight and a possible Game Nine were going to be played on the same day, and the only way to do that fairly was to do it at a neutral site, so they picked Caguas.

In Game Eight, we were down in the ninth inning with two outs and nobody on when Cordero hit an opposite-field home run to tie it. In the bottom of the inning, with Roberto Hernandez pitching and Chad Kreuter catching, a two-out, two-strike pitch which was a passed ball/wild pitch allowed Alomar to score the winning run.

We won the regular season again in 1995–1996. There was a new playoff system where the number one and four teams would play a best-of-seven series to face the winner between the two and three seeds. That year the semifinals seemed like the finals because we played in San Juan. It went all seven, and we won the final game in 21 innings. Jose Hernandez had been hitless but grounded one through the hole at shortstop to drive in the winning run.

We went through our entire bullpen but still had to open the championship series the next night against Arecibo, which was the Cinderella team that year. We lost the first two games and lost in eight.

On the first day of the 1996–1997 season, I told the players, "When these exhibition games are over and our real season starts, we're going to end up playing San Juan again, so let's take extra note of the games against them. You mark my words, after losing game eight the last two years, this year in San Juan we're going to clinch our birth in the Caribbean Series in game eight."

Pedro Muñoz had a so-so year and we traded for a first baseman, Boi

Rodriguez, who had a good season for us. When it got to Game Seven, it was the only time that I sat Muñoz because his stats against the opposing pitcher weren't as good as Boi's stats were. Pedro was so pissed off at me that he said, "Well, if I'm not going to play in this game, I don't want to play in any of the rest."

I said, "Pedro, it's one game. You've got to put the team before yourself. I know your pride is hurt. This is the first time I've ever not played you." I felt that for the sake of the team, I needed Boi Rodriguez in the lineup more.

We won Game Seven to go up, 4–3, and in Game Eight Pedro was back in the lineup as the DH, hit two solo home runs, and we won, 2–1. Roberto Hernandez got the save in front of 25,000 people in San Juan. With the tying and winning runs on, Pedro Valdez grounded to first. Our first baseman fed Hernandez, and Roberto slammed his foot down on the bag for emphasis as he pounded his fist in his glove. We finally did it. We overcame the Game Eight jinx.

Amidst all the celebrating, Pedro bearhugged me. He said, "I never forgot that back on the first day of practice you said we would win in eight games. I thought about that coming to the park today."

I said, "Pedro, you made it happen."

We went to the Caribbean World Series in Hermosillo, Mexico. The series is always in the first week of February, and some of the American players didn't want to go because it was getting close to spring training. We were able to add some players, and I had the pleasure of adding Roberto Alomar to play second base and hit third. Just managing Roberto for one week was a personal thrill for me. Getting to watch him play for a week was something. He was like an extra coach on the field. He was a consummate leader of the team on the field, in the clubhouse and away from the ballpark.

Just to give you one idea of what Roberto brought to us, he was the three-hitter for us and had been a two-hitter for most of his career. He was a five-tool player and had the ability to steal a base when needed, and just the threat of the stolen base gave hitters better pitches to hit. In one of our games, Alomar homered from the left side to give us an early lead, and we tacked on some runs by the time he came up in the fifth inning. The other team brought in a lefty to make Alomar bat right-handed with Armando Rios on third and one out. Robbie called me over to the on-deck circle and said, "Hey, give Rios a heads-up because I'm probably going to drop down a bunt."

Alomar dropped down a bunt to plate a run and he reached first.

Then he stole second and came around to score. Most ballplayers would've been thinking about trying to homer from both sides, and here he was thinking about pushing a bunt to catch the defense by surprise. That's just the kind of mindset he had.

Sandy Alomar, Sr., had been one of the original Los Angeles Angels when I was a kid. So Roberto's dad was not only a ballplayer but also one of six players in the history of the Puerto Rican winter league to collect 1,000 hits. And that came in a 50- to 60-game season. That means Robbie grew up in a baseball environment, being around his dad and probably being a batboy in the Puerto Rican league.

Roberto gave me the ultimate compliment on the flight back. After playing on the Mayaguez team for a week, he said he saw why we won year in and year out. Unfortunately, we didn't win the series, but it was a privilege to manage him.

The 1997–1998 season was another good one. Guy Hansen was back as pitching coach. In all four years with Guy, we led the league in ERA. Guy did a fabulous job. Twice during his tenure we had the "Rookie of the Year," which happened to be a pitcher. The fans want to win, but Guy and I would sneak in a development guy each year who we knew was good and thought could handle the pressure.

In 1994–1995 it happened to be Armando Rios, later an outfielder with the White Sox. He was a Single-A player when we got him, but we made him the leadoff hitter. In 1995–1996, it was Jose Rosado, a Class-A pitcher for the Royals. Guy thought he could be the fourth starter, but I was very reluctant to put a Single-A pitcher in that situation. Rosado was "Rookie of the Year" and made it to the big leagues two years later. In 1996–1997, the "Rookie of the Year" was Enrique Calero, a right-handed pitcher. He was also a Class-A pitcher who Guy had high belief in. Enrique was a big part of us winning the pennant. Even though he was a starter for us and in the minors, he was a middle and late-inning reliever in the majors.

The 1997–1998 season was one that we really took pride in. Nobody had repeated as champion until we did that season. We knew going into the season that we had a really good team, and we won the regular season title. But in the playoffs, anything can happen, and we were darn near upset by a Caguas team that had not been to the playoffs in ten years. They actually had us down three games to two in a best-of-seven, and it took a ninth-inning home run in Game Six by Wil Cordero to tie it before we won that one in extra innings. It took another ninth-inning homer by Cordero in Game Seven to tie it, and an 11th-inning homer by Cordero to win it. That got us back to the final, and for the only time in my career it took us all nine games to win it. We won Game Nine, 10–0.

A note on Cordero and his home runs: I've read "Moneyball" and Bill James' book that fostered the Moneyball philosophy about the importance of stats and getting on base. You certainly can't argue with a lot of the stats about how getting on base is important. The object of the game is to win, to win you have to score more runs, and to score more runs you have to get on base. The one and only thing I had a big problem with was regarding stolen bases.

The statistics they brought up showed how, strategically, the stolen base is one of the worst plays in baseball, and Oakland took it to an extreme by not even taking big leads off bases for fear of being picked off. More than anything else in my career, managing Wil Cordero during the 1997–1998 season in Mayaguez, I saw the effect of both the stolen base and just the threat of a stolen base that allowed us to win that second championship.

In my tenure in Mayaguez, we had two legitimate power hitters in Wil Cordero and Pedro Muñoz. We always had speed, and our ability to win was centered around the fact that we knew that we could manufacture runs. With the strength of our pitching and our defense, we knew that even up against good pitching, we could manufacture runs to make our pitching stand up.

But in the 1997–1998 season, we stole so many bases that the hitters got better pitches to hit. Catchers take stolen bases as an embarrassment. They take it as a personal affront. Pudge Rodriguez was the catcher of the Caguas team we played in the semifinals. Pudge would rather call seven fastballs in a row, to give him a better chance to throw out a base stealer, than call breaking balls, even to a dead-red fastball hitter like Wil Cordero.

In that series our speed guys, whether it was Armando Rios, Alex Diaz or José Valentín, were better as decoys but not running, so as to get Pudge to call fastballs that they were trying to spot away from Cordero. He didn't go the other way often, and usually on breaking balls he would roll over. But in the seven games against Caguas and nine against San Juan, Cordero hit nine or ten home runs. He did that because he was getting pitches that he never would've gotten to hit but for the fact that we were a threat to run, which totally goes against Bill James' contention. If we were not noted as a running team, I have no doubt that they would've been feeding Cordero a steady diet of breaking balls, in which case he wouldn't have hit all those home runs.

The speed guys would tell me after an inning that they had the pitcher read well and that they could steal second even with Pudge behind the plate, but I gave them the hold sign. I said, "Yeah. We gave you the hold sign for two reasons. Number one, if you steal the base then they'll go back to throwing Cordero breaking balls, or two, they'll walk him intentionally with a base open." That was probably the hottest stretch for any player that I managed.

Another note on stolen bases. One time late in his career and late in my tenure in Puerto Rico, Roberto Hernandez said, "Do me a favor. Don't ever trade me to another team down here" after he saved yet another playoff game. I asked why, and I learned something from this. He threw 98 mph and had an overpowering fastball. He had a nasty slider and a split-finger that was nasty, but he never had control of it. He would use it when he was ahead in the count as a chase pitch because he didn't throw it for a strike very often. He told me that our team ran so much that he would never want to pitch against our team. A guy stealing second didn't bother him, but we would take third as well. As a closer, Roberto felt that with a runner at third in a one-run game, that he was now down to two pitches instead of three because he didn't want to risk giving up the tying run on a split-finger in the dirt that would get away from the catcher. As a manager, that made me believe even more in how important it was to steal third, because if one of the top closers of his time felt the pressure, then certainly other guys would feel it.

After beating San Juan in Game Nine, I thought we were destined to win the Caribbean World Series. But we had won that series in nine games in nine days, traveling back and forth across the island, and some American players left to get ready for spring training. We were hard-pressed to replenish our pitching staff with replacements because we had to leave for Venezuela the next day.

In the first game, we led 7–4 in the 14th inning but we ran out of pitching. Our bullpen coach, Rafy Chavez, came in to pitch and gave up four runs. That Dominican team had four major league shortstops, including Miguel Tejada and Tony Batista. I was watching the team take infield practice and thought, "where else would you see four shortstops in one infield?"

During this series, I got to manage Pudge Rodriguez in the prime of his career. He caught for us along with Bengie Molina. In that first game, I assumed Pudge wanted to come out after nine innings because as much as I wanted to win, my first thought is for the players and their careers. Pudge looked at me like I was crazy and said, "We're winning this game. I'm winning it for my country. I'm not coming out of it." He caught all 14 innings. He was a gamer and a manager's player.

Going at it with an umpire during winter ball. I never came out to put on a show, and allowed myself to get animated only when I knew I was right. (Note the back-of-jersey product placement for Medalla Light, a Puerto Rican lager.)

During the series, we also had a game against Venezuela which Valentín won with his base running. We were tied at four in the bottom of the tenth, and we had two outs and nobody on. Oscar Henriquez, a 6'5", 240-pound pitcher, was on the mound for Venezuela. He threw in the mid–'90s with a slider and a nasty split which was tough to hit but moved so much that it often ended up in the dirt. Valentín got hit in the back with a fastball. The next hitter saw a slider that the catcher blocked and kept right on home plate. It didn't even leave the catcher's box, but Valentín moved to second. A 1–2 split was in the dirt and the catcher blocked it, but Valentín's read and jump was so good from second that the catcher picked it up and rushed the throw to third. The throw went into left field, and we left them standing on the field. We won a game in an inning in which we didn't make contact with the ball. I was in the third-base box thinking who would believe it if they didn't see it?

We did get a little revenge by beating the Dominican team, but that was their only loss of the series. They went 5–1 and we went 4–2. We finished second, which seemed to be our M.O. in the Caribbean Series.

I knew my days in winter ball were coming to an end because when that season ended, I flew back to my home in California for one day to unpack, repack, and go to the dentist, and the next day I was driving to Mesa, Arizona, to commence spring training with the Cubs. It was my first year as third base coach with the major league team.

As excited as I was, when I saw the enthusiasm of all the other coaches after I had just gone through 90 games with one day off, I thought, "Oh my God, I'm going to be doing this all the way through the first Sunday in October," and I knew I needed a break from winter ball.

When I was with the Royals in 2001, Ivan Mendes asked me if I would come back again. I went back because of my friendship with him but told him that I couldn't go back for the whole three and a half months. I needed a month off after the major league season, so I came in mid-season for one final time in Mayaguez. Our players had aged and our dynasty had come to an end. We did not make the playoffs, and I felt somewhat guilty because I wasn't with them from start to finish, which also wasn't fair to the guy who started off the year.

I was done until Valentín called me a few years later. He lived in Manatí in Puerto Rico and bought his own team with all the money he made as a player. The city had never had a team, but Tony bought a team and moved it there. They finished in last place in 2005, and he asked me if I could come down and bring the Mayaguez magic to Manatí.

Out of respect for him and everything he did for me as a player, I felt I owed it to him. I went down there, and it turned out to be a real fun season because we went from worst to first. To see the jam-packed crowd before the playoffs, I put my arm around Tony and said, "I can't imagine what it feels like to be in your shoes, to have lived and grown up in this city, bought your own team, playing on it, and you brought all these people here."

Doug Glanville

This is my favorite development story of all time. Any longtime baseball person loves this story because this is what the minor leagues are about.

I became the Cubs' minor league field coordinator in 1995, and Doug Glanville was in Triple-A. The Cubs took him with the 12th pick in the 1991 draft, one spot ahead of Manny Ramirez. When I got to the Cubs, I didn't look to see where people were drafted. I'd hear things as I went along, but I've always been known to treat everyone the same. I don't like to look at draft lists and pick out the ones, twos and threes. I just evaluate with my own eyes, and then sometimes I'm shocked when I hear something about that guy Glanville being the number one pick. Really?

Then I find out someone else who I know is going to play in the big leagues was taken in the 13th round. Once you put on the uniform, it's all about results.

In Triple-A Iowa, Glanville hit .270 with 13 stolen bases and was caught stealing nine times, which was criminal for a guy with his talent. He had been in the Fall League, and at that time you had to be a Double-A or Triple-A player to go to the Fall League. It was MLB's way of trying to create a winter league within the states that would be like Puerto Rico, Venezuela, Mexico and the Dominican.

It was set up for development, but there's nobody there to watch the games. So it's really like the Instructional League with older players. Outside of a few snowbirds and retired people, when you go to a Fall League game you're lucky if there's more than 200 people at the park.

Glanville was only there because he was a former number one pick. He wasn't there on merit. Being the field coordinator, I made four trips to every farm team. Having been a scout for ten years, it was obvious Glanville had athletic ability, but none of it was coming out. He was 25 and he didn't really have any stats in Triple-A, nothing to warrant him being a big league player.

At the end of season, the farm director, Jim Hendry, and I handpicked the Instructional League team. Instructional League teams are usually made up of your top draft picks and top performers from the rookie league, but they're young players. It's like having a good student and sending him to summer school to help him advance and graduate early. I picked Glanville to come to the Instructional League after he had been in the Fall League the year before.

Naturally, on the first day Glanville asked me what he was doing here. It was like he was going backwards. I said that we didn't know each other that well. It was my first year as coordinator, we had six teams, 150 players, I ran the whole spring training camp and had seen every team four times, so I felt that with my scouting background, I had a good handle on everybody.

With Glanville, I knew he had athletic ability, but here's a guy who is virtually a failed number one pick. Even Hendry asked why I wanted to take Glanville. I said that I wanted to see if we can teach him to play, to utilize the skills that he's got.

What bothered me personally was that Glanville was always a safety-first guy when I watched him play. If the bases were loaded with two outs on defense and somebody hit a shallow fly ball to center, he was the type of guy who would coming running in and then, rather than risk a diving attempt and missing it and having all the runs score, he would put on the brakes, let it bounce, catch it on a hop, and let two runs score while holding the runners to first and second.

He was the type of guy who would be given the steal sign, and the hitter would end up going to a 3–2 count because he would never run on any of the pitches. When you asked him afterwards, it was like he had an excuse on each pitch for why he didn't go. The basic thing was the fear of being caught. For me, everything was back asswards.

I've always been a guy who preached "when in doubt, be aggressive." I don't want to wait for things to happen or throw shit against the wall and see if it's going to stick. My philosophy is to make things happen, take chances. Managing and decision-making is about having the courage of your convictions, which is something I tell to young managers I train. When you have it, your players buy into it. Guy Hansen said I had "the guts of a burglar." I wouldn't hesitate to call a double steal down by one run in the ninth, because I wanted a hit to win the game, not just tie it. But Doug didn't know me that well. Doug was around 6'1", 175, tall, thin, like a gazelle. He could really run, but you'd never know it from the 13 stolen bases.

I closed the door and said, "You're here because you've done just enough to go through the system. You were the number one pick out of the University of Pennsylvania. You're a very smart kid. You're a passive-first guy and that's not getting you anywhere. Brian McRae is the leadoff guy in Chicago with the Cubs now." They were looking for a leadoff guy, and Glanville should've been that guy, but he just wasn't. "You don't know how to play, you don't know how to utilize the God-given skills that you got, and you're only going to be here for three weeks. I'm not going to make you stay here the whole time, and then I have a job for you in Mexico."

I had just come from the Padres, so I had connections in Latin America because of my time there. I was going to send Doug to Culiacán, but now that I was with the Cubs and having a successful winter career managing in Puerto Rico, I was taking five Cubs players with me, guys that Doug played with in Iowa. I needed a center fielder, but I was taking one from the Padres.

I told Doug,

> For the three weeks that you are here, anytime there's a decision on offense or defense to make that's aggressive or passive, I always want you to take the aggressive one. I don't care if we're getting beat 10–0. It's Instructional League, the games don't mean anything. You need to learn how to not be a safety-first guy and if it doesn't pan out, if you get thrown out trying to take an extra base or trying to steal a base, or dive for a ball and you miss it and all the runners score and we lose the game, I promise you I will be the first guy patting you on the ass for doing what I want, which is to be aggressive. If I see you passive in any facet of the game, I'm going to be the first guy waiting for you when you come off the field to talk to you when you come in the dugout.

That was the first building block. We developed a relationship and a trust of me meaning what I said. A lot of managers will tell a guy one thing, but if he gets thrown and it costs the team a game, then their emotions get the best of them and they want to criticize the player. They want to have their cake and eat it too, and it doesn't work that way.

I also told Doug that he would be going to Mexico after the three weeks. He had never been to winter ball. He knew I was taking five of his teammates to Mayaguez, and he told me he would rather come with us. What I didn't tell him was that they have no concern about development in Puerto Rico. They were paying me a lot of money to win, which we did my first six years in a row. I didn't want to tell him that he wasn't good enough to come with me. Darrell Sherman, a center fielder from my Padres days, was a better player at that point in time, and that's who I was bringing with me.

At the first staff meeting on the first day of practice, I told the staff that we would take turns, but every single day for three weeks one of us was going to feed a machine, not in the cage but on the field, with breaking balls, and Glanville had to hit 100 balls to the right of second base. He was a notorious pull hitter. He had done well against left-handed pitching but he didn't do well against righties because he did not know how to hit the breaking ball, how to let it get deeper in the zone and instead of trying to roll over on it and hitting it to short, hit it with the break the opposite way. I said, "We've got a gifted athlete here and we're going to do everything in our power to try to teach this guy how to hit a breaking ball. We'll rotate. I don't care if it's done in the morning before we practice or after the game. Just figure it out and we'll get it done."

We all took turns doing that. As the three weeks went by, naturally with his athletic skills he got a better feel of it. I always used to teach guys three principles in hitting the ball to the opposite field. I called it wait, lean, and drive. You have to let the ball get deeper because if you don't, you're going to do just what the pitcher wants, roll over and top a ball to the third baseman or shortstop. Number two, you want to lean into it with your front shoulder. And third, you want to drive it the other way, you don't want to lift it. Nobody is going to have as much power to the opposite field as you have to your pull field. So I always used to teach guys, mentally, to use your top hand just like when you play ping-pong and somebody lobs a ball on your side of the table, you slam that ball back in his face to win the point. That's the feeling that your right hand has to have driving through the ball so that you don't lift it up in the air and pop it up to second or to the right fielder.

In Instructional League, you're there for six days a week with only Sundays off. So he was getting a ton of reps because this was in addition to the cage drills, batting practice and the games. This was an extra hundred on top of that.

My favorite memory of that Instructional League is that we had a bunch of young kids and we were playing .500 ball, but all of a sudden everything came together as it sometimes does with a team, and we won nine games in a row. It's only the Instructional League, the games don't really mean anything, but they do as far as camaraderie goes, and as long as you're keeping score, someone might as well win.

It finally came down to Glanville's last day. We were on the nine-game winning streak but we were losing, 5–0, to the Angels in the ninth.

Then we started to rally. I've always had a philosophy, whatever team I'm with, that we won't ever lose a game. A lot of days we'll run out of innings, or we'll run out of outs and we won't have a chance to catch them. But the great thing about baseball as compared to football, basketball or hockey is that in those sports there's a clock that tells you the game is over even when there's time left. There's not enough time to come back. But in baseball, as long as you have an out left, anything can happen. Any longtime baseball person has seen miraculous things happen.

In this game, we rallied and scored a couple of runs. Right away I'm thinking about the next day to praise the kids that it was okay that the streak ended because of the way we came back in the ninth and didn't give up. All of a sudden we rallied to score four runs and had the bases loaded with two outs, and Glanville was the runner at second base.

The hitter at the plate rolled over on a breaking ball and hit a slow ground ball in the hole at shortstop—the Derek Jeter play where the shortstop has to backhand it running toward the third base dugout and throw across his body to first base. The player on the Angels made a fine play, but the throw was too late to get the runner. I thought, "Oh my God, we tied the game." But not only did we tie it, a moment later the first baseman was throwing the ball to the plate and Glanville slid in safe.

He scored from second on an infield single to win the game. I never got so excited at an Instructional League game. It was everything that I had been preaching. Doug to me was like a stallion with unlimited potential and athletic ability who just didn't know how to play.

Doug felt that the traditional baseball people were holding him back. Doug is a very gifted guy, mentally as well as physically. His father was a psychiatrist, his mother was a teacher, and Doug writes an occasional column for the *New York Times* and has written a book. He's very articulate on TV. So where most baseball people were reading the *Sporting News* or *Baseball America* on bus rides and planes, Doug always had a novel or something about the economics of inner-city Chicago. A lot of baseball people refer to people like Doug Glanville in a derogatory way. Like when guys are getting on the bus and they see Doug reading about the latest on economics in inner-city Chicago, it would be like, "Oh, Joe College is going to get smart on this trip."

When I was a coach on Tony Muser's staff in Kansas City, we happened to have three Stanford graduates on our team at the same time: the first baseman, Dave McCarty, A. J. Hinch, who is now managing the Astros, and Jeff Austin, a pitcher. In team meetings, Muser would always jokingly refer to those three guys as "Joe College" as though they were baseball players but were nerdy guys who were smarter than the rest of us. Muser meant it as a joke in his humorous and sarcastic way, but it wasn't always received in the way it was meant.

When seeing a team for a few days, you can evaluate the players, but sometimes you don't get the true picture of what's going on day in and day out. What I didn't know was that the way the Cubs' Triple-A manager had dealt with Doug had caused him to be like a turtle and go into his shell for fear of being singled out or ridiculed in front of the group. He felt like he was walking on eggshells. He was already "Joe College" just because he didn't read the baseball newspaper. He was going to be engrossed in a novel or something historical because that's him. To each his own is what I would say.

But I remember Doug telling me about an incident early in the season when he had a green light and tried to steal a base but was thrown out and the team lost the game. He felt he was ridiculed in front of the team as being the reason that the game was lost. It made him withdraw to the mindset of "I'm not going to make a mistake where I'll be singled out." He may not have believed me at first, but if he was on first, waited three pitches and didn't run, and the hitter ended up grounding out, I was as consistent as the day was long. I'd say, "Hey, you had three pitches to run, why didn't you run?"

He would make up whatever the excuse was, and then I would say, "Doug, you're only going to be here for three weeks. I want us creating as many opportunities as we can. The more that you run, the more adept you're going to get at reading pitchers and getting better jumps." When he saw that the times I confronted him were only in teaching things and not to get on him, but pushing him to be aggressive, we built a bond and we built a trust.

After he scored the winning run, I brought him into my office, and not only did I congratulate him, I said,

> A lesser guy would've just gone through the motions here with these kids. But you got a lot out of these three weeks because I know what you put into it, and I know how hard me and the staff drove you to try to get to understand. This Instructional League game will be forgotten tomorrow, but this game will never be forgotten by me. Something you bring to the table that other people don't have is the kind of speed and aggressiveness to not just be content to go to third, but knowing that it was two outs and two strikes. You were going on the swing and the ball happened to be topped in the hole and you never stopped going around third. I mean, who scores from second on an infield single? But that's what aggressiveness can do, and that intimidates other teams.

After the game, I called Culiacán and told them I was sending them left-handed-hitting center fielder Darrell Sherman because I was taking

Glanville to Puerto Rico. When I handed him his ticket, I didn't have to say anything. He knew that I knew that he was a winning player. Three weeks earlier, he wasn't good enough to go with me. I was going to take a guy from my former organization, and now he's going to come with me to be my leadoff man and play center field in Mayaguez.

Every time I see that MasterCard commercial where they have three things and then they go "and this is priceless," I think of the look of pride on his face. The fact that he had been accepted by me to come to Puerto Rico with the five other guys, that was awesome. When we got to Puerto Rico, he was our leadoff guy.

We also had José Valentín. In Puerto Rico he goes by Tony, but in the States he was known as José Valentín. He played shortstop for the Milwaukee Brewers and Chicago White Sox. He was with me for about six years in Puerto Rico. Valentín and Robin Yount were probably the two best baserunners I think I've ever had on a team. I told Glanville from the first practice to watch everything that Valentín did. Glanville had more speed, but Valentín was the best that I've ever seen to this day at being able to read the ball out of the pitcher's hand out of the stretch. Any by watching it every time, he knew when the pitcher holds on just a hair too late and the ball is not going to go 60 feet, six inches in the air. Valentín just took off because catchers are taught to drop to their knees and block the ball, not catch it.

In my era, we were taught that when you took a lead at first base, you studied the pitcher and then, when you were sure that he went to the plate, you shuffled off the base, looking at the hitter. If the ball was in the dirt and the catcher blocked it in front of him, you stayed, and if the ball went off the catcher to either side you would advance to second or third.

When I first went to Puerto Rico and had Valentín, I saw him advance on balls that the catcher blocked right in front of him, picked up and made a good throw to second base. I couldn't figure out how he was doing it. As a coach, sometimes we learn from the players, because Valentín taught me. He said, "I don't look in at the plate, I stay with the pitcher until the ball comes out of his hand because when I do that all the time, I can tell right away when it's not going to get there and I just run. I don't care whether the catcher catches it or not because I know he's taught to go to his knees, and even if he catches it on the short hop it's pretty tough for him to throw me out."

So I learned that from Valentín and started teaching it to players, but Glanville took it to another level. He had the speed to do it on pitches that the catcher would short-hop clean, but his jump was so good that often times the catcher would rush the throw into center field and he'd end up on third base. As a big leaguer, that became part of Glanville's game.

The second thing Valentín was phenomenal at was awareness. At all levels of baseball, you teach players that when they get to first base, five things should automatically go through their head. The inning, the score, the number of outs are the three factors are going to dictate whether you're going to be an aggressive or a conservative base runner. Assuming the team is tied or ahead, I'm going to be aggressive going first to third. The fourth thing you do is pick up the coach for the sign. The fifth thing is something all big league players are guilty of forgetting sometimes. Yount and Valentín would look where the outfielders were before the pitch was thrown, so if a Texas leaguer or a ball was hit in the air, they knew without having to stop and read the ball that the outfielder was not going to make the catch.

When I first managed Valentín, I remember a right-handed hitter breaking his bat and hitting a looping fly ball to right field. In the third base box, I didn't know if it was going to be caught or not. But the moment the ball left the bat, Valentín took off even though there was only one out. The ball ended up dropping for a pop-fly double. It didn't even get past the outfielder, and Valentín scored from first base. I told him after the inning how lucky he was. I said, "You thought there were two outs, didn't you?"

And he goes, "No. I knew there was one." I asked why he started running like that. Valentín said, "Because I saw that the outfielder was playing over in right-center for the guy to pull the ball, so I knew as soon as it was hit, the fact that it was over my head leading off first base, I knew it had no chance to be caught."

I thought, "Wow. I learned something." Then I started preaching to everybody about it. You can preach it, but a lot of players don't absorb it, they don't see the importance of it. To Glanville's credit, playing with Valentín made him see just how crucial these things are. Seeing is believing.

Within the first ten days of the 1995–1996 season, we had a game where we were trailing, 7–6, but had the bases loaded in the eighth. This game was when Glanville became a star in the eyes of the fans at Mayaguez.

We were down by one with the bases loaded and one out with Muñoz, our cleanup hitter, at the plate. I remember this game like it was last night. Pedro drove a ball 400 feet to the wall in center for a sac fly that tied up the game. I'm coaching third and, as I've been preaching to Glanville since

Instructional League, don't be content at just going base to base because your speed can intimidate. He was sprinting like he should be, and I'm coaching third and see him coming towards me.

Now when I coach outfielders, I always tell them that on relay throws, if you miss the infielder, miss high. Make his feet be driving back toward the infield to help him make a stronger throw. On cutoff throws, you want them to be low, but relay throws should be high. The center fielder threw a ball that made the shortstop go further out to get it, and the moment I saw the shortstop's feet going towards center field I just kept pinwheeling early, trying to score Doug all the way from second base.

Just the difference of the shortstop having to go out towards center a couple more steps to catch that throw, he had to turn and throw flat-footed with no momentum coming toward the plate. Glanville beat that throw to the plate, and Pedro Muñoz got two RBI on a sac fly. Roberto Hernandez came in and got three outs, we won the game, 8–7, and Glanville could do no wrong in the eyes of Mayaguez fans from that point on.

When we got to the finals for the Puerto Rican championship I said, "Doug, you're going to lead off this game with a base hit today. I already know that's coming. They're probably going to throw over three, four, five times to shut you down. They're going to try to send a message. I don't care if they throw over eight times in a row, the first time they make a pitch to the plate I need you to steal second. If they throw you out it's on me, but I want to send a message to them from the first hitter of this series."

Sure enough, Glanville led off the game with a base hit. They threw to first base eight times in a row. When they went to the plate for the first time, Glanville stole second. Wil Cordero singled him in, and we were off to the races. As a coach and a manager, it's so exciting to be able to dictate the manner in which the game is going to be played. You have to have the talent that can pull it off, and they have to have the confidence that they're going to be backed up by the manager and not get criticized or browbeat should it not pan out.

That's my observation whether somebody teaches in a classroom or tries to be a baseball coach. There are a lot of people who make rules, and then they don't follow them up themselves because when it doesn't work out, they want to have somebody to lash out at. When I train young managers, I tell them that they have to be consistent all the time so that their players can trust and know and have confidence in what they're doing.

Not only did we win the Puerto Rico winter league, but Glanville beat out Roberto Alomar for MVP of the league in his own country. And this was a guy that I took to Instructional League four months prior to this. Even I underestimated him. I knew Glanville had abilities, but he exceeded my own expectations. Watching him mature into the player that he was capable of being was very exciting.

In 1996, I was running the Cubs' major league spring training. I wasn't on the staff yet, I was still the field coordinator. Glanville came back with me after this phenomenal winter. He got to lead off in the first spring training game. He led off with a base hit. Then he advanced to second and third on balls that didn't even get away from the catcher, they were right in front of him. The guys in the dugout couldn't believe it. Mark Grace hit a lazy fly ball to shallow left, and Glanville tagged and scored. I felt just like a proud father. Here's a guy who had been so passive the year before, and now in the first inning he's doing things that are getting people talking. I remember Grace coming over and saying that was the easiest RBI he could pick up.

Doug made the big league team that year. He was in left field and played against lefty pitchers. Luis Gonzalez was the left fielder who played against righties. This was before Luis came up with his big-time power. Brian McRae was in center, and Sammy Sosa was in right.

When I made the staff for the 1998 season, I was excited that I was going to be with Doug for 162 games, but we needed a second baseman and the Philadelphia Phillies needed a center fielder. In the winter, Glanville got traded for Mickey Morandini. Morandini did great for us. He was a great guy and we became real tight, but it hurt to see Glanville, who had a big league season under his belt and had developed a bit of confidence, go to the Phillies as an everyday player.

In September 1999, we were in Philly and Glanville took me out to lunch. He wanted to take me to the original Philly Cheesesteak place because that was where he was from. After lunch, he dropped me off at the hotel the Cubs were staying at, and our general manager, Ed Lynch, happened to be standing outside. Ed gave me a funny look when he saw me get out of the car, although he didn't say anything. I felt a little weird.

That night, Glanville got his 200th hit of the season, which was a three-run homer. I had mixed feelings. I wanted us to win, but by the same token here was a guy that we had and traded, and now he's blossoming into a player. This doesn't look good for us. It's an achievement for a player to get 200 hits in a season.

Doug finished second in the National League in hits. Luis Gonzalez was first although he was in Arizona by that point. We could have used them on our 95-loss team. Imagine an outfield of Gonzalez, Glanville and Sosa. In fairness to Mickey Morandini, we wouldn't have made the playoffs in 1998 without Mickey. He hit second all year and was a good infielder who could turn the double play.

One of the things I got a kick out of during my lunch with Glanville was what he learned from Valentín. He had 34 steals that year and was caught only twice. He said ten of the steals weren't really steals but because he got such a good jump reading that the ball was going to be in the dirt, from the press box they must've thought it was a delayed steal when he was really just advancing on a ball in the dirt.

In his book, Doug said the first time in his career that was all about winning was in Puerto Rico. In the minors, you're on a team but a lot of it is about individuals. In Puerto Rico, it's like already being in the big leagues. It's a team with a history and tradition. It's all about finding a way to win the game each and every night. Players at Mayaguez lost themselves in the team. There was no worry about individual stats. Doug thrived in that family kind of environment. He had a high intelligence level. In one year, he taught himself to speak fluent Spanish while other guys would lie around during the day. Doug bought a book and would walk around the town and converse with people. He's just a terrific person. He entered the majors for the first time with tremendous confidence because he had played against Pudge Rodriguez, Carlos Delgado, and Roberto Alomar, and he knew that he could play with these people.

Jose Hernandez

After Glanville, Jose Hernandez is the subject of my second favorite player development story. People always talk about fear of failure, but Jose taught me that players can have fear of success. There are guys who like to stay in the background. What will be will be, don't rock the boat, I'll just chew my sunflower seeds and watch from the dugout.

In 1990, my second year in Mayaguez, Hernandez was a utility infielder for Ponce in the Puerto Rican league. He'd play against us and he'd rarely start, but if they had the lead he'd be in the game at third or short because of his defensive skills. His arm strength was off the chart. He could run, throw, and field. He just could not hit at all. He played a few games with the Rangers and Indians before ending up with the Cubs.

My third year in Mayaguez was 1994, and in the interim, my owner had traded for Hernandez. I remember asking my owner why we traded for him, because I didn't think much of Hernandez. He had this big swing and couldn't stay back on anything off-speed or breaking. Now getting a chance to work with him on a daily basis, I saw that he had unbelievable power for a guy who was about 6'1", 175 pounds. He had wiry strength. He was certainly not an impressive physical specimen to look at until you watched him throw a baseball or field his position. When I saw what he had, I wanted to exploit that to the fullest.

In batting practice, he would hit balls out with regularity. As I got to know him better, I learned as a coach that some people are their own worst enemies. He was more content to be in the background and not have the pressure of being an everyday player. For whatever reason, that's how he was. As our relationship grew when I was with the Cubs and he was the utility infielder, I challenged him to be as good as he could be.

Wil Cordero was our captain in Mayaguez and was in the prime of his career. I told Jose that I didn't see any difference between him and

Cordero other than Cordero was the guy and wanted to be the guy, and Jose was content to stay in the background. He owed it to himself and his family to be as good as he could be.

Being a long-term development guy, my coaches found a way to get him in the lineup every day at Mayaguez, and he certainly had his holes. Everybody knows everybody in Puerto Rico. There are no tricks. It's not like the big leagues where there are 30 teams. With only six teams, you can't hide any flaws. He couldn't sniff a breaking ball or a change-up, but he could hit anybody's fastball from his nose to his toes. He really didn't have a strike zone. It was just a daily thing to harness it, and he got better and better.

We had a great team so there wasn't pressure on him to be "the guy." We had Wil Cordero, Pedro Muñoz, José Valentín, and Alex Diaz, plus all the Americans on the team. Jose blended in nicely and continued to improve, and he excelled on defense.

I told Cubs manager Jim Riggleman that "this guy Hernandez is way better than any of us give him credit for. There are tools that just need to come out." Nobody talks about the mental part of the game. My co-captains, Cordero and Roberto Hernandez, both saw in him what I did, that he could be an impact player at the big league level. But he had zero confidence.

He is the only player I've ever done a drill with that goes against everything I believe in. I try to make my drills as game-like as possible. I cringe when I see people doing the soft toss drill where the coach is on a knee and tosses the ball to the player, who hits it into a screen. That drill is at a 90-degree angle from the side, which is not how the ball comes at them. It comes from the front.

Jose lunged so badly at pitches. When he strode into the ball, his weight went on to his front leg and his hands came forward immediately when the ball came out of the pitcher's hand. I was forever telling him that when the pitcher throws a pitch to you, only he and the catcher know what pitch they're throwing and where in the strike zone they're throwing it. You can only know when the ball is in flight, and you've got a split-second to make an adjustment to it. Except in your case, you're swinging right out of the pitcher's hand and don't give yourself any adjustment period. That's why he'd occasionally swing at a pitch that would bounce three feet in front of home plate or at a fastball at the bill of his cap.

I invented a soft-toss drill with him where I stood behind him, where the umpire would stand, and underhand the ball out towards the mound. I knew that would keep him from lunging. If you lunge, the ball is never going to get out in front of your body. I wanted him to take a short stride, like he was stepping onto a carton of eggs and not breaking any of them, leaving the weight on his back leg. The drill automatically forced him to do what I wanted. That allowed the underhand toss of mine to get out in front of his body, and *then* he could extend his arms and whack it. We did that drill every day for a week, and he got it. And when he got it, he took off.

In the winter of 1997–1998, Jose set a Puerto Rican league record with 20 home runs. And that's in a 54-game schedule. That went a huge way toward him believing in himself. Even at the beginning of his 20 home run season, there was a game in San Juan where Jose struck out in all four of his at-bats, and he was crying like a 15-year-old in the dugout. This was coming off a night when he was 0-for-4 with three strikeouts.

Guy Hansen and I sat down with him. I said, "Jose, look. The last time I checked, I'm managing this team, and your name is going to be in the lineup tomorrow, and the day after that, and the day after that, and the day after that, regardless of what you're doing. You're going to help the team win with your defense, with a stolen base, throwing somebody out. If I'm going to hang with you in the bad at-bats, you cannot choke like this and hang your head and pout like it's the end of the world. I'm showing more confidence in you than you're showing in yourself."

There's one game from his Mayaguez season that stands out in our minds. Our paths haven't crossed a lot, but he called me last winter and in the course of conversation brought up this one particular at-bat, and I remembered it like it was yesterday.

We were trailing by one run in the late of innings of a playoff game, and Jose was up with runners on first and second, and nobody out. Jose, to put it politely, was not the best on signs. He was our cleanup hitter, and I wanted him swinging away. I went through a bunch of decoy signs, and he wasn't sure what I wanted. A bunt would put the tying and winning runs in scoring position. He called time so we could meet halfway between third and home.

He said, "I'm bunting, right?"

I said, "Heck no! We came here to win the game and win it right now. They probably think you're going to bunt, and you may get a fastball to hit. Just make sure you don't go outside your zone."

Sure enough, he got a letter-high fastball and tomahawked it over the center field fence for a three-run homer. We won the game and series, and went to the Caribbean Series.

Everyone anticipated a showdown between Puerto Rico and the

Dominican Republic. We played the DR in the first game and went to extra innings. In the tenth, Miguel Tejada said, "Gamby, I think the team that wins this first game is going to win the whole series."

I said, "I think you're right."

In the 14th inning, Jose hit a three-run homer to the opposite field. We went up 7–4, but unfortunately we were out of pitchers. At the time, Puerto Rico was the only country in the world where the final was best-of-nine. The games were sold out, the owners liked making money, and that happened to be the only time in my nine years in Puerto Rico that we went all nine games. We won, but had to go to Venezuela the next day. We didn't have any opportunity to get additional players on our team. Our bullpen was shot, and we put in the bullpen coach. He gave up four runs and we lost, 8–7. They went 5–1 to win the Caribbean Series, and we finished 4–2. It was a shame that Jose's homer didn't stand up as the game-winner.

Ponce struggled to make the playoffs, and here was a guy that was a utility player on that team becoming a star in Mayaguez, which was a perennial pennant-winning team. The newspapers in Puerto Rico called us "The Team of the Decade," and Jose was a huge factor in that success from 1994–1997.

In those days in Mayaguez, we would have a brief meeting before the team stretched. You're never going to get anything accomplished with Knute Rockne speeches in baseball. That's a football thing. I believe if I was captain of the *Titanic*, that after we hit the iceberg, I'd have told everybody, "Hey, don't anybody panic. We're just stopping for ice." The constant positive attitude. At Mayaguez, we will never lose a game. There might be some nights where we run out of outs. Our team, to a man, really did buy into that philosophy. Our fans would never leave the park early because they always knew we'd come back to some degree.

Jose, over time, went from a negative, unconfident guy to buying in, and he knew whether he did good or bad that he'd play every day as long as he didn't quit on himself. As long as you've got skills and you get an opportunity to play, they have to surface. In those days, they didn't have mental skills coaches. Now every organization has a full-time mental skills coach because a certain number of players need constant reinforcement or they'll beat themselves down.

In 1998, the Cubs got Jeff Blauser, who was an All-Star the year before with Atlanta. He was the everyday shortstop with the Braves when they were winning the division every year, but when we got him in Chicago, he was towards the end of the career. He was scuffling so badly in mid–

June, and Riggleman came to me and said, "You better have your talk with your boy Hernandez because I'm going to start him, not just today but for a stretch of games. Even if you have to trick him into pretending that he's hitting Puerto Rican pitching in winter ball. I want to see the results of what he's been doing in winter ball."

I went to his locker and said, "Jose, this is a big opportunity for you. You've got to get yourself in the mindset confidence-wise and approach-wise like you were in winter ball. This is your chance to shine." Jose responded well and homered in each of the next three games.

That helped take some of the pressure off, but he was a guy who always put self-induced pressure on himself. When he took an 0-fer and struck out three times, it was almost like a self-fulfilling prophecy. *Yeah, well, I know I can't hit, I just proved it again.* It took a long time to get out of that mindset. Everybody's going to strike out, everybody's going to have a bad day, but you have to trust your ability. Day by day you can help the team by stealing a base or making a fine defensive play, throwing someone out on a relay. It was fun for me as his coach, and manager, to see him blossom and become a leading player.

I give Riggleman credit because he found a way to get Jose into the lineup. He started games at first, second, short and third, and after we traded for Gary Gaetti, Hernandez started games in center field. His versatility got him a lot more playing time. What team doesn't like a guy who can play everywhere and hit 23 home runs? As a utility player, he had double-digit home run seasons, so the Cubs knew he had power. He just never made enough contact to be considered an everyday guy.

He showed some power and hit 23 home runs in 1998. Consequently the bad news for the Cubs was that once he showed his power and drove in runs, it looked like he was going to leave in free agency. Jose was going to be a free agent at the end of the 1999 season, so Andy MacPhail and Ed Lynch talked to me personally because of my relationship with him. His agent was telling him that his value would never be higher on the open market than it was, so he turned down a three-year, $9 million contract offer from us. Rather than seeing him leave and getting nothing in return, we traded him to Atlanta at the trade deadline.

Then he signed a three-year, $10 million deal with the Brewers. In Milwaukee, he hit homers and played defense, but the strikeouts became unlivable. One season, Jose's manager sat him out the last few games so that he wouldn't break the single-season strikeout record. He was a high-maintenance guy who needed someone, a father figure to take the time with him each and every day to keep his confidence going. I never got to see him in Milwaukee. I'm guessing that he never developed a personal relationship like we had.

During my time in Kansas City, we had a series in Colorado and I got to see Jose and his wife, Melanie, for the first time in years. Melanie cornered me after a game one night, and she felt frustrated as a wife that he hadn't met anybody with Colorado or Milwaukee that he developed a rapport like the one he had with me. She wasn't making excuses for him.

You try to groom players to coach themselves, but there are some players who are followers as opposed to leaders, and Jose was definitely a follower. He'd be the first to tell you that. And he's the type of person that succeeds more when he has a father figure around. Now that he's in the pro game as a coach, he's seeing the game from my side. He said it made him think of our time together. I hope he can establish a bond with his players like we had.

When you're basically a lifetime minor leaguer like I've been, it's satisfying to have stories like Glanville and Hernandez, when you can catch a guy at the right time who's willing to listen to you and develop a trust and a bond. They're the ones that have the skills, you're just the jockey trying to point them in the right direction to the finish line.

I wish we would have been able to entice him to stay in Chicago. I think if Jose could do it over again, he would've gone against his agent and stayed with the Cubs. That was my gut feeling from the conversation I had with Melanie in Colorado. She was saying there just wasn't anybody who took him under his wing the way that I did, and how I knew that Jose needed that.

Some people are just that way. There can be hardliners who say you're supposed to outgrow that shit and do it on your own. And most people do. When we raise our kids, we raise them to be independent. There are some followers who need guidance, and he was one of them.

I told Jose that he didn't owe me anything. My job was to help him, which I did. But you're playing at Wrigley Field in an unbelievable environment with the Cubs. His success led them to offering a multi-million dollar deal. If it was me, I would definitely want to stay here. He had already been with Cleveland and Texas, so why would you want to walk? And if he didn't sign, he'd probably be moved before the season ended.

He wanted to maximize his value. I don't blame him. I was fortunate enough to grow up in an era when you mentioned Robin Yount, George Brett or Carl Yastrzemski, and you knew right away what team they were with. You didn't have a Randy Johnson situation where people were wondering what team he should be representing in the Hall of Fame. I never blamed Jose, but I thought it was best for his long-term future to stay with the Cubs.

He bounced around a lot in his last few seasons. His career started and ended as a utility player, and he had some real good years in the middle. You don't see many guys getting 15 years in the majors.

The Padres Years

Getting fired by the Tigers was a plus because I became field coordinator with the Padres, who trained in Yuma, which was only two hours from my home in Palm Springs. Once spring training is over, you spend the whole year roving the six farm teams. All the Tigers' teams were on the East Coast, and it made it tough to get home. The Padres' Double-A team was in Mobile, Alabama, and the Class-A team was in Rockford, Illinois, but the other four teams were on the West Coast.

Joe McIlvaine became the Padres' general manager in 1991 and wanted to bring in his own people, so I came in as field coordinator.

I had never been to Yuma, Arizona, so I went early on my first day of spring training to find the park. There was a staff meeting at eight and I got there at seven. I pulled into the parking lot, and Tony Gwynn was already in the batting cage with Merv Rettenmund, the hitting coach. It was an old facility with the batting cages right next to the parking lot, so when you pulled into a parking space, you were looking right at the batting cages. Gwynn was already doing his drills, and I sat in my car for a minute and I thought, "no wonder he wins the batting title every year." Boy, if people could see this. Some people think that you just show up, and here's a guy that was the best hitter in baseball and was the first guy in the cage. He was also famous for being one of the first guys to study video of his swing. He really worked at his craft.

Tony was one of the last guys to regularly walk more than he struck out. Strikeouts are much more prominent now. Mike Trout, one of the best players in the game, struck out more times in his first three full seasons than Yogi Berra did in his entire career. Berra grew up when kids played stickball and over-the-line, and everything was about hand-eye coordinator. Now kids are obsessed with computers, laptops and video games. The only time they're on the field is when it's required by the coach or travel team, as opposed to back then when it was a way of life. Guys took pride in walking more than they struck out, but we're in an era where strikeouts are accepted.

When I managed, I tried to foster an attitude of "the first two strikes belong to you, the player, but the third strike belongs to the team." That means choking up or shortening the swing a little bit to put the ball in play, particularly with men on base. Once you make contact, it puts pressure on the defense. Somebody has to catch it, somebody has to throw it, and it has to be caught at the other end. There's nothing that can be productive from a strikeout, and yet it's nothing for players to strikeout 150 or 170 times a year. In Berra's era, the tough pitchers were the starters. Basically, if a guy pitched in the bullpen, it was because he wasn't good enough. The hitters got to face the starting pitcher more times. Now we're in an era of specialty relievers. The Royals expect a starter to go only five or six innings. They have a specialty guy for each of the seventh, eighth and ninth innings. Wade Davis comes in and throws 98 in the ninth inning. You can see there being more strikeouts, although not as many as we're getting. You only see these relievers one time, and the edge goes to the pitcher.

Jim Riggleman was the Padres' manager in 1993 and had me run the major league spring training camp as far as organizing all the workouts, which was the first time I ran a camp. There are about 50 to 65 players, made up of the 40-man roster and non-roster invitees. It takes quite a bit of organization to keep everybody moving and busy. Organization was always a forte of mine.

In a bunting talk one day, I mentioned, whether it's sacrifice bunting or base hit bunting, using the very end of the bat to deaden the ball no matter how hard the pitcher threw. Gwynn was interested in that concept and came out early the next day. We did some bunting where I actually demonstrated it, and of course it was easy for him. He didn't base-hit bunt a lot because he was such a good hitter. It was fun watching him with the bat because it was like watching an artist.

To break up the monotony of spring training, especially being in Yuma where we didn't have other teams to play, I always had a game I called the "Offensive Execution Game" that I had used in the minor leagues. Tony had heard about it from some of minor league guys and asked if we were going to do it. Riggleman told me to go ahead and put it in. It's a game that's designed to make guys think about team baseball. It's a ten-inning game, and you get points for sac bunts, for base-hit bunts, for getting a guy over to third with nobody out, scoring a guy from third with the infield in, and a squeeze play. A lot of things you would expect a one- or two- or eight-hitter to do. There were points awarded for hitting the ball out of the ballpark to balance it out for the power guys. Tony was a three-hitter but could do everything, and he obviously scored the most points. People gravitate to what they like, so he got a kick out of winning. With his personality, work ethic, and willingness to work with the younger guys, Tony was a leader on the field and in the clubhouse. He was a real people person.

There were some very talented guys on the Padres in the early 1990s, like Tony Fernandez, Fred McGriff, and Gary Sheffield. When Tom Werner bought the team, they spent some money to get these guys, but then being a small-market team, it quickly went the other way. Guys were traded and left as free agents. They went with more homegrown, budget-salary guys. The big club had 84 wins in 1991 but lost 101 games in 1993.

It was funny to see Bruce Hurst, whom I had scouted years earlier, on the Padres. It just shows what a small fraternity baseball is. I had also scouted Sheffield. And some of my minor league Tigers, like Bean, Livingstone, and Clark, were on the 1994 Padres. We even had Phil Clark's older brother, Gerald, when I got there in 1991.

Despite the budget-cutting, McIlvane had pretty much kept the minor leagues intact from the previous regime. Bruce Bochy managed the High Desert team, the high class-A team, in the California League. In the first month of working with him, there was no doubt in my mind that he was going to be a big league manager for all of the reasons that people see today. It was evident back then. He was early in his managing career at that point, but he was a former backup catcher and a big guy who had a presence about him and had charisma. His personality and his people skills were on display. I remember telling him at the end of the year in the Instructional League, "You're going to be doing this in the big leagues and it's not going to be too far off." You could just see it. His High Desert team won a championship with some future big leaguers on the rotation. The 1–2 punch in the rotation was Scott Sanders and Tim Worrell.

Our roving infield coach was Gene Glynn, and after one week of watching him work with infielders and seeing his drills and communication skills, I asked him how he came to be with the Padres. He told me that he was a journeyman player in the Montreal system, got to the Triple-A level, and they made him a coach and started him with the rookie league team. Delino DeShields was a high draft pick that they had high hopes for. Gene went from rookie league to A-ball to Double-A as Delino's mentor and coach. Then they let Gene go. I asked why he got let go, and Gene told me that Montreal just said that they were going in a different direction. I had already been in the game for 15 years with three different organizations. I said, "Gene, let me tell you something. Any organization that's going in a direction that doesn't include you is going in the wrong direction." I regret that I only got to work with Gene for a year or two before Don Baylor, the manager of the expansion Rockies, took Gene as his protégé. They made him the field coordinator for a year and then brought him up as the major league third base and infield coach. Gene followed Baylor to the Cubs, and then Felipe Alou took him to Montreal and San Francisco. Now he's the Twins' third base coach.

When you're the field coordinator and you've got guys like Bruce Bochy, Gene Glynn and Jim Riggleman coaching in the system, it made my job a lot of fun to watch those guys in action. Riggleman and I had known each other because we managed Mayaguez to championships in consecutive years. We formed a good bond getting to work together in San Diego that would continue on to Chicago.

My favorite development story from my Padres days involved a pitcher, which is kind of ironic because I prided myself on being a hitting and a base running guy. Todd Worrell may have been the most famous closer in that era when he was with the Cardinals. His younger brother, Tim, had gone to Biola College, which stands for the Biblical Institute of Los Angeles. It's a small, Christian college. Although he had a good pitcher's body, he wasn't as big and certainly didn't have the arm strength that his brother did. But Tim had an uncanny ability to throw strikes. The minor leagues are full of guys with good arms who are trying to learn to get the ball over the plate, and Tim just had a gift. On the scouting 20-to-80 scale, Tim had about 65 control from the first day that he came into pro ball. He could throw any of his three pitches, fastball, slider, change, for a strike on virtually any count.

But because he came from a small college, he was a low draft pick, we sent him to our low, class-A team which was in Burlington. In my rounds as field coordinator, I made Burlington my last stop because it was cold in Iowa in April. By the time I got there, Worrell was pitching well, with very few walks, and his ERA was microscopic. I saw him pitch a gem, and it didn't take a genius to tell our farm director, Ed Lynch, that Worrell more than had his feet on the ground. You like to push the college guys, so we sent him to High Desert with Bruce Bochy's team.

By the time I made my rounds and got to High Desert, I was living in Palm Springs, where the Angels happened to have a team. I would try to see the High Desert team in Palm Springs because it gave me extra time at home. The trip to Palm Springs was a commuter trip from High Desert. Worrell's first two starts with High Desert were horrible. His ERA was over 10. He had zero success. I happened to walk into a restaurant while

Tim and his dad were in there, and we ended up having lunch together. Tim was almost embarrassed to see me in the restaurant because he had been pitching so bad and was going to pitch that night. And he was facing the Angels, who were the best-hitting team in the league. I hadn't seen him pitch, but looking at the stats I saw that his walks were up and he had more hits surrendered than innings pitched. Granted, it was only two starts, and the Cal League is a hitters' league because of the light air.

I said,

> Tim, we did not send you here to High Desert for you to fail. We're in the business of knowing what we're doing. Without even seeing you pitch, my disappointment in you, from looking at the numbers are telling me that you're not pitching the same way that you pitched in Burlington. Because the plate is 17 inches wide in the Cal League as it is in the Midwest League, but with all the walks, you're giving people things that they're not entitled to. The number of walks is also telling me that all these hits you're giving up, I'm willing to bet that more than half of them are coming from counts that are in the hitter's favor. When you're not walking them you're pitching from 1–0, 2–1 and 3–1 counts. When you're giving up these doubles and home runs, you're giving the league too much credit rather than evaluating that your performance is giving these guys pitches that they should never see in the first place.

From that point on, I found over my career that when a lot of guys move up a level, instead of trusting what got them there they immediately have a brain fart in their mind and start assuming "Oh my God, this league is going to be way better than where I'm coming from." They try to pitch differently and then wonder why they fail.

Over lunch I said, "In this game tonight, I'd love to see, even if you have to play mind games with yourself, punch the strike zone and pitch the way you're capable of pitching, and then see what kind of results you get. Because there may come a time in your career that you need a pitching coach to teach you a different pitch or something to add more movement, but until you fail you need to pitch the way that got you here."

It was fun watching the game that night. I was sitting with his dad and watched Tim pound the strike zone with his God-given ability to throw strikes. Bochy pulled him for the last two innings because he wanted to give the bullpen some work in a blowout. The rest was history. Worrell and Scott Sanders led the team to the Cal League championship. Worrell went on to pitch 14 seasons in the majors. It was a big teaching moment. One of Yogi Berra's famous lines was "90 percent of the game is half mental." The truth is that any sport can be a mind game. Worrell got shell-shocked in his first couple of starts, and I think he let it mentally beat him down to the point where he wasn't pitching the way he was supposed to pitch. I was glad I was in the right place at the right time because we didn't have the mental skills coaches that they have now.

I think there's a lesson, not just in baseball, but in life, from the Instructional League of 1992. I had Bochy managing the Instructional League team. Tim Flannery, a popular former Padre, was handling the infield. Tim was a broadcaster who wanted to get into coaching. He became Bochy's longtime third base coach with the Padres and Giants. Ty Waller, who happens to be black, was our outfield and base running instructor. One day, I was setting up a pitching machine to throw breaking balls to the guys in batting practice. The guys were playing pepper down the right field line. While I was putting the machine up by myself, Flannery, Bochy and Waller were joking around with the position players. They were joking about inviting each other to each other's house. The players and coaches were laughing while I had my back to all this.

When I got done, I walked over to the three coaches, because with my sense of humor I always liked there to be a good atmosphere. I asked what I missed and they told me to look at the players. We had 15 position players playing pepper in three groups of five, while we stood and watched at first base. I looked and told them that I didn't get it. Bochy said, "Well Tom, look at the pepper games."

I said, "Yeah, I'm looking, but what you guys are missing is I had my back turned when the joke was going on." Then I made a joke because to put the tripod on the machine, I had to screw in these legs. So I said, "I had my back to you guys. I was setting up that machine and that's probably the first thing that I've screwed in a month." And they all laughed. I used a sexual connotation in relation to putting the pitching machine up.

Then Flannery said, "Tom, look at the pepper games." I looked at the pepper games again. And Tim Flannery looked at me and said, "You really don't get it, do you?"

I said, "No. I really don't."

They pointed out that it just so happened that when we picked the best players in our organization to come to Instructional League, ethnically there happened to be five whites, five blacks, and five Latinos. And that's exactly how their pepper games were.

I bring this up because the coaches and players were joking about it. I didn't get it even when they tried to point it out to me. When I looked out there, all I saw were 15 Padres in dark blue jerseys. When I walked out to the pitching machine, I thought that I'll probably never live long enough, but what a much better world it's gonna be, if and when the time comes when everybody is like me and just looks out there and sees players, instead of three different racial or ethnic groups.

Three intelligent guys saw something that I didn't. I could've stood there for a half-hour, and I never would have figured out what it was they were joking about.

Flannery once hired a stripper for me on my birthday in the middle of the morning during spring training. This would've gotten us all fired in this day and age. This cop car came on the field, and a woman dressed as an officer got out and announced that she was looking for Tom Gamboa. I panicked, thinking that something happened to one of my kids. I said, "That's me." She came over and immediately slapped handcuffs on me, and I said, "What is this about? I paid my child support." She told me I was being detained and the next thing, she sat me down and cuffed me to a bench. Then she went back to the car and turned the music on. And of course everyone knew about it except for me, and everybody circled around, and she went through her dance and taking her police uniform off. It was a gag gift from Tim. Only Flan would do that. He was a prankster, and that was the all-time prank on me.

During my time in San Diego, there were some good teaching points for young coaches and managers. Tim Flannery exudes passion for family, baseball and music. Maybe music and then baseball. That's what Flannery's all about. When we made Flan a manager in 1993, he managed the rookie league team in Spokane. He had never managed before, had just started his coaching career the previous instructional league, when we hired him to get some experience on the field. We knew right away that he would be terrific at managing because he had so much passion, and the team usually takes on the personality of its manager. But when you've never managed for anybody before, it's amazing how fast the game goes. To the average person watching at home or in the stands, some people criticize the game for being too slow. But for a new manager, the game can move like a movie on fast-forward.

When Flannery started his managing career, he won his first two games and was all excited. We were out having pizza and beer when he opened the door, so to speak, and asked what I thought of his managing. I said, "Tim, you're going to be real good at this. You just have so much passion and enthusiasm and energy, the kids are going to feed off that. But on the other side of the coin, there's one thing that, to tell you the truth, I'm really shocked it got by you."

He asked what I meant. I said, "Well, in both of these games, the same nine guys that started the game, finished the game. (Not counting pitchers who were on pitch limits.) Using your personnel is something that takes experience, but I'm only surprised because of the type of player that you were in your career." When Flannery played for the Padres, he was the backup second baseman behind Alan Wiggins, a real speedster. "For example, you had the college first baseman behind the high school kid that was the prospect, and after the kid had his three or four at-bats, you could have got the college guy in for defense for a couple of innings, maybe even an at-bat to get his pro debut and get his nerves out of the way."

The team had played on Friday and Saturday night, and there was a Sunday afternoon game. I said, "I know you're going to catch the backup catcher tomorrow. Just think of how nervous that kid's gonna be in his debut. If he caught a couple of innings today and got an at-bat, regardless of what he did with it, he might've had a chance to get those jitters out of the way, which just might've helped him in one of those at-bats tomorrow."

Flannery slept on it, and the next day at the park he said, "I thought about what you said last night, and playing for Dick Williams, I always knew that I would play the Sunday day game after Saturday night to give Wiggins a day off. When I think back on it, it seems like Dick Williams always found a way to get me into the game on Saturday night, whether it was to pinch-hit for the pitcher, or an inning on defense, or to pinch-run, especially if I had sat for three or four days."

I said, "Well, there you go. Case in point. Lesson learned." Those are the types of things you usually pick up with experience. And he caught on to it right away.

When Riggleman was managing in Vegas in 1992, we acquired Jeff Gardner from the Mets. Gardner was a 5'10", 165-pound, left-handed-hitting second baseman. He didn't throw hard enough to be on the left side of the diamond but was a good second baseman. He didn't have a lot of power but could hit and played parts of two years in the big leagues. After being traded, he played a year-plus at second for the Padres in the big leagues.

Gardner led the Coast League, which was an offensive league, in hitting. In my travels as field coordinator, I was sitting behind the plate one night and watched Gardner go 0-for-4 without ever getting a good pitch to hit. I'd already been coaching for many, many years and never took the time to think of how important it is for contact hitters to be selective at what they swing at. I had never consciously thought of this before, and I had a talk with Gardner the next day about it. I could see that he hadn't thought much about it to that point.

I said, "You know, I didn't see you really get a good pitch to hit last night." He asked what my point was. I said, "Anybody can go oh-for-four, my God, you're leading the league in hitting. But I think the critical point here is that more than anybody else on this team, you need to really be selective at what you swing at, because a lesser guy would've swung and missed at some of those pitches and maintained their at-bat. But your hand-eye coordination is so good that, to my mind, the whole night you swung at strikes that were better for the pitcher than for the hitter. Consequently, you grounded out three times and flew out to center."

My point was that if he didn't swing and made the pitcher throw again, the next pitch might not be on the corner, but rather over the plate, and Gardner might've had his usual hit or two. That was a very big teaching point for me as a coach.

There was another teaching moment for me and Riggleman. We had Kevin Ward, a guy who was every manager's dream. Kevin was a right-handed-hitting outfielder, had some power but not enough to be a big leaguer, and not enough speed to steal bases. When you're a corner outfielder who doesn't hit for power and doesn't steal bases, you're fighting an uphill battle to get to the big leagues, and if you get there, to stay there.

With the Padres on the team trip to Taiwan, 1992. I was the field coordinator and had the pleasure of working with Tony Gwynn, Fred McGriff and Gary Sheffield.

Kevin had a terrific makeup, and everybody on the team gravitated to him. He was a local San Diego boy. After nine years at the Triple-A level in pro ball, somebody got hurt and Kevin got his call-up. He wasn't in the big leagues very long although he doubled in his first at-bat. He got a taste of it, but when he came down to the minor leagues I think he was still on cloud nine from having been there, and was not the same guy when he came back. When he was done hitting with his group, he would go into the clubhouse a get a cup of coffee instead of shagging fly balls with his teammates. It was big league-itis.

I came into town about a week or two after he returned. The first day there, Riggleman was telling me how excited the whole team was about Kevin getting brought up. The whole team was thrilled. But Riggleman went on to tell me that since Ward got back, he was kind of a pain in the ass. I asked how that could be with Kevin being the most-liked guy in the whole farm system. Riggleman told me several instances of how Kevin was about "me, me, me" instead of "we, we, we." I asked Jim what he did about it, and Jim said he did nothing.

When you let little things slide, they do in fact become big things, and they become cancers that can tear apart your team. Here was a guy who was a catalyst on the club but had changed. So as not to rock the boat, or not to pick on a guy who had always been a manager's player, it was becoming a thorn in people's sides.

The next day, I said, "Jim, I think the common sense thing to do is to get Ward in the office and praise him for how happy you, and the coaching staff, and all of the players were that he got to the big leagues. But now he's back in Triple-A and he needs to go back to being the guy that he's always been." It's that same old story that everybody thinks their shit don't stink and, in fact, it does.

When Riggleman called him on it, right away Kevin couldn't apologize enough for not being the guy that he was before. When we went out for beers that night, Riggleman felt better that the issue had been addressed, and you could see with the atmosphere with the team that everything was back to normal.

I just think it's a lesson for all of us, whether it's raising kids or managing a baseball team or a 7–11, that you have to conduct business. You can't let something slide just because the team is winning, and by the same token you don't want to come down too hard on something little when the team is losing, just because you as a manager are frustrated. It's about the consistency of policing things.

Like I've mentioned, Riggleman and I were two baseball fanatics and old-school guys. He learned his baseball in the Cardinals' organization and really idolized George Kissell, and rightfully so. Kissell worked as a field coordinator and head of instruction with the Cardinals for about 40 years. I can't even tell you how many times Riggleman brought up Kissell's name over the years.

When Riggleman managed the Triple-A club, I was the field coordinator. I would make four trips to every club, and on my fourth and last trip to Vegas, Riggs and I went out for some beers after the game. He did a terrific job. Riggleman has always been the type of guy who is thinking about the seventh, eighth and ninth innings in the first, second and third, and going over scenarios in his head of what matchups he may want later in the game. He was on top of it.

Riggleman said, "Hey, you've made four trips in this year. I've got a lot of respect for you. Give me some feedback."

I said, "Jimmy, I have no doubts you're going to be managing in the big leagues." He was well known in the baseball fraternity as an up-and-coming manager. I said, "My opinion isn't the only one, but since you're asking, there's only one thing I think you're missing the boat on."

He asked what I meant. I said, "There's no doubt that the position players in Vegas would run through a wall for you." Jimmy really cared about his players, was a player's manager, communicated well, hit fungoes every day, and was always around the batting cage. He had the utmost respect for virtually anyone that's ever played for him. But I said, "I don't think that you know the pitchers on your staff at all."

At first he got kind of defensive. I said, "From my take, basically when they see you is only when you come to mound and take the ball from the starters." He had a real good pitching coach, Jon Matlack, but asked what I would suggest. I said,

> Ever since I started managing, I would take one day of the week where I didn't hit fungoes or throw BP. I would roam the outfield during BP, and I would spend the whole hour with the pitchers while they were out there shagging fly balls. It might be two minutes with one guy and it might be seven or eight minutes with another guy, whatever I thought that they needed. But it was just to give them my impressions of their outings and what I think they've done. Nothing that had to do with mechanics that would override the pitching coach, but just so that they got to know me better, and for me to know them better and what made them tick to bring the whole team together.

To Jim's credit, when we got to the park the next day he said, "I thought about what you told me last night, and you're 100 percent right."

To finish the story, we skip ahead a few years to when we're living together in downtown Chicago, he's the Cubs' manager and I'm the third base coach. We'd been living together for about a month, and one night we were out at his favorite place, PJ Clarke's, a popular burger and beer place on Rush Street. Jimmy said, "You know, I'm disappointed in you that you haven't given me a compliment."

I didn't get it. One day during the week, Jimmy would avoid the press during BP because when he was at the cage, all the writers would be around, especially in a big market like Chicago. Jimmy would go out behind the screen behind second base. Usually, the pitcher who started the night before would sit on a bucket where all the balls would come in, so he'd be protected by the screen. Jimmy would be behind the screen and would call the pitchers in one by one and chat with them. I had noticed it, but I hadn't thought to say anything to Jimmy about it.

I took it as a compliment that something I recommended in the Vegas days was something that he took and put in his arsenal as a tool to make sure that he reached out to all the players. As a manager, even if it's not by design, you're going to come into contact with the position players every day. You're doing infield, you're hitting ground balls during BP, you're throwing BP. You're always around the cage. In the minor leagues, as third base coach, you're always coming into contact with runners. But it takes a plan to communicate with the pitchers, otherwise you could go days off the calendar and only see them when you go to the mound to take the ball out of their hands.

I thought Tony LaRussa did something interesting, and who didn't admire Tony, he'll certainly go down as one of the best managers of all time. His thing was that he had all 25 of his players' names on index cards. And every day, for the top card on his desk, Tony made it his policy to make sure that he spent some time with that player. Then that card would go to the bottom. It was his way of having a checklist to make sure that he came into contact with each and every player on his club, rather than leaving it to chance. When I heard that, I got a kick out of it because I thought here's a guy I really admire and idolize, so I'm glad I'm on the right track because it was something I prided myself on doing during my career.

Ed Lynch was the farm director when I was with the Padres, but in 1995 he became general manager of the Cubs. The first two things he did were getting permission from San Diego to take Riggleman with him, because he had been managing the Padres, and bringing me over as the field coordinator. I was down in Puerto Rico, and I had three sleepless nights because I was trying to decide what to do. I really liked the Padres and living in Palm Springs, I liked the closeness of training in Phoenix, and all but one of their teams were on the West Coast. But I was already so close with Lynch and Riggleman, I thought that's probably better for my future. I was open to both options. I was under contract with the Padres, but they said they wouldn't hold me back from going with Lynch. And it was going to be more money, so that's when I went.

After three seasons as Cubs field coordinator, I was named the third-base coach for the 1998 season.

Coaching Third at Wrigley

I had spent so long in the minor leagues. I had been doing it for so long that, if anything, I was more surprised in how long it took. My teams had won pennants at several minor league levels and all six of my years in winter ball up to that point. I couldn't have possibly been more prepared. If anything, I was over-prepared.

Ironically, I was offered two big league jobs on the same day. One was to be the third base coach for the Cubs, the team I was currently the minor league field coordinator for, and then one of my best friends, Tony Muser, wanted me to be the hitting coach of the Kansas City Royals.

I chose to stay with the Cubs. In hindsight, it was actually the wrong decision to make because I was with the Cubs for two years and then we all got fired when we finished last in the 1999 season. Had I gone with the Royals, Tony Muser's tenure lasted a few more years, so I would have gotten more time.

But it was historic. It was a Cinderella year for baseball.

When I was hired, the Cubs moved Dan Radison from third base coach to first base. Rad and I had worked together with the Padres. Tony Muser was the third base coach, and at the All-Star break he was hired to manage the Royals, so the Cubs moved Radison from first to third, but he had coached third in the minor leagues for only a short amount of time.

So he, by his own admission, was uncomfortable there, especially in a big market like Chicago. He was kind of relieved to get back into his element at first base because there's less pressure and decision-making at first. I had coached third my whole life, on every minor league team I'd ever had from rookie league to Triple-A, and all my years in Puerto Rico.

I laughed when a writer asked me if I could handle the pressure of coaching third base in a big market like Chicago. I've coached third base in winter ball in Puerto Rico. If you've never seen a winter league baseball game, just turn on a European soccer match because that's what the atmosphere is like. Not any more, but that's what it used to be like. For an American who's never been down there, they don't care how many games you've won in a row. They expect you to win when they pay their money.

My first year in Puerto Rico, my team lost on Opening Night and then set a record with 14 straight wins. That had never been done before. We didn't play three-game series like they do in the majors. It's a commuter league, so we'd go back and forth playing one game at a time, traveling two-and-a-half hours across the island.

The night the record ended, we were blown out. I went through two or three pitchers in the first inning. At Mayaguez, we had eight to 10,000 fans every night. When I went out to coach third base from the third inning on, our fans were throwing oranges and beer cans at me. They had to keep cleaning the debris, so in the seventh inning, the home plate umpire stopped me and told me they didn't want me coaching third any more. I said, "You can call the game and I won't say anything, but these people aren't going to intimidate me." They were too intimidated to call the game, so they just kept cleaning the debris.

The American players had never been out of the U.S., so everybody was kind of shell-shocked. I called off stretching because it felt like somebody had died. They had never experienced anything like that.

Nothing, *nothing,* in minor league baseball can mentally prepare a player for what's going to happen when he gets to the big leagues in Boston, New York, Philly or Chicago, except winter ball. So they kept throwing stuff because they were pissed that we weren't winning that night.

I called all the players and explained to them that now they could see why their respective teams wanted them to come to winter ball—to get more experience against better competition, but also for the first time in your life to experience adversity. When they pay their money, they don't care if we won 50 games in a row. They're with us win or tie. There's no such thing as losing in the Latin American vocabulary. Doesn't exist.

And they don't ever want to hear development, a guy being brought to Puerto Rico or the Dominican to get better on his fielding. They want the finished product. Fuck development. Give us the better player because we want to win. They weren't developing in the '80s and '90s. They wanted guys to be at least Double-A and preferably Triple-A and had good stats, or they wouldn't take them.

As a joke, I told the players that I had met with security and they were going to start screening the fans for weapons. We're 14–2. Let's get back to stretching and have some fun. We're on a Caribbean island. We came here to have some fun and play baseball. We went on to win the championship. We won everything there was to win. We won the season, then we went into a round-robin playoff and we won that. The top two teams went to a best-of-seven finals, and we won in five games.

So I had experienced all this before I ever got to Chicago. If we were getting beat in Chicago, they would throw those little red salad tomatoes. It was nothing. And in Boston they throw change at you. They throw nickels, dimes, and quarters, so I'd always walk across the field at Fenway Park with my head down because I didn't want to get hit in the eye.

Did I play in the big leagues? No. But was I prepared to be a third base coach? I had been prepared long before I ever got the job. I was disappointed I wasn't managing in the big leagues, let alone just being a third base coach.

My teams had won everywhere I'd been. We won at rookie ball in Paintsville. They moved me to Beloit, and we won in Beloit. We won at High-A Stockton. I don't know anybody else with a resume like that who wasn't ready for the big leagues.

It was my first year as third base coach, but I had already been running spring training the three previous years for Riggleman. Riggleman and I had met in San Diego in 1991. There was a new regime, he was hired as Triple-A manager, and I was hired as the field coordinator. When Riggleman got the managing job, he hired me to run the major league spring training for him as the minor league coordinator.

This was because I'm super-organized, and Jimmy's not three-dimensional, as in knowing what's going on at three different fields at the same time. I was running the major league spring training, organizing the work day for Tony Gwynn, Tony Fernandez, and Fred McGriff. Riggleman gave me free reign.

When Riggleman and I went to the Cubs, he wanted me to do the same thing because he trusted me. I had already run three Cubs spring trainings, not as a coach but as the field coordinator. I was working with Shawon Dunston, Mark Grace, and Sammy Sosa. Then when the season began, they went to Chicago and I roved the minor league farm system. In 1998, nothing changed except that I was going to Chicago too. I knew all the players from the previous three years.

When we left spring training, we flew to play an exhibition game in Texas on the way to Florida. The coaches always sat up front, and the players sat in the back and played cards. As Sosa walked by me, he stuck out his hand to congratulate me for being in the big leagues, and I could tell there was something in his fist when we shook hands. He had given me a thousand bucks. I said, "I can't take this."

He said, "No. I want you to buy a couple of new suits on Sammy Sosa." You had to wear suits in the big leagues. I never forgot that. He bought my first two suits for me being in the big leagues. He was a great guy.

With regards to my wardrobe, I'm always Mr. Stylish on the golf course. But in the rest of my life, I've been referred to as a guy that's all-class but it's a shame that it's all third. I worked with Tony Muser with five different teams, and he's like a brother to me. He's always referred to me, in public, as "Joe Shit the Rag Man." When he managed the Royals, he always liked saying substance mattered over style, and he'd use me as an example of that. When I was with Kansas City, I once spent the day in Cleveland, and when I got back to my room there was a layout of clothes all over my bed. I found out through the grapevine that Carlos Beltran learned what size I took and had bought half a dozen shirts, some pants, a pair of shorts and a pair of shoes.

During the dynasty years in Puerto Rico, I was notorious for horrible dressing because you're on a tropical island and you're driving back and forth every day. I had a pair of old, white casual loafers, a pair of white shorts that were smeared with ketchup and mustard, and I usually wore a sleeveless tank top. One night, I was sitting in my office and I smelled smoke. I walked into the clubhouse, and there was a bonfire on the floor with all the players were circled around it. I thought it was a bonding thing or maybe something like Jobu from "Major League." I got closer to the bonfire, and I recognized that it was my clothes that were on fire. All of a sudden it wasn't so funny. Wil Cordero and Roberto Hernandez stood in front of everyone and said, "We're tired of having a first place team with a manager that dresses like we're in last place." Somebody reached into one of the lockers and pulled out some real nice clothes and shoes. It was their subtle way of telling me that they wanted the leader of the ship to be a bit classier.

Sosa also told me before the season that he didn't want to high-five me after he hit a home run. He said, "I plan on hitting a lot of them this year. When I come by third, just make a fist and I'll pound it." I didn't know it was going to happen 66 times.

We opened the season in Florida against the defending World Champion Marlins. The team had been dismantled after winning the title. Everybody respected them as the defending world champs, but everybody went into the season knowing they weren't the team of the year before.

Florida won the first game, but then we took the next two. In the third game, Jeff Blauser singled to left in the ninth inning with two outs, and I waved Mark Grace home with go-ahead run in an 8–7 win. Then we flew to Chicago for the home opener.

That was a huge thrill for my dad. He was born and raised in Chicago and was a huge Cubs and Ernie Banks fan. My dad flew in from California because he wanted to see his son coach third base for the Cubs on Opening Day in Chicago.

I always thought getting to the big leagues would be real exciting. I had paid so many dues and had been so successful that it was more like "it's about time." I was 50 years old. It wasn't like when I was a kid, where you're all excited for Opening Day and there's this disbelief.

I'd like to tell you there was excitement, but there just wasn't. It was almost like it was just another game to me because I had been doing it for so long. I had been running major league camps for five years, and I was there for 30 spring training games each year.

Even when I went to Yankee Stadium for the first time, it wasn't a big thing. The only place that was different was when we went to Los Angeles to play the Dodgers. When I went out to coach third at Dodger Stadium, I looked at the bleachers and behind home plate. I grew up in LA. When that stadium was built, I was 14. If priests and brothers at my high school weren't using tickets, they'd give them to me, and I'd take the bus and sit behind home plate. If I wanted to go and didn't have tickets, I would take the bus, get a ticket in the cheap seats and sit in centerfield.

The reality of being on the field at Dodger Stadium was a neat feeling. Wow, when I was a kid I was on the outside looking in, and I always hoped to play here. That never happened, but at least I'm here coaching. That was like fulfilling a boyhood dream.

The Dodgers spoiled my homecoming by scoring nine runs in the second inning. Kerry Wood got knocked around, but he made up for it a few starts later. In a game at Wrigley Field in early May, Wood struck out 20 Astros in his fifth start in the majors. That was amazing.

Being the field coordinator, I knew Kerry Wood from the day we signed him. I knew that this wasn't just another guy. This was one of these one-in-a-million guys you hear about. Bob Patterson, the lefty reliever, got hurt, and Wood was brought up. It was supposed to be for a couple of starts when Patterson was on the Disabled List, but I knew he'd never go back because he was just a different guy. He should've made the team out of spring training. He dominated all spring.

The Cubs announced that he wouldn't start the year in the majors even though he was pitching well. He had never pitched in Triple-A, and he was only 20. The day it came out in the newspapers in Arizona, we

Coaching third base for the Cubs at Wrigley Field. Wrigley had "38,000 fans packed in like sardines" during games that summer for the McGwire-Sosa home run chase and pennant race.

played the Angels. Terry Collins was managing Anaheim, and when we were walking across the field, Collins came up to Riggleman, shook his hand, and congratulated him on winning the division. Collins said, "I just read in the paper that Kerry Wood's not making your team, so if you have five guys better than him, I'm going to pre-congratulate you because you're going to win your division."

We all laughed. Wood was pitching great. He made his debut in Montreal, almost like they were protecting him to take the pressure off. He was out of the country and in front of a small crowd. I was up on the railing when Wood took the mound. Hitting coach Jeff Pentland and Dan Radison said, "Hey Tom, we can't see." I said, "Get up here and watch this. This guy's going to strike out thousands. *Thousands.* We're going to see the first one right here."

Wood struck out Montreal's leadoff hitter, Mark Grudzielanek. I wanted to see that first strikeout because I knew. Unfortunately he got hurt or else he would've been one of the biggies. He still was but for a short frame of time. Patterson was on the DL longer than expected, so Kerry got four starts, and of course his fifth one in May solidified that he wasn't going anywhere. When he struck out 20, there was no way they were sending him back. The fans wouldn't have let him go back.

The first pitch of the game was 98 miles per hour. It was one of those things that every athlete dreams about. He had his best stuff and control. He was locked in, and his stuff was electric. It's amazing that seven guys didn't strike out. That was fun to watch. It was exciting being there and witnessing it first-hand.

That was when Houston won the division by 12½ games. They had an awesome team with the Killer Bs: Craig Biggio, Jeff Bagwell, Sean Berry, and Derek Bell. Bell was the 20th strikeout victim. They had those four guys at their prime. After the game, Mark Grace was running up and down the clubhouse, shouting about how we just saw the greatest game ever pitched in the history of baseball. The clubhouse is very antiquated, very long and very narrow with lockers on both sides, and Grace was running back and forth like a high school kid.

Ron Santo, our radio broadcaster, was right behind him and said that he'd been around the big leagues three times as long as Grace and agreed that this was the greatest. Billy Williams was my locker mate, and he calmly turned around and said that this might be the second-best game. As soon as he said that, Ronnie said, "That's right. This'll be the second greatest game ever pitched." Grace asked what could possibly top Wood's performance?

Santo said, "Billy and I played in it. Sandy Koufax threw a perfect game against us and struck out 14 batters." That's when I told Billy that I had just started my senior year in high school and was sitting in the first row at that game. I was right behind the plate, and I didn't know how anybody was hitting the ball. The people who say a ball can't rise wouldn't be saying that if they were at that game.

Billy, who was a good guy and a great friend, said, "Tommy, I was a pretty good hitter when I played."

I said, "No shit. You're in the Hall of Fame. You hit 426 home runs."

He said, "I actually had some good days against Koufax but I never faced anything in my career like that night. He struck me out in the first and I told Ron 'if this man's going to throw like this for nine innings, guys are going to have a tough time fouling one off, let alone hitting it.'" Billy later made a comment that hitting against Koufax was like trying to drink coffee with a fork. Koufax's next start after the perfect game was a rematch against the Cubs, and Billy hit a homer, but he didn't tell me that part. That's how humble he was.

I had seen the perfect game as a fan, and now I heard it from my Hall of Fame locker mate. Years later, I got another perspective on the same game. When I was with the Dodgers in 2000, all the coaches were having dinner one night at Vero Beach during spring training. Tommy Lasorda happened to be telling Koufax stories. Claude Osteen interjected and talked about his rookie season, and as soon as he started talking, I knew it was going to be another view of the same game. He was in the whirlpool with Don Drysdale, and they were listening to Vin Scully on the radio when Drysdale told Osteen that they had to get out of the whirlpool and get on the bench. He could just tell it would be something special. After seven innings, Koufax was perfect and leading, 1–0. Sandy was sitting right next to Claude, and of course nobody was saying anything because of the baseball superstition about not talking to a pitcher when he has a no-hitter.

Koufax told his catcher, Jeff Torborg, not to call any more curveballs because he couldn't get a feel for it. Torborg said there was pressure on him because he was calling it to change speeds so that the Cubs couldn't sit on one pitch. Koufax, who had no sense of humor, said, "If someone gets a hit these last two innings, they're going to earn it. Don't call it any more. If you want me to change speeds, we'll just start changing off my fastball because we'll start adding to it." Claude was sitting there trying not to laugh because he'd never seen a human being throw as hard as what he'd been watching, and Koufax just said with a straight face that he'd start adding to it.

Koufax had a stylish delivery, like Fred Couples' golf swing. He was fluid as could be, but the last two innings he was throwing every pitch as though it would be the hardest and the last that he was ever going to throw. There was so much effort and violence that his hat kept falling off. The Cubs had no chance in the ninth. Harvey Kuenn, a former batting champion in the AL, was the last out. He actually made the last out of another Koufax no-hitter. Kuenn was at the end of his career. Joey Amalfitano made the second out and told Kuenn, who was pinch-hitting, that he didn't need to take a bat up because he had no chance. He struck out.

Everyone in Chicago claims they were at the Kerry Wood game, but it was one of those typical cold, shitty days. Even though we usually filled the park every day, there were only about 15,000 fans at that game. I'm from California, so my dad had told me about the fans, but until you experience it first-hand, this whole loveable losers thing and the fanaticism of Cubs fans is pretty amazing. On the West Coast, it's the Dodgers-Giants rivalry, but because of the proximity of North and South Side Chicago, it pales in comparison to Cubs-White Sox.

I remember they gave me an Explorer in Chicago. They gave me a car. I don't even remember signing anything for it. The dealership just gave me the keys. Of course, their license plates and the logo advertising the dealership were all over the car because when you get to Wrigley Field, there's a parking lot for players and coaches. These fanatical fans are there to get autographs at all hours of the morning as you pull in. As coaches, we would usually get to the ballpark at 7:30 or 8:00 in the morning for a 1:20 game. I remember some guy from Springfield, Illinois, who was standing in the rain with his umbrella just to get autographs. I mean, this is really going overboard for anybody's autograph. Certainly not mine, but even for Sosa's or Grace's.

When I got to the big leagues, I also didn't know about the Cubs-Cardinals rivalry. From the first time we went to St. Louis, I felt like I was at a Nebraska football game. When you're standing in your blue uniform in the third base coaches' box and you look around the stadium and see 50,000 people dressed in red, it's like a college football atmosphere. I've often read that Cardinals fans as a whole are extremely knowledgeable about the game. I would have to concur. A lot of cities have rabid fans and support. We of course did in Chicago, and the Yankees and Red Sox have passionate fans, more so than I was exposed to growing up on the West Coast. St. Louis fans really seem to know the inside of the game. A guy would hit a weak ground ball to get a runner over, and the fans would acknowledge that it was a team at-bat. It was fun going there, and with us being in contention it made the games dramatic.

A few weeks after Wood's performance, I took part in a far less enjoyable game. We took a 7–1 lead against Curt Schilling and the Phillies, but Philadelphia came back and led, 8–7, heading into the bottom of the ninth. Sosa was on first with one out when Grace doubled off the ivy. I was trying to stop Sammy, but he was running with his head down and didn't see me. On the relay to the plate, Sammy finally put on the brakes and tried to get back to third but was thrown out. That was a painful loss. I had to answer a bunch of questions after that. I was also the base running coach, so it was my job in spring training to do a better job of teaching everybody to make eye contact with me at all times. I felt directly responsible for that loss.

As the third base coach, it is your fault. You've got to find a way. Sammy still had speed at that point, but he had a habit at times of running with his head down. Guys like Willie Mays and Pete Rose were always given credit for their awareness because they always knew where the ball was. There are other players who tend to more or less have blinders on,

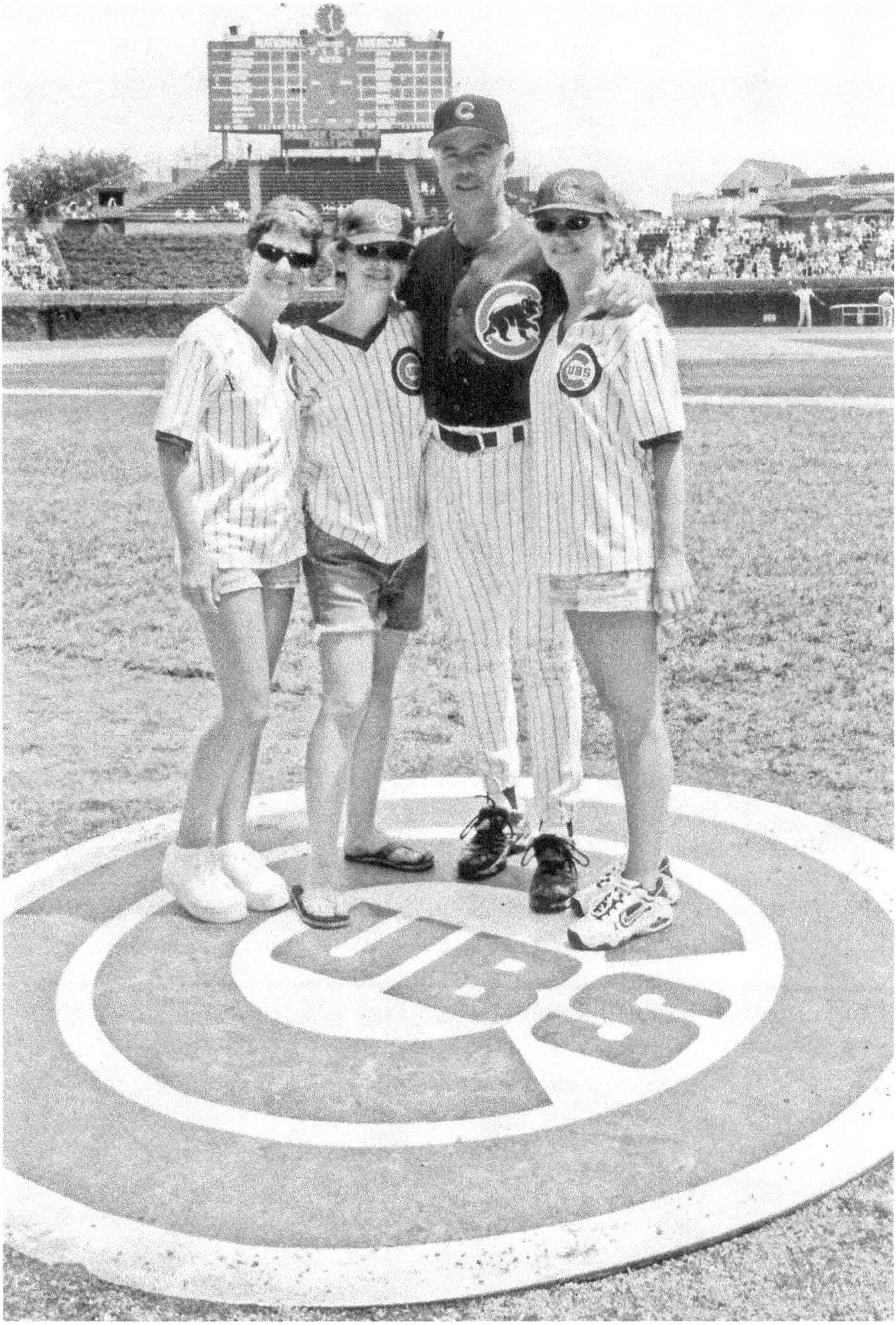

Shannon, Jamie, Rebecca join me before a game at Wrigley Field.

who don't have a field awareness of where the ball is. Grace had gotten such a big hit, and we should have had runners on second and third with one out. I took the hit from the press. There's no third base coach who doesn't make a mistake. You're a traffic cop. You take enough pride that your good decisions are going to far outweigh the bad ones. And a player can't hear you verbally because there are 38,000 people at the park.

Nobody cared about Sosa's running in June. After hitting six homers in April and seven more in May, Sammy hit 20 in June. It was fun to watch. The Cubs hadn't made the playoffs since 1989, and in June there was a reality that we were in the race. Dan Radison commented that if Sosa could keep hitting homers like this, then we'd finally have a chance to be in the race. I thought that Sosa would keep hitting them. Radison said, "Well he's not going to do this all year long. Nobody could do that." I just knew that he was so strong. We didn't know what he was on. There was no attention paid to steroids at that time. It just was what it was. I told Radison that Sammy would keep hitting them, and Rad noted that "if he keeps hitting them then he'll break the record. I never thought I'd see the record broken but unless he gets hurt, I just don't see that he's not going to keep hitting them." He improved his hitting technique so much under Jeff Pentland, and he was so strong that he didn't have to hit them good. When he hit them good, they went out of the stadium. When he just hit it okay, it went over the fence.

People ask me what the biggest difference with Sosa was that year. To me, the single biggest difference was the 1–1 pitch. The 1–1 count is the most critical, in my opinion. Even if the umpire misses the first pitch and calls it a strike, you still have two left. Prior to 1998, Sosa was so aggressive and such a wild, free swinger that he struck out a lot and basically was a .260 hitter. On the 1–1 count, they would throw a slider or a chase pitch, and he would check his swing or go after it. Now you've really changed the whole count because at 1–2, you're not going to get a good ball to hit. The pitcher's in the driver's seat now. When a hitter swings at a bad pitch, there's a good chance the pitcher is going to throw the same thing again. If he chased it once, he may chase it twice, and Sosa would strike out. Or Sosa knew he'd looked real bad on a slider in the dirt and was expecting them to do it again, and then he would strike out looking on a fastball right down the pipe.

Pentland came on board and hit it off with Sosa immediately in spring training. Pentland and I had grown up together. He was a great college hitting coach at Arizona State, where he had played. I knew he was going to be a good addition, but I didn't know just how well he and Sosa were going to click. He got Sosa to double-tap. Instead of one step into the ball, it was two. He could let the ball come to him and hit it deeper, which would open up the field for him instead of just pulling the ball. What I saw right from April was that on the 1–1 pitch, Sosa would take the slider down and away. He was so strong and in such a good hitting position that it made me back up deeper in the coaches' box. I thought, "Oh my God, if he gets a strike it's going to happen again." That's why I was so confident when I told Radison that he was going to keep doing it all year. He was in such a good hitting position it didn't even matter what they threw. If it got in the strike zone he was going to kill it. Pentland deserves a lot of the credit for that. Sosa hit .251 in 1997 and improved dramatically to .308 in 1998.

It got to a point where men would be on base and he wouldn't chase, and the count would get to 2–1, 3–1, where they had to throw a strike. There would be times where I told the runner at third base to be careful because "if this ball gets in the zone it's going to be killed." I don't want him to be killed because this is going to be a rocket somewhere. It just kept happening.

Rene Lachemann was the third base coach for the Cardinals, and he'd always be right against our dugout railing at Wrigley when Mark McGwire came up. We would tease him and told him that he might as well come into the dugout with us. He'd say, "Well I'm sure as hell not gonna be in the box if McGwire turns on one. I'd have no time to get out of the way." I never gave it a thought when Sosa was up. I mean, I probably should've, especially when there was a runner at second base and I'd be in front of the third base box so I could get a better angle and help the runner. I just never gave a thought about being hit, and yet I was 75 feet away. I should've been worried, but I was too stupid to ever think about it.

Believe it or not, you're totally oblivious. They used to mic me for the FOX Game of the Week, and they were always trying to remind me that they had to bleep me a lot because of the obscenities. The problem was that the moment that the game starts, I'm so focused on the game and talking to the runner at third about situations, I'm totally unaware that I'm wearing a microphone.

We went on a ten-game win streak from late May to early June. It's great when something like that happens. You can't wait to get to the park when you've got that kind of momentum going. It began with a win over the Braves in a game Tom Glavine started. Brant Brown hit a walk-off homer for us. We swept Atlanta, Florida, the White Sox, and took a game from the Twins. Henry Rodriguez was big in that stretch. He hit 31 home

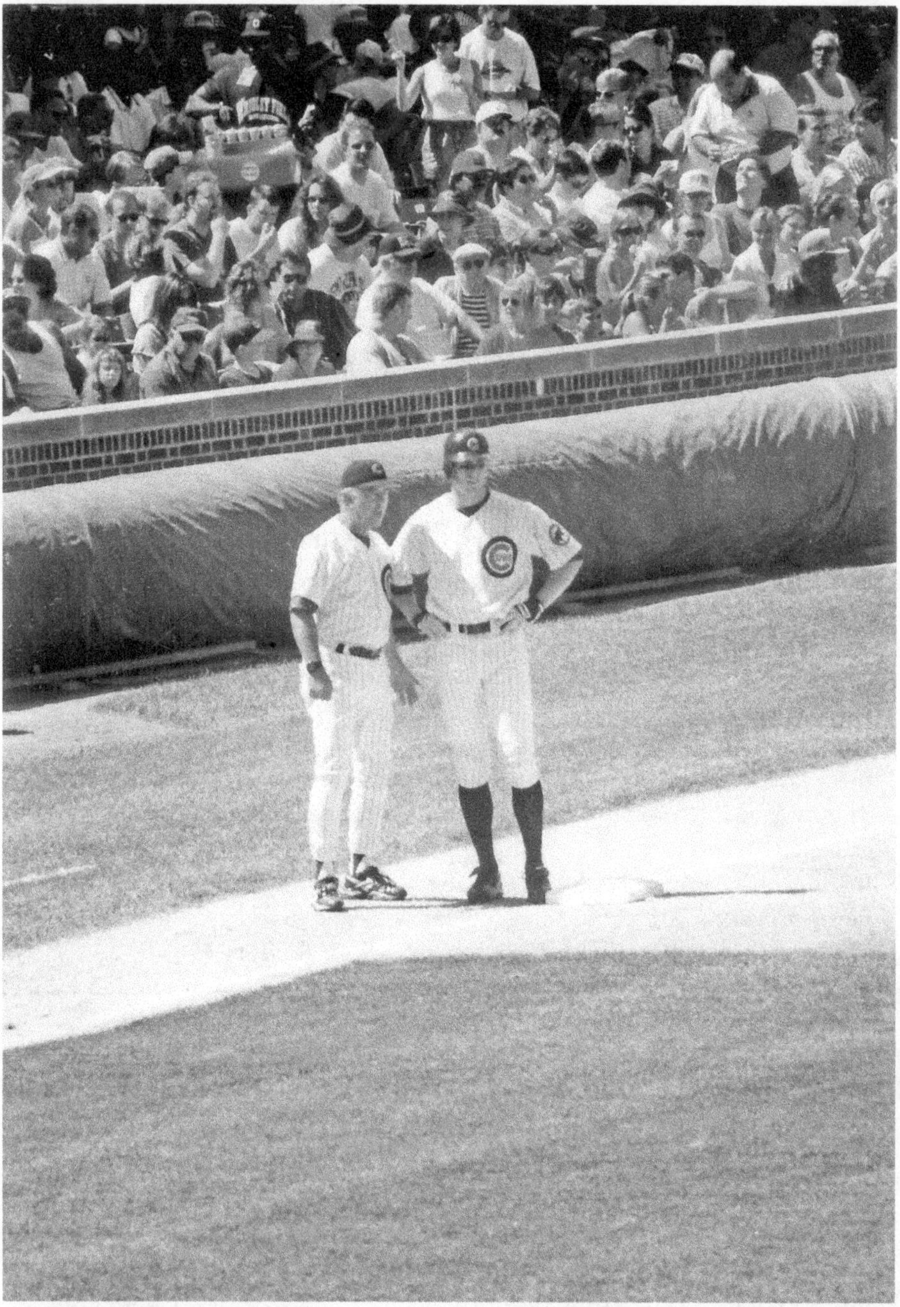

Talking with outfielder Brant Brown as I am coaching third base in 1998. Brown hit 15 homers before being traded to Pittsburgh in the offseason.

runs in 1998. It may not have gotten national attention, but the guys on the team knew it. Henry was the protection behind Sosa, a left-handed hitter with big-time power to all fields. He was a great guy too. Real quiet with no ego but a great run producer. Limited range in left but real good hands.

Jose Hernandez hit 23 homers for us. He was one of the stars on my team in Puerto Rico and was a utility player with really good tools but very low confidence. I had kept telling everybody with the Cubs that he was better than we thought he was. He played against me, and all he could do was play defense, and then my owner traded for him and I couldn't believe the power that he had. A lot of strikeouts but big-time power. You just had to keep his confidence going. He set the record with 20 homers in one season in Puerto Rico. Before the White Sox series, Riggleman told me that Hernandez was going to start, so I should have a talk with him and get him to produce. He homered in three straight games, two against Chicago and one against Minnesota. That got him off to a nice start, and he did a good job.

The only player still on the roster from the 1989 playoff team was Mark Grace. Grace hit .309 in 1998 and actually finished the decade with the most hits of any player in baseball. He was a terrific hitter with an incredible sense of timing. We got to talk a lot in the clubhouse because most players and coaches were married and left early, but we were single and didn't have to rush out. We'd have a couple of beers, and he'd always have a few cigarettes. He was an intelligent guy and very articulate, so I was curious as to what he would do with his post-playing career. Grace told me he thought about broadcasting or coaching. He asked what I made, and I told him $100,000. He looked at me in total disbelief and said, "You can live on that?"

In addition to the salary, we were getting $100 a day in meal money on the road, and you get licensing money because every player, coach, trainer and manager shares in a royalty fund for anything that sells with a big league logo on it. One year I got a check for about $35,000. In addition to my home I have a rental house in California. Compared to my friends in my peer group at age 50, I was considered to be doing well, and Grace was asking me if I could live on that. He'd been in the big leagues so long that this was like Monopoly money to him. He told me that he forgot what the real world was like. He later got into broadcasting and coaching. Grace announced for the Diamondbacks, and then after a DUI he became a hitting coach in the minors and is now the hitting coach for the big club.

Of course, the main guy in 1998 was Sosa. He hit grand slams in back-to-back games against Arizona in July. Sammy hadn't hit one in over 4,400 career at-bats and then hit one two days in a row. What are the odds of that? In the game where he hit the second one, he had flied out to deep center in the first inning. He told me that the pitcher was going to try to get him out with that inside pitch again and that he was "going to hit it so fucking far that they'll never find it." I was thinking about that when he came up with the bases loaded. Sammy hit this prodigious bomb. He goes, "I told you." I go, "Yeah you did."

It amazes me how easy it was for some guys. A few years earlier, one of our first spring training games was against the Giants at Hohokam Park in Mesa. Barry Bonds had some new shoes, and when he went to the plate he was hitting the cleats with the bat, as if they didn't have enough attention. They were black with orange stripes. Our catcher was Scott Servais, and he said, "Nice zebras, Barry." Barry said, "Watch this zebra leave the yard." Frank Castillo throws a slider, and Bonds hits it out to right-center. It's the first week of spring training. A few days later, we went to Scottsdale to play the Giants at their park. Bonds hits another one out of the park. Servais comes back to the dugout shaking his head. They were talking when Bonds told him that there are only a few guys that can hit it out when they want to, and that on the first strike he saw he'd do it again. This is the kind of shit that we all did in the backyard when you're playing wiffle ball with your friends, but not in the big leagues. Some of the guys are just that talented.

The other guy that I've heard similar stories about was Ken Griffey, Jr. I actually got to manage Mackey Sasser, a former teammate of both Bonds and Griffey. He was coming up through the minor leagues when I was starting my managing career. Mackey really didn't have a position, but he could fucking hit. He played against me in a few different leagues, and once I managed him in an All-Star Game. Down by two runs, I brought him up to pinch-hit with two on and two out. I said, "Mack, just pretend you're playing against Beloit." We could never get him out. He went to the plate, saw one pitch, and lined a ball up the gap for a two-run double. I told the guys in the dugout that he did that to my team all the time. I had Mack at the end of his career, and during a rain delay I asked him to compare Bonds and Griffey.

We're talking about arguably the two best guys in the game. I only saw them as opponents. Sasser said that Griffey played the game like an 18-year-old. The game was just so easy for him, but he did something that kind of freaked his teammates out. Griffey forgot it was Mothers' Day until he got to the park and everybody was talking about it. He called his mom from a clubhouse phone and apologized, but said he'd hit a home run for her. Who says that? This is the big leagues. And then he went out and hit one. The next month, it was Fathers' Day, and his dad was the first base coach for Seattle. He gave his dad a big hug and told him he'd hit a home run, and then came through. Guys in the dugout were just looking at each other like "who does this?" The only way I can relate to stories like that is that I used to do this kind of stuff when I played over-the-line with my friends, and you could kind of control what you were doing. The guy that's pitching to you is on your team, so you're just going to wait for a pitch that you can fucking drive out there. But it's not competition in the big leagues, when a guy is out there throwing 95.

We had some good arms on Chicago. Kevin Tapani was a master of pitching and won 19 games in 1998. He was our version of Greg Maddux. Tapani worked fast, threw strikes, kept the ball down and never threw a pitch without knowing what the next one was going to be. Like Maddux, he didn't have overpowering stuff or an ideal pitcher's body, but he had pinpoint control. Before we got him, I admired him when he pitched in Minnesota. He was on the 1991 World Series champs. I knew we were getting a class guy that younger guys could learn from because he really knew how to pitch. He was our ace. Kerry Wood was the guy everybody wanted to see because of the stuff, but Tapani was like the professor that Wood and all the guys on our staff were learning from.

Steve Trachsel was a real good competitor, a great guy but very hard to play behind. There's a reason he was known as "The Human Rain Delay." We couldn't get him to see that. Trachsel had no idea how slow he worked. He was very analytical. He was the kind of guy that players prayed wouldn't pitch on getaway day on the road, because you knew you were in for a long one. I told him that there was a reason we played better defense when Tapani pitched. As a former center fielder, I tried hard behind everybody, but he's the type of guy that psychologically, the players are expecting him to go into deep counts on every batter. When a ball is hit, I might be a step late as opposed to Tapani, who worked so fast and threw so many strikes that it was almost like batting practice. You're assuming that every pitch has a chance to be hit to you, and guys have a better first-step jump on balls.

As we got into August, we were really in the race. Rod Beck was doing a great job as closer, but we were struggling in the set-up role. We traded a prospect, Jon Garland, to our crosstown rival for Matt Karchner. Garland would become an All-Star and World Series champion in 2005. Karchner had good stuff, but the White Sox were out of it and it was a big jump going from the White Sox to where 38,000 people packed in like sardines every day at Wrigley in the middle of a pennant race. I think the pressure of that got to Karchner. He was victimized a bit by the home run ball, which could happen to anybody. There was a writer for the *Chicago Tribune* who was like their version of Jim Murray at the *Los Angeles Times*. He made a living off of sarcasm. He wrote that when the Cubs gave up Garland for Karchner, all we heard about was the tremendous movement that Karchner had on his power sinker, but so far the only movement he'd seen off Karchner's pitches "are when they're taking the first bounce off Waveland Avenue." The players hated it, but as a guy with a sense of humor I thought it was funny. The poor guy was just in a rut, and it got on his mind. He'd be hoping to get by, and he'd make one bad pitch and sonofabitch, they'd hit it out again.

The same writer also made fun of Scott Servais. Scott called a good game and could hit a little bit, but was inconsistent behind the plate. So this guy wrote on the front page of the paper that he wasn't sure which was worse: his mid-winter bout with the flu or sitting behind the plate at a Cubs game, trying to watch Servais throw out Expos runners. It was funny, but it also wasn't funny because you're ripping players on our team who are trying their best.

The nation was captivated by the home run chase between Sosa and Mark McGwire, but our focus was on trying to get that wild card. Baseball is such a team game, the new regime was in its fourth season, and the Cubs had done nothing but lose. As the days grew fewer, everyone had been eliminated except the Mets, Giants and us.

Still, the home run thing was nice. It was exciting to witness it firsthand. We had a two-game series with the Cardinals in early September with McGwire sitting on 60 homers. Flying into St. Louis, I knew we were going to see it. Not just that it was going to happen, but that I was going to see it in person. I remember saying on the plane, "God, I never thought I'd see somebody break the Maris record, and we're going to see it." Dan Radison said, "It's obvious he's going to break the record but it's not going to happen right now." I said, "Yeah it is. I know it's going to."

In the first inning of the first game, he hit number 61. The next day in batting practice, he took 15 swings and hit 14 of them out. He was just locked in. It was like watching a professional golfer hitting balls. When McGwire came to the plate in the fourth to face Trachsel, I got off the bench and was hanging on the railing. Wood and Tapani told me they couldn't see. I said, "Get up here and watch. This is going to be history."

Tapani said, "Well, he's not going to do it right now." I said, "Yes he is. It's going to happen in this at-bat. I know it is." Except it was so totally different than what you expected, because usually McGwire's home runs were majestic bombs that could be appreciated. This one was just a rocket line drive into the left-field corner, just barely fair and just barely over the fence. It happened so fast that I think it caught everybody by surprise. It was like time stood still for a second, and then everybody realized it just happened. Then you saw all the flashbulbs going off.

We still had a game to win. When McGwire came to the plate in the sixth with the game tied at two, an intentional walk was given. Then Ray Lankford hit a three-run homer to give the Cardinals the lead. Go figure. St. Louis won, 6–3, to finish a two-game sweep.

It wasn't the first premonition I had about a home run. In 1974, I was coaching a high school team in LA, and after practice I told all my players to watch the Dodgers-Braves game that night. I told them that the second time Hank Aaron came to the plate against Al Downing, he would hit career homer 715 to break the record. I don't know why I knew that, but I knew it. I was watching the game on TV with my wife, and when Aaron came to the plate for his second at-bat, I told her it was going to happen. Sure enough, he hit a homer over the left field fence. As McGwire ran around the bases, Wood came up to me and asked how I knew that was going to happen. I just knew.

The Cubs players were shaking hands with McGwire as he rounded the bases. Even though you're in a competition, you're acknowledging something historic. Sammy ran all the way in from right field to celebrate with him. Sosa passed Maris' mark five days later.

We began a three-game series with Milwaukee with Sosa sitting at 58 homers and the Brewers trying to play spoiler. We lost the first game, 13–11, even though Sosa hit number 59. The next day, the Brewers took a 10–2 lead but Sosa hit his 60th home run of the season as we fought back to tie the game. Orlando Merced hit a three-run homer to give us a 15–12 win. The rubber match may have been the craziest game. Sosa hit his 61st homer, but Milwaukee took a 10–8 lead into the ninth. Sosa hit his 62nd homer, and Gary Gaetti's RBI single tied the game 10–10. Sammy didn't get a chance to hit number 63. Mark Grace hit a walk-off homer in the tenth for an 11–10 win. There were 72 combined runs scored in the three games.

Sosa came to me and said, "You could've gotten a little more excited. Sammy Sosa broke the home run record today." I mocked him and said, "Oh, I saw that last week with McGwire."

Less than two weeks later, we went to Milwaukee for a two-game series. We won the first game and then took a 7–0 lead in the second game with Sammy hitting his 64th and 65th homers. The Brewers fought back to cut the lead to 7–5 and loaded the bases with two outs in the ninth. Rod Beck got Geoff Jenkins to hit a routine fly ball to left, but the wind was blowing in. Brant Brown went back on it and then when he turned, the wind started knocking it down. When he came in, he actually should've made a basket catch. It hit the heel of his glove, and he dropped it. All three runs scored and we lost, 8–7. That was a long walk in. I felt so bad for Brant after that one. He was primarily a first baseman but played a good left field when Henry Rodriguez was hurt. He was never a big power guy, but he hit 14 homers that year, and they all seemed to come at big times. He hit two walk-off homers and another shot that tied a game in the ninth.

Brant took it like a man, faced the press, and didn't make any excuses. I felt really bad for him, but I admired that he owned up to it because that's really all you can do. Everybody sympathized with Brant because it's no fun to be the goat. It's not like it was a tough play, but he just missed it. He would've caught that 99 times out of 100, but because it was such a big game everybody was aware of it. That's the nature of the game. We've all been there. I felt the same way after Sosa was thrown out against the Phillies. It's one thing to lose a game in the minors in front of a few thousand people, but when you're fighting for the playoffs and you have Cubs Nation watching on WGN and something like that happens, you're on the big stage. Ron Santo had the famous "Oh No!" call that was replayed for years. Ronnie sat behind me on the plane, and I told him it sounded like someone was dying in the broadcast booth. He said, "They were, it was me."

He lived and died with the Cubs.

With two games left in the season, we were tied with the Mets and Giants for the wild card spot. The Mets lost their final two games to Atlanta and were eliminated. We were playing in Houston, and the Giants were playing in Colorado. Sosa hit his 66th homer in that series. It was one of the longest home runs I ever saw, into the upper deck of the Astrodome. Could a baseball really go that far? I just kept looking at the spot.

We lost the final game in 11 innings after leading 3–1 in the eighth. I remember the letdown of feeling that we worked our asses off all season, and now we're out of it. We were walking up stairs to get to the clubhouse when we heard cheering inside. Between the time we left the field and walked into the clubhouse, Neifi Perez hit a walk-off home run off Robb Nen to give the Rockies a 9–8 win. San Francisco had blown a 7–0 lead just like we had done four days earlier. Instead of our season ending, there was going to be a one-game playoff.

A coin-toss determined that the game would be at Wrigley Field instead of Candlestick Park. Steve Trachsel got the start and pitched the game of his life. There was a lot of speculation in the press that he wasn't up to a game of that magnitude. I always liked Trachsel. He had a great work ethic, and he had plus major league stuff. He was one of those anal types. If he wasn't a baseball player, he'd have been a CPA. I could see why he pitched slowly. The way his mind worked, he was going to think of all the possibilities.

I have to tip my hat. Trachsel was terrific against a Giants team that had Bonds and Jeff Kent. They had a good team, and Trachsel took a no-hitter into the seventh. Gary Gaetti hit a home run off Mark Gardner. Gaetti was a third baseman who had a great career but was at the end of it that year. We picked him up late in the year and actually signed him on his 40th birthday. His hands were great, but he didn't have the range. He came up with some big hits for us that year.

After Trachsel was taken out in the seventh, we used Karchner and Felix Heredia to finish the inning. Tapani came out of the bullpen to pitch the eighth. We led 5–0 going into the ninth. Then we needed Tapani, Terry Mulholland and Rod Beck to record the final three outs to hold on to a 5–3 win. Beck finished the season with 51 saves, not bad for his first year as a Cub. He had a fabulous year for us, and we never would have sniffed the playoffs without him. Getting Rod Beck was a lifesaver.

Beck died in 2007. I remember he had a big party in spring 1998 with his wife, Stacey, and two beautiful little girls. Because of the drugs, the lifestyle, and the hard partying, I can't say I was shocked, although it was sad. Beck had the perfect make-up for a closer. Barrel-chested, beer-belly, beer-drinking, had his little Fu Manchu. He had the menacing look like Al Hrabosky. The out-of-shape, fun-loving guy who was also unbelievably competitive. He was just determined that he was going to find a way to get you out. When he lost his stuff, he went back to the Cubs and was pitching for their Triple-A team and living in his motor home in the parking lot. That didn't surprise me because he loved to compete. He was the type of guy who would've kept playing baseball even if it was in a beer-drinking park league. He just loved everything about the camaraderie, the competition during the game and the beer drinking after it.

Another pitcher who passed away was Kevin Foster. He was a Cub, and later in his career he pitched in Puerto Rico, so our paths crossed. He had a loose arm and was a good teammate. There was one year where he started off great and then struggled to win in the second half. He pitched up in the zone and was a fly ball pitcher. In April, May and early June, the wind comes in off Lake Michigan, and it's cold and damp when the wind is blowing in. The fly balls, even by Sosa, are cut in half, and they become easy outs. Then in June, July and August, when the summer winds come, they're blowing straight out from behind home plate out to the outfield, and now routine fly balls get blown right out of the stadium.

Back in the 1970s, you could count on one hand the players who could hit home runs on a semi-regular basis to the opposite field. Dale Murphy, Mike Schmidt, Steve Garvey. But when the winds blew out in the summer of 1998, Mickey Morandini, who weighed 165 pounds and hit three home runs a year, hit a home run in the basket in left-center field and I couldn't believe it. You just can't be a fly ball pitcher at Wrigley Field in the summertime.

I'm a traditionalist. I wasn't for the wild card when they put it in, but they knew what they were doing. It created a lot of excitement in New York, San Francisco and Chicago in 1998. There's no excitement if Houston just runs away with the division. It was thrilling until the last day of the season and even a 163rd game. On the night of the playoff, the beer and restaurant sales had the biggest one-day take in the history of Chicago. Only 38,000 people could be in the park, but the atmosphere in the city was such that nobody wanted to be at home. If you couldn't be at Wrigley, you wanted to be at a sports bar with other people. That's when I realized the magnitude of it all. It was something when they finally won the World Series in 2016.

It was on to the NLDS to face the Braves. We knew it was going to be an uphill battle facing John Smoltz, Tom Glavine and Greg Maddux. But gosh darn it, we had them in Game Two. After Atlanta took Game One, Tapani had a 1–0 lead in the ninth inning of Game Two. Javy Lopez tied the game with a one-out homer. Just one bad pitch. Chipper Jones had the walk-off hit in the tenth, and that was basically the series. That was the one game we were in. I didn't get to wave many runners home as we scored four runs in three games. The series might have been different if we had won Game Two and stole the home-field advantage.

It was a fun season. Once the weather got decent, we had 38,000 fans at every single home game. You could feel the electricity and energy when you're on the field. There is something different about Wrigley Field and

Fenway Park. I don't know if it's nostalgia, but you can feel it before the game starts. Wood was named NL Rookie of the Year and Sosa won the MVP Award. In addition to the 66 home runs, Sammy had 158 RBI. Wow. Nobody else on the team had 90.

At the time what I didn't know, because I was naïve on the subject, was the steroid thing. That was an era where there wasn't much talk, even in the clubhouse, about steroids. That was before it all became exposed and talked about. The first time it came to my attention, we were on a plane and our team doctor passed around a pamphlet amongst the coaches with a picture of Barry Bonds. There was a picture of him early in his career with the Pirates and one of him with the Giants. It was like looking at a normal person and then The Incredible Hulk.

There was an article by a team doctor about what to look for in people on steroids. It talked about acne, both on the back and face, and said it made your head expand. And of course your muscles became humungous. Strength and stamina improved, and there was weight gain.

The first day of spring training, it was obvious that Sammy was bigger. I remember saying, "Oh my God, what did you do this winter?" He said, "Sammy worked out hard on the weights this winter." He referred to himself in the third person.

Sosa was as strong as a bull. I just assumed that he was in the weight room all winter, pumping iron. As strong as he was before, now he was just incredibly strong. When he started taking batting practice, he was hitting balls off the scoreboard. In Hohokam, there was a concourse in left field and then a video board. He'd hit balls off the netting that was protecting the scoreboard. They looked like Titleist twos going out of there instead of baseballs.

I was naïve about the whole thing even after the fact. In my career, major or minor, the only time I ever saw anybody taking anything was when I managed in Mexico in 2004. I would occasionally see guys taking shots in the buttocks before the game. When I inquired as to what it was, they told me it was B12. I don't even know what B12 does.

Between my time with the Cubs and Royals, there was getting to be some talk about steroids. When I saw Jason Grimsley, he was a hard-throwing, sinkerball relief pitcher with good stuff. His command was so-so, but his stuff was real good. He had quite a few years in the league and was a former number one draft choice of the Phillies. He was a good guy, a good teammate, and was well-liked by everybody on the Royals.

I'd go in the weight room to work out, and I'd see him get on a stationary bike and peddle that thing so fast. Not just for five or ten minutes but for a half-hour at an incredible pace. I just couldn't believe it. Something that you or I could do for 60 seconds, Grimsley could do for 30 minutes. It's not like he did interval training where he'd peddle hard and then coast for awhile. He just went balls-out for 30 minutes. There'd be smoke coming off the bike chains. It was really something to watch.

I just couldn't believe it. He was in really good shape, but he was 35 at the time. I was just amazed. I never had that kind of stamina in my 20s, let alone my 30s. I never thought anything other than that he was just in great shape. He was lean and had no body fat.

A few years later, he became one of the first players busted for performance-enhancing drugs. He had them sent right from the factory to his home and the clubhouse. There was no hiding about it. He retired and disappeared. I had no idea that something man-made could increase your stamina. I thought you did that by running and walking, the conventional ways.

That's what made me so sure in my own mind that Lance Armstrong had to be on something when he was winning all those cycling titles. That explained how Grimsley was able to deny the law of diminishing returns to peddle that bike. Armstrong won the Tour de France every year and was passing drug tests, but I told my friends that it wasn't possible.

Everyone was talking about it when Bonds was doing what he was doing. McGwire's 70 was incredible, and now here's a guy hitting 73. And he was setting records for intentional walks. That's when sportswriters and fans got on the bandwagon. Then there was Rafael Palmeiro pointing his finger at Congress and then, lo and behold, he failed a test.

McGwire has returned to the majors as a hitting coach with the Cardinals and Dodgers, and a bench coach with the Padres. The Sosa-McGwire battle, and that whole 1998 season, really brought a lot of fans back who had been turned off by the strike several years earlier. They liked the home runs and all the runs scored. At the time, you never saw sportswriters writing about anything regarding drugs. That home run chase of two charismatic guys with two different personalities grabbed the public. McGwire was more on the shy, introvert side, and Sosa was the total extrovert. It was like when I was a kid in 1961 with the Roger Maris–Mickey Mantle chase of Babe Ruth that captivated America. It certainly put baseball back on the map and popularized it again.

Everybody expected to build off 1998. We assumed we were going to be right there, and we were until we were in Arizona and it went south. And when it went south, it was a long season from June until the end of September. The optimism of spring training, April and May quickly faded, and it got completely ugly.

We were bringing back most of the players from a 90-win team and had traded Brant Brown for Jon Lieber. That was a great addition. Lieber and John Smoltz had the two best sliders in the league. Lieber had good command and was a great teammate and competitor.

Kerry Wood would miss the season. He was born with a weak arm, and it had nothing to do with how much he was used or wasn't used previously. The doctors thought it would go at some time.

Rod Beck, who closed out 51 of our 90 wins the year before, really struggled. He had lost his command and was walking a lot of batters. The fans loved him so much because they could relate to the beer drinking, overweight guy who competed his ass off and loved to play, but I think the game just caught up with him in 1999, health-wise and stuff-wise.

With Beck struggling, we acquired Rick Aguilera, who had won titles with the Mets and Twins. He was a proven commodity. We thought he was going to be a good addition because he'd been a good pitcher, but Wrigley's a different park. Aguilera really struggled. Everybody felt bad for him.

We were always looking for a left-handed reliever. In the spring of 1998, we had a chance to trade for John Rocker. I had a vast knowledge of non–Cubs because of my time in the minors and in Puerto Rico. Braves shortstop Walt Weiss was injured in spring training, and they needed a replacement. They came to us, asking for Manny Alexander. Manny was a good, all-around utility player and a veteran who knew how to play.

Atlanta gave us a list of players to choose from. I was called off the field to go in with Ed Lynch and Andy MacPhail. Through 1997, John Rocker had never pitched above Double-A and had not been successful in the Braves' system. Guy Hansen was in the Royals' system, and the general manager had been John Schuerholz, who had gone on to Atlanta. He asked Guy for a favor, getting Rocker into winter ball because he wasn't cutting it as a starter and they thought maybe he could convert to a reliever.

Guy told me he wanted to do it, and I said that we could always use a left-handed reliever. As it turned out, Rocker's makeup was ideally suited to it, getting three or four outs, a sprint as opposed to a marathon. His velocity was going up, and he was a very competitive guy. Rocker helped us win a championship and was more of a factor the more that he did it, when we could start using him on back-to-back days.

When I went into the office and saw Rocker's name on the list, I couldn't believe it. I said, "They're really going to give us any name on this list for Manny Alexander? We ought to call them right now because this guy Rocker's going to be a stud." I told them what he did for my Mayaguez team against major league hitters like Juan Gonzalez, Pudge Rodriguez and Bernie Williams. Plus the Cubs were looking for a lefty in the bullpen.

When we did not make that deal, I was in shock. Ed felt that we couldn't trade a big league infielder for a guy who hadn't been successful at Double-A yet. I was trying to tell him that John was just in the wrong role as a starter and was the real deal. Not only did Rocker make the roster in 1998 but MacPhail saw him pitch, came to my locker and said, "You're not really going to tell me this big guy, this is the guy we had a chance to get for Manny Alexander?" I told him it was. He had instant success and became the newest sensation, but it started the previous winter in Puerto Rico. We went through a lot of lefty relievers in my two years in Chicago. We had Bob Patterson at the end of his career, and we had Felix Heredia, a young kid we got from the Marlins. But we had a chance to get Rocker before Atlanta realized what they had.

Lance Johnson was picked off first base to end a game in Arizona, and from then on you could just sense the air was out of our balloon. That was early June, and by mid–July there was a conversation between the coaching staff, MacPhail and Lynch about starting to build for the future. Not that it was the wrong decision, because if you're not in the race, what's the point of playing people who aren't going to be with you the next year? Might as well take a look and see what your needs are going to be. But the attitude and the chemistry of the team were going to go south.

Because we had so many free agents and we fell out of the race, management, rightfully so, wanted to play younger guys, except we were caught at a point where we didn't have a lot of prospects in the system. To sit down guys like Benito Santiago, Gary Gaetti and Mickey Morandini, it was like a lack of respect shown to veterans with long-term careers. Now they're sitting on the bench in favor of lesser, younger players, knowing they're not going to be back the following year. And none of the younger guys really panned out.

It was the first time in their careers the veterans were sitting. They understood it was a business, but none of them liked it. As free agents, how were they going to attract attention for the next year? You can't put statistics on the board if you're not getting the opportunity to play.

Veterans can take sitting behind a young stud. If it's Kris Bryant or Kyle Schwarber or any of these guys the Cubs trot out now, it becomes easier to accept from the veterans' standpoint. But that wasn't the case in 1999. And all that did was add fuel to the fire in terms of the attitude of the whole team going in the tank.

The whole thing created a real sour atmosphere and attitude in the clubhouse. It's very tough when you're on your way to losing 95 games and you're not building anything for the future. It was painful to endure. Our young guys couldn't really compete. We were outmanned before the game started. Riggleman handled the situation the best that he could. He didn't want these guys to completely die on the pine, so they were getting at-bats here and there.

Everybody could see that there was nothing anybody could do about it. It was a problem that couldn't be fixed. When Riggleman and I would go out for dinner, there weren't decisions to make on how to fix this. We understood why management didn't want to play the veterans. It was just a shame that we didn't have better players to give at-bats and innings pitched to.

The media was tough on us. In Chicago, it's everywhere, so you can't really avoid it. I would hear some of the players and staff talking about these sports talk shows, but I was never one to listen to them. That's not good or bad, it just doesn't appeal to me. I always liked reading the *Sun-Times* and the *Tribune* because I liked to have a pulse of what's going on in the big leagues, and I liked checking the box scores. But when you're spending more time at the ballpark than you are with your family, which is what a 162-game schedule is, it can be a long, long ordeal when you're not winning.

The fans at Wrigley weren't happy with us, and I don't blame them. We were coming off a Cinderella year and we lost 95 games. After June 8, we went 35–72, basically losing two of every three. We didn't win a series for two months. It couldn't get over fast enough. Once we were out of the race, it became a total clusterfuck.

In Morandini's spot at second, we put Chad Meyers. I don't mean to disparage Meyers, but he was indicative of "this is the best we've got in the system to replace Morandini" yet it wasn't an upgrade, and as time would tell, Meyers wasn't the guy.

Jose Nieves played the final third of the season at short after we traded Jose Hernandez. It was another example of "this is the best we've got," but Nieves was another guy who didn't pan out. Meyers and Nieves got very marginal big league time.

When we sat Benito Santiago, we used Jeff Reed, a veteran, and Sandy Martinez. Martinez got a little bit of time in the big leagues and had a bazooka for an arm. But he never flourished to become a big league player.

We acquired Shane Andrews after he was cut by the Expos, and he played some third base for us. Roosevelt Brown was one of our better outfielders out of the system. He had some tools but he didn't really pan out. Bo Porter was a poor man's Bo Jackson. He had pro football potential as well as pro baseball. Porter was a gifted right fielder with a live body who could run, throw and field, but he spent three years in Single-A with us because it was a mystery as to whether he would ever hit a breaking ball. His athletic ability got him to the big leagues, but he didn't pan out either. Then he became a manager with the Astros.

Glenallen Hill was a bright spot in limited time. Hill hit 20 homers in 99 games. He had been our tenth guy in 1998, and he would DH when we played in AL ballparks. But he was another guy who had his at-bats curtailed in 1999.

Mark Grace played well in 1999, and of course Sosa was great again. He followed up his MVP season with 63 home runs.

There was a sense of gloom and doom, and when it got to September we all felt like we were lame ducks. Somebody has to be accountable, and you take the good in 1998 with the bad in 1999. The futility was so bad for a big-market team coming off a big season. Out with the old and in with the new, and that's what happened.

It was too bad because I think anybody that's ever been with the Cubs would want to spend their whole career at Wrigley Field. I'm always shocked when a free agent leaves, because of the environment at Wrigley Field and getting to play so many day games. But there is a certain sense of relief once it happens, when you know it's impending.

The last game of the season was in St. Louis. Mark McGwire hit his 65th homer and Sosa hit his 63rd. It was the last game for Willie McGee, and he got a big hand when he came off the field in the fifth inning. I was thinking how wrong I was that I turned him down all those years ago, although I was glad that one of my closest friends in the scouting fraternity, Wayne Morgan, signed Willie to the Yankees. Willie had a hell of a career and will always be a beloved figure in St. Louis.

My big league managerial career wasn't happening. In 1998, Steve Stone, the Cubs' TV analyst, came up to me at an airport terminal and said, "Who do you know with the Marlins?" I said I knew a few people but didn't get his point. Steve said that he had heard through the grapevine that I was going to be on a short list of the people they were considering for the manager position. Jim Leyland had let it be known that he wasn't returning as Marlins manager in 1999. I knew a couple of assistants to the GM, including Dick Egan, who had been my pitching coach in Puerto Rico. Dick was always a big sponsor of mine. He believed in my ability to motivate people and to run a ballgame. A week later, the *Chicago Tribune* had an article that mentioned that Tom Gamboa's name was on a short list of people to succeed Leyland. Nothing ever came of that. And when you're out of the big leagues, it's out of sight, out of mind.

The only other time I thought I was close was after the 2000 season, which was one of the best jobs I ever did. I was in Albuquerque, the Triple-A affiliate of the Dodgers, and at the end of the season they fired Davey Johnson as big league manager. I thought for certain that I was going to get an interview for a big league managing job. And I thought that if I didn't get a job, for sure they would want be to be the bench coach. When I didn't even get an interview, I gave up any aspirations to manage in the big leagues. I was content to get back as a coach.

Managing in Albuquerque

A day after the season ended, we were all asked to go to the ballpark. Riggleman told us that he wasn't being brought back. The Cubs kept Jeff Pentland because he had so much success with Sosa. The rest of us were told that the new manager would pick his own staff, so we were free to look elsewhere. That was a polite way of telling us that we were fired along with Riggleman.

Looking for a job is never a fun time, but on my drive home from Chicago to California, I got a call from the Kansas City Royals, who were managed by my friend Tony Muser. Allard Baird, who was the general manager, told me that the coaching staff had been re-signed for the 2000 season, so they would create a job roving in the minor leagues so that I could get to know their talent for a year, basically knowing that I'd be on the staff in 2001.

I was going to take it, but the Dodgers contacted me about managing their Triple-A team in Albuquerque. I called Tony and said, "Muse, obviously I want to come with you to the big leagues, but rather than for you guys to create a job for me, I would much rather manage Triple-A with the Dodgers and come with you guys next year. But I don't want to burn any bridges by saying no." It turned out that the front office was okay with that.

I knew how big the Dodgers were on loyalty. People worked for the organization for a long, long time. When I went to Dodger Stadium to talk about the job, I knew the three people interviewing me. Kevin Malone, the general manger, was a longtime friend. Bill Geivett was the Vice President of Player Development, a former Gaucho from Santa Barbara as I was, so we knew each other. And Jerry Weinstein was the farm director.

I told them up front, at the expense of the job, even having grown up as a Dodgers fan and loving the thought of managing in Albuquerque, that it certainly looked like I'd be in the big leagues with the Royals the following year. "If you're looking for somebody long-term, I understand." I wanted to be up front. I didn't want to take the job, leave after a year and have people asking why I even bothered coming. They appreciated the honesty and said they wanted me for the one year.

Being a Dodgers fan, seeing Vero Beach on TV, and hearing all the stories, I admit it was an exciting thing for me at 52 to be living at Vero in the barracks. Everybody lived on site at Dodgertown. Rick Burleson, the Double-A manager, and I were roommates, and we hit it off from the first day. Burly was a longtime major leaguer with the Red Sox and Angels. He was fairly new in his managing, and I had never played in the majors, but having been a longtime manager, Burly and I became inseparable. Between having dinner, shooting pool, and talking baseball in our room, we really became close friends.

The Dodgers have a big commissary with terrific food, and at night it was a real treat to sit at the table and listen as Tommy Lasorda would command the room with his storytelling. He was a terrific storyteller, and he had a million of them from his lifetime as a Dodger. On a personal note, it was fun for me being there.

As Triple-A manager, most of the Triple-A players are in big league camp, so I spent a good part of the camp with Davey Johnson and his big league staff. The Triple-A team is like the taxi squad of a pro football team. You're there to provide whatever the team needs. Having a mostly veteran team, the best thing that happened to bring my team together was a game late in spring training.

I was trying to get the whole club to be aggressive, not just the speed guys. We had a game towards the end of spring training against the Mets, who had six starters fighting for five spots. We were playing the Mets' Triple-A and big league team on the same day. Davey Johnson and Bobby Valentine were both watching the first game from the front row. As luck would have it, Bobby Valentine picked Dennis Springer, a knuckleball pitcher, to start in the morning game. The other guy competing for the spot would pitch against the big league team in the afternoon.

Before the game, I told my team that facing a knuckleballer was a chance for everybody to learn that seeing is believing, of how running can change the complexion of a game. We were going to steal everything that wasn't nailed down. I was always mystified by the few knuckleballers that came through. It was my observation that when Tom Candiotti, Wilbur Wood, or Phil Niekro pitched, it still seemed like the traditional game was played. If a guy has a good knuckleball, a catcher has to be basically be flat-footed and stay with it the whole way, or else they'd miss it and it'd go to the backstop. Because of the movement on the pitch, there's no opportunity to get your feet started early and cheat when a guy is about to steal a base.

I told the guys that catchers do not like to get embarrassed. The catcher against us happened to be Todd Pratt, who I worked with when I was with the Cubs. I really liked Todd, and he was known for his defense. I told them that Springer probably topped out at about 85, which is like a batting practice fastball for pro players. He had a real good knuckleball. I said, "we're going to steal enough bases and with a catcher not liking to be embarrassed, at some point in a running situation, somebody is going to get a mediocre fastball right down the pipe. Just make sure you don't miss it."

Our leadoff guy was Mike Metcalfe, a little switch-hitting second baseman. He led off the game with a drag bunt single, and two pitches later he was standing on third. We stole seven or eight bases in the first four innings.

When I went out to coach third base in the fifth inning, Pratt stood up and said, "Jesus, Tom. You're embarrassing me in front of Valentine."

I jokingly said, "Well, that's the penalty you pay for catching a knuckleballer."

In the fifth, we had runners on the corners with one out and I held the runner at first base. Because we had run so much, Pratt called for a fastball with Chris Ashby at the plate. Ashby was a big, right-handed hitter, and he hit a three-run homer to left. At that point, I knew I had proved my point to my club about how we were going to play. That turned out to be a huge thing for me personally, getting some veteran guys to realize that we'd play aggressively when we had the opportunity. That was the most meaningful game as a manager that spring.

At the beginning of the season, I addressed the team and said, "Hey, everybody would rather be in the big leagues than in Triple-A. That goes without saying. But if you're the type of guy who is always going to be focusing on LA and who got hurt and when am I going to get called up, you're going to let days go off the calendar. Make the most of the experience where you're at. It's the only thing you can control. You can't control what moves the Dodgers make."

On that club, we had a few guys who made quite an impact as big league players. My opening night starter, and number one starter, was Eric Gagne. I tip my hat to whoever it was in the Dodgers system who had the thought of making him the closer. I never thought of that. His stuff was so good that I saw him being a real good guy in the big leagues, but he became a closer, had 84 consecutive saves and won a Cy Young Award. It was incredible. You're talking about a dominating closer.

Paul Lo Duca was my catcher, although at that time the Dodgers had a big time prospect who never panned out, Ángel Peña, they wanted to catch. Lo Duca led the Dodgers in hitting that spring, and he was pissed when he got sent down. He was a fiery, competitive son of a gun. The Dodgers had Todd Hundley as the catcher and Chad Kreuter as the backup. (Hundley came down to Triple-A to rehab for a few games to get some at-bats after an injury.) And it was Lo Duca's last option, the last time they could send him down without losing him.

I said, "Paul, nobody's going to tell you that you did not deserve to make that team. You proved it on the field and behind the plate. You had an option left, and this is the business side of baseball."

He told me that he wasn't going to play at Triple-A because they wanted Peña to play. Because we had a trust in each other from spring training, I joked that, "Oh, so now you're going to manage the club here. You're telling me that you're not going to play, and I know that we're a better team with you in the lineup and probably hitting second or third. You just have to trust that I'm going to get you in there."

I had an okay from the Dodgers to play him occasionally at third and first, as well as using him as a designated hitter. Paul had actually been a shortstop in high school. Sometimes he would catch, but they wanted Pena to play. Paul found out very quickly that he was going to be an everyday player. I was true to my word, and he had a very productive season for us.

It turned out that I was the last manager in the nearly 30-year history of the Albuquerque Dukes. Pat McKernan was the owner, and it was one of the last family-owned Triple-A clubs when everything was going corporate. Pat and his wife had a lot of kids, and all were involved in the team with ticket sales, advertising and other jobs. It was a lame-duck situation because the city had voted down a bond to build a new ballpark, and the Dodgers made it known that if they were going to pull out if they didn't get a new park.

Pat owned a small restaurant in town, and before the season I said, "I feel bad for you losing the franchise, but I feel real good about the fact that you're going to go out a winner because I think we're going to have a real good chance to win the division with the team that we have. " He said that he would just be happy to finish over .500 because they hadn't had a winning season in a few years.

A few months later, we had breakfast again, and at this point we were 34–32. In the middle of breakfast, Pat said, "Don't take this the wrong way, because I'm happy we're over .500, but you actually told me we were going to win this year and I'm not seeing it."

Then I told him with unbelievable confidence, "Pat, we had so many guys that are 29 and 30 years old, that had been to the big leagues but were now like an insurance policy in Triple-A. Because of so many veteran guys, it's taking me longer than it's ever taken me to get everybody to lose themselves and their stats in the team and not worry about call-ups."

It took longer than I anticipated getting everybody to buy in. But I saw it happening. I told Pat that he wouldn't want to miss any of the games from here on out.

I knew the ability level was there, but the teamwork and the camaraderie was taking longer. To be specific, Kevin Malone had taken a kid named Hiram Bocachica, an infielder from Puerto Rico who had played against my Mayaguez teams. Bocachica had a lot of talent but had not been well-coached or bought into the team concept. We had Alex Cora leading off, and I wanted Bocachica to hit second. If Cora was on second with nobody out, the job of the hitter is to get him over to third. But Bocachica was the type of guy, even at the Triple-A level where you're supposed to know how to play, who would swing and hit the ball hard but it would be a one-hopper to the third baseman or shortstop. And then he would almost question me when I said, "That's not what you're supposed to do." His attitude was, "well I hit the ball hard, I can't control where it goes."

It finally got to a point where I brought him into the office and said, "Look, the next time we get a guy to second base with nobody out in a close game, make sure you look for it because I'm going to put the bunt on. If you don't get that guy over with the bunt, the next thing will be for me to start hitting you eighth or ninth." With nobody out, a player wants to hit. Nobody wants to hit at the bottom of the order, and it was better for the team for him to be batting second.

Later in the season he said, "I get it now. Let me try getting a guy over." As the season went on, Bocachica started not just hitting balls to the right side, but driving balls with authority into the gap in right-center and some balls out of the ballpark. He hadn't been on a playoff team in Puerto Rico, and before a game he told me, "Now I see why your team was always winning in winter ball." It was all about the team and doing what it takes to win the game.

It's not about asking a player what to do, it's telling him what he's going to do or you're going to find other options. That was the year that Bocachica put it all together, and he was called up to the majors and made his debut in September. Kevin Malone called me up because he felt vindicated. Bocachica had hit .322 with 23 homers for us in 2000.

After that breakfast with McKernan we went 52–26. That's two out of every three. It was unbelievably fun. There was one downer, although it may have helped guys get their heads straight. We had won eight of 11 and had Nashville, a last-place team from another division, come in to play us. Right from batting practice and infield, I could tell we were just there, but weren't focused. Complacency had set in. It was almost as though we're in first, they're in last and all we have to do is show up. When you play 144 games, you have nights like this, because players aren't going to be up every night like they are in football, where they play once a week. But part of being a professional is being focused day in and day out.

We were very blasé. We were trailing, 2–0, in the fourth inning and I told our trainer that I wanted him to go into the clubhouse and write on the chalkboard that win or lose, we were having a meeting after this game. When you'd walk in the clubhouse, there would be a chalkboard staring you right in the face. While we were hitting and I was coaching third, my trainer, Jason Menke, told a couple of players that I was mad and that there would be a meeting. The intensity level immediately changed, and we were more focused. Chris Prieto hit a walk-off homer in the 12th inning to give us an 8–7 win. (Prieto had 25 stolen bases that year and became the leadoff guy after Cora went to the big leagues.)

After the game, I met with a couple of writers in the dugout and then walked up the ramp and into the clubhouse. It was on the blackboard that we were having a meeting, yet guys were in the shower, getting food, and playing music. It was like there was an assumption that the meeting had been called off because we won. As a manager, it's nice that we won, but winning is an attitude. And as a manager, you're always thinking about the next game.

I got guys out of the shower and got everybody at their lockers. I said, "Winning, and the process of winning, is an all the time deal. Tiger Woods expects to win every golf tournament. It used to be that if a guy won a tournament and had a couple of top-10 finishes, it was considered good. This guy only thinks it's good if you win all of them. Not that that's going to happen in pro baseball, but it's the mindset, the attitude. You don't need me to tell you that we weren't really there today when we came to the park. It was kind of going through the motions."

I added that we wasted three innings of relief pitching that we might need tomorrow in a close game. As I rambled on, I could see from the looks on the players' faces that they were shocked that I was pissed after a win. I said, "I'm not an idiot. I know we've won nine out of 12 but the difference is, I look around this locker room and see people complacent that we've won nine out of 12, and I lay awake at night wondering how the fuck we lost the other three." That's when I slammed the door and went into my office. It's funny now, but it wasn't funny at the time.

At the end of the year, Chris Donnels made a statement about how funny it was the night I got the red ass at them. I had a goal not to snap that year, and I asked what he was talking about. He brought up the incident and added, "When you said in all seriousness that we were complacent and you lay awake at night wondering how we lost the other three, you were so pissed, but it was hard not to laugh at the expectation of that. Fortunately, your office door slammed so you were out of sight."

I think my point was proved, and it was certainly a great group. Alex Cora was with us only a part of the season before getting called up. Bocachica had his best season and developed a lot that year regarding the team concept. To me, that's what it's about. When you lose yourself in the team, the stats take care of themselves. Paul Lo Duca was a great, versatile team player who had a good year for himself. Chris Donnels had a huge year for us with 27 home runs, and he was called up before the season ended.

I think that anyone would tell you that Triple-A is the toughest level to manage in the minors. The majors are the toughest level because of the media scrutiny and the money the players are making. What makes Triple-A is all the different factions you have on the team.

If you look at rookie ball and the Single-A level, all the players are young, enthusiastic, and they see their careers in front of them. They're not in high school any more. They're in pro ball, which is something they've wanted to do since they were five years old. At low-A and high-A, they are still young and naïve and learning how to play the game. You're still teaching basic things about the game.

Double-A is the first time that you have guys on your team who know that they're starting to level off. You've got youngsters coming up who are going somewhere, and one or two that have been to the majors but might be on a rehab assignment or hanging on and hoping for a chance to get back.

But at Triple-A, you have many different factions. You didn't have to be a scout to know that Alex Cora, Eric Gagne, and Paul Lo Duca were going to the big leagues at some point, whether it was that season or the following season. On certain teams, there can be a little envy from other players knowing that these guys are on the fast track.

Then you have your second group of guys, the homegrown players that signed in the system, and the journeyman guy that has fought and worked his way to each level in the system to get to Triple-A. He might be 26 or 27 and has achieved a great amount by getting to Triple-A, but he's got enough maturity and experience to know that he's just an organizational player. He's still got a hope of getting to the big leagues in some type of role, but the reality is it's probably not going to happen. He's seen too many people pass him by. I don't want to say they're trapped, because they love the game, but they're making enough money at Triple-A and don't want to give up the uniform. And between that and whatever they do in the winter, they're doing enough to make a living even though they know it's going to come to an end at some point.

The third group is the six-year free agents making pretty good darn money and hoping for the brass ring. Your club got them in a bidding war, it usually means an invite to big-league camp, and it means more money than you're paying to your homegrown Triple-A guy that you just promoted from Double-A. The fact that you had interest in him means you have a need if your big league guy gets hurt. When I was with San Diego, we had Matt Clark from LSU, and he went through the system, hitting a lot of home runs at each level, but he couldn't make it to the big leagues. He was slow-footed and couldn't play anywhere but first, and the major league club had Adrian Gonzalez. He ended up with the Binghamton Mets in 2014 and had a clause in his contract that if he didn't get to the big leagues by a certain date, he would become a free agent. He walked away and signed with the Brewers, and after somebody got hurt, Matt Clark got to go to the big leagues for the last month of the season and hit some homers, although he didn't get resigned.

The fourth group is made up of the guys who have already been to the big leagues and have their careers in the rearview mirror. Maybe they're there to learn another pitch or better control, or for the love the game. They're still playing Triple-A, hoping for that ten-day call-up to get some more pension time and to get back to the big leagues again. The Mets had a guy like that in Buddy Carlyle. He made his debut in the late 1990s and was in the Royals' system when I was there in the early 2000s. He hung around long enough to pitch for the 2015 Mets team that won the pennant. In 2014, he pitched 31 innings and had a 1.45 ERA. That's what experience can do. He was like a Four-A guy.

With all the different groups, if the manager doesn't have experience bringing these people together, you can go through a five-month, 144-game season with people just playing for themselves. But when it all comes together, like it did for us at Albuquerque, it can be a lot of fun.

Ron "PaPa Jack" Jackson was our hitting coach and a few years later was the Red Sox hitting coach when they won the World Series. He did a real good job with the guys in Albuquerque. My pitching coach was Dean Trainor, a longtime minor league pitching guy who now manages in Triple-A. I had a real good, passionate staff. When I'd try to mold young managers and coaches, I'd tell them, "You show me a manager that doesn't have passion and I'll show you a dead ass team." I think that in any sport, given enough time, the team takes on the personality of the guy running it. Look at the teams Pat Riley had with the Lakers. His overabundant passion reflected itself in the team. Tom Landry was a real stern guy, and the Cowboys played with that passion. If you saw Landry's eyes on the sidelines, he looked like a serial killer with the focus that he had. If you have coaches who have passion for what they do, your players are going to feed off that.

Because of the success we were having, I picked a date that I thought we would clinch the division on and joked that it would be a struggle to motivate everyone once we clinched. We clinched the division on August 26 at Colorado Springs, and a few guys reminded me that back in June I had picked that date.

We had a lot of good guys that weren't as well known as Lo Duca and Gagne. Chris Ashby was a guy that the Dodgers had gotten from another organization. He was a tall, lean left fielder with some pretty good tools. He ended up becoming the classic 4-A player, a guy who can put up numbers in Triple-A and just can't quite get over the hump to get to the big leagues. He could hit some but would struggle with right-handed breaking balls, so his hitting was limited and he had some power, but not enough to be a prototypical left fielder in the big leagues. But he was a great teammate and he did real well for us.

It was the same story for my first baseman, Kevin Grijek. He was a grinder. He played balls out and could do a good job at the Triple-A level, but just didn't have enough home run frequency to be a big league guy.

The consummate guy on that team was Shawn Gilbert. He was a veteran guy who was 35 years old and was like the unofficial captain of that team. Gilbert was a team player who could play center field, second base, shortstop and third base.

A big-time Dodgers prospect at one time on that club was Adam Riggs. He was a second and third baseman who was very strong with plus power. The longer he played and the more he moved up the ladder, he was a guy that could really rake left-handed pitching but had some holes against righties. He had limited range in the field. Riggs played for a little while in the majors and then played in Japan.

I had Gregg Olson on rehab. He was with the big league Dodgers, had an injury and came to us for a few weeks. He was terrific with us because he didn't come down with the typical big league attitude. He really molded in what we were doing. Before he left, he told me what a great atmosphere there was on the team. With my experience, I'll take some of the credit for trying to create that atmosphere, but it ultimately comes from the players that you've got.

We had Tony Mota, who was Manny's son. Manny had the all-time pinch-hit record until Lenny Harris broke it. Tony was a switch-hitting right fielder who could run and throw. He started the year hitting third and had a strong, powerful body. Tony did not have a lot of loft in his swing, he was more of a line drive hitter so you didn't see the power reflected. Manny was a hitting coach for the Dodgers at the time. They may have been the first team with two. Ben Hines worked with the American players, and Manny Mota worked with the Latin players.

Curtis Pride joined us in mid-season, and what a pleasure he was. He was deaf, and my concern was on possible collisions in the outfield, but Curtis was very adept with hand waving. He could run, make contact and play defense.

Chris Michalak is a guy who was a career minor leaguer (with a few cups of coffee in the big leagues) and had the single best pickoff move I've ever seen for a left-handed pitcher. He claims that he never pitched a game in his pro career without picking off at least one guy. We had a game where he picked off two guys in one inning. It got to a point where guys in the dugout would be focused on it and predicting the pickoff. Chris was a great competitor. He was short on stuff, but really knew how to pitch. And he was an extra weapon with his bat. He had excellent hand-eye coordination, so we had a standard deal that in any bunt situation with a runner on first or runners on first and second, if the pitcher fell behind the count, we would automatically convert to a hit and run. Late in the season, we had a game where Chris was up in the fourth inning of a tie game with runners on first and second with nobody out. It's a no-brainer that you're bunting. The pitcher went to ball one, and we went to the automatic hit and run. And Michalak was a left-handed hitter, so if he swings and misses, the catcher has an open window to throw the runner out at third by 20 feet. He lined a two-run double to left-center to break a 1–1 tie. He factored in winning his own game. And then he pitched a complete game.

In the bullpen, Bobby Ayala led the team with nine saves. Al Reyes, who I liked a lot, pitched well out of the bullpen. Another huge factor was Trevor Miller, a guy who went on to have a long career as a situational lefty. Trevor was another consummate team player who got a lot out of the year. Dean Trainor did a good job with him. Chad Ricketts was a prospect we were trying to develop and groom. He kind of gained confidence and eased into that role as the season went along.

We lost to the Memphis Cardinals in five games in the playoffs. We could've won in four games. We were actually one out away from winning, but they came back in Game Four and then won Game Five. Memphis actually called up Albert Pujols from Low-A to Triple-A for the series.

It was very satisfying year. When you finish nearly 30 games over .500, it's hard not to have fun. I told the team, "Guys, I thought coaching third base at Wrigley Field was the best job that I ever had, but if I can't be in the big leagues you guys have made this immensely fun. One, with your ability level, and two, our success because of the way you guys bonded together with the team."

When the season ended, Kansas City wanted me on the staff for 2001, but Kevin Malone refused the permission. I went to Kevin and asked what happened because I had been up front about leaving when we spoke at the beginning of the year. Kevin said that Kansas City wanted me as the bullpen coach, and that this team was moving to Las Vegas and they wanted me to manager. I told him that I didn't have that much time in the majors and although the bullpen isn't ideally what I'm suited for, it is the big leagues. Kevin told me he'd like me to stay but that he'd grant me permission to leave. That's what opened the door for me to get back with Kansas City.

Kansas City

One of the most memorable things in Kansas City was getting to watch Jermaine Dye on a daily basis. He was a gifted athlete and physical specimen. He was our right fielder and a scout's dream. Jermaine had a great, live athletic body, could run, throw and field, and had power and a quick bat. I just loved the way that he played the game.

We had Joe Randa, a third baseman that most would consider a journeyman. You're talking about an overachiever who maximized his ability. When you look at tools, he didn't stand out like a Jermaine Dye. He played a fantastic third base for us, making diving plays in games when we'd be behind, 7–1. He just left it all out there. I admired the way he played the game. He carved out a nice career for himself.

Mike Sweeney was the favorite son in Kansas City. The people just loved him. Mike could really hit and was a run producer who put up some really big years in Kansas City.

Carlos Beltran became the biggest star from that team but was still young at the time. I had seen him play in Puerto Rico, and his talent was very apparent. My pitching coach was Guy Hansen, who was also the Royals' coach, and I questioned him. Beltran had been a second-round pick, and the first-round pick for the Royals was a big outfielder named Juan Lebron, who had the body type of a young Juan Gonzalez. Beltran and Lebron were still young and over their heads against the competition in Puerto Rico, but looking at their skills I told Guy, "Your organization is lucky you ever got Beltran because he should've been the first pick."

Beltran had all five tools and was a switch-hitter. He did everything so easy. The gifted ones make it seem effortless. He had won the Rookie of the Year Award in 1999. Carlos had a poor first half when I was there in 2001. We had a bet going on in the bullpen because you can't keep a good athlete down, and Beltran started to come on. I made a friendly wager with some guys that Beltran would get to 30 homers and 100 RBI. He didn't get to 30 homers, but he was on fire in the second half. In the last game of the season, in Detroit, he made an out in the late innings and somebody told me, "He did great but there just weren't enough games for him to get to 100."

I said, "Well, the game isn't over yet." He ended up coming to the plate with the bases loaded and two outs in the ninth, with 97 RBI. I said, "He's gonna do it. I just know he's gonna do it." And he drove a ball past the bullpen at Comerica, just a rocket out of the park for a grand slam. Everybody got excited. We lost 97 games and were hopelessly out of it, but it was a thrill watching a young guy of that skill set come around. He was also a great base stealer. Carlos had a long stretch with a lot of stolen bases and was caught only once, on a pitchout. Guys like Rickey Henderson, Lou Brock and a young Carlos Beltran could get to top speed on a second or third stride.

In Kansas City I was reunited with Roberto Hernandez. We hadn't seen each other in three years, but when I was hired by the Royals, my first phone call was to Roberto, telling him that we were reunited. He was at the tail end of his career but still threw hard. He didn't get as many opportunities because there wasn't much winning.

We had a very prolific offense that could score runs in bunches, but other than Jeff Suppan, who was a reliable and productive starter, we struggled in the pitching department. Brent Strom, our pitching coach, was fired and replaced by Al Nipper. It's the old adage of "you can't fire the players." We had the offense. We had no trouble scoring five or six runs. Unfortunately, we would give up seven or eight, and Brent took the fall.

We finished 65–97. The season ended a week late because of the attacks on September 11. On Sunday the ninth, we had finished a road trip with a game day in Texas and then we flew back to Kansas City and got in that evening. And we had no game scheduled for Monday. I was at the Plaza in Kansas City, which is kind of an upscale place with restaurants. I went to Tomfoolery's to eat and get a couple of beers, and the next thing I knew my phone was ringing. I was so sound asleep I didn't even know who it was. I just said hello and they told me to turn on my TV. I saw the replay of the plane hitting the tower, which I thought was a movie or something. Then I came awake and realized it was really happening. Major League Baseball responded by pushing games back, and nobody played until the 17th.

After we started the 2002 season with an 8–15 record, Tony Muser was let go. It was tough for me when Muser was on the hot seat, and what really wasn't good was that you could feel the tension in the clubhouse because once the papers start speculating on the manager, even though Muser was a big enough and strong enough man to take the pressure off the players and take the heat, it starts creating tension. Even though it was only April, there was so much written in the papers about it, it's almost like you're waiting for something to relieve the tension. And what relieves the tension is when a change is made, right or wrong.

John Mizerock, our bullpen coach, was made the interim manager, and then they brought in Tony Peña. That boded well for me. Everybody is on pins and needles when a new manager comes in, but he had a barbecue for the team and he told his wife that he knew one day he would be a manager and that I would be on his staff. I liked that his passion and energy for the game was just so out there, you couldn't help but be infected by it.

Paul Byrd had a terrific year in 2002. He was our ace. Suppan went 9–16 with an ERA over five. He was usually our most dependable starter. He threw over 200 innings. I never knew Suppan to miss a start when I was there.

We got Chuck Knoblauch, who had helped the Yankees make the World Series four straight years. I was the outfield coach in 2002 and it was fun working with Knoblauch in left, Beltran in center, and Michael Tucker in right.

Our fourth outfielder and primary DH was Raul Ibanez, who went on to have a fantastic career and is a class person. He's very humble and has a great work ethic. I think I knew what we had in Raul before the Royals did. Raul had won a batting title in Puerto Rico when he was still in the minors and facing big leaguers. He could hit, but he never really had a position and wasn't much of an outfielder. He came up with the Mariners and never established himself. I don't think he felt comfortable. He also didn't play as much for Lou Piniella because the Seattle lineup was loaded.

What's amazing is that in 2001, we sent Raul not once, but twice to the minor leagues because we needed the roster spot. He could've been claimed by any team in baseball, twice. Once he came back up, Muser started hitting him against righties. Once he got his feet on the ground, he played more like he did in Puerto Rico. When Peña took over, he thought "screw the platoon" and started playing him against left-handers. Raul started to hit for average and power and drive in runs. Plus he worked his butt off every day in the outfield when we did drills, and he became a decent outfielder.

In September 2002, we were in Oakland when they were on an historic winning streak. They won their 18th and 19th in a row against us, and then we played the final game of the series on Sunday Night Baseball. They were on fire and came out and were just burying us. It was 11–0 in the early innings. And then all of a sudden we started scoring against Tim Hudson. I remember being proud of the guys for battling back and not laying down. And then we ended up tying the game.

As soon as we tied them up at 11, Scott Hatteberg hit a pinch-hit homer off Jason Grimsley, just a blast to right-center which left us on the field at 12–11. That was a long flight back to Kansas City. It was one of those things where you're proud of yourself for overcoming an 11-run deficit, but we couldn't finish it off.

We lost 100 games, but then we started the 2003 season 16–3. We were the talk of baseball. Tony did a great job. Every move he made in the month of April paid off. We had a lot of momentum and a lot of confidence, and although we came back to our level as the season went along, we did finish over .500, which was the first time that happened for the Royals in nearly a decade.

Jose Lima was brought in, which started "Lima Time" in Kansas City. He was a 20-game winner with the Astros but was past his prime, but really knew how to pitch and was a showman at the same time. Even on days he didn't pitch, he was like a tenth player on the team in the dugout. He brought a lot of the enthusiasm that Tony liked. Lima did pretty well and went 8–3.

Even though we finished 83–79, the team ERA was over five. We always had offense but not enough pitching to hold the other team down. I was actually reunited with Jeff Pentland, who had become the Royals' hitting coach.

We had Angel Berroa, who was a real exciting player and had all the skills to play shortstop. He was inconsistent at the plate but still very young. He won the AL Rookie of the Year Award in 2003. He got some time in the big leagues but never improved enough with the bat.

Desi Relaford was an established big leaguer who had played a lot at short but was a very good teammate and gracefully moved to second base to kind of tutor and nurture Berroa.

Brent Mayne was a good catcher with leadership qualities. He was a real good signal caller. He was like a jockey riding a horse that would get the most out of whatever a pitcher had to offer.

Starting pitcher Darrell May went from 4–10 with an ERA over five in 2002, to 10–8 with an ERA under four in 2003. It's time to get your feet on the ground in the big leagues. I'm sure a lot of it is that when you first get to the big leagues, it's natural to pitch away from contact. When you do that, your walks go up, you get behind in the count, and you get hurt. In 2003, Darrell was more aggressive in the strike zone, gave up fewer walks, pitched ahead in the count, and did a solid job for us.

Chris George went 9–6 with an ERA over seven. We scored a lot of runs when Chris pitched. Sometimes that happens. Chris was a former number one pick of the Royals. He didn't throw too hard, a crafty left-hander, kind of a poor man's Jamie Moyer. Velocity was not his strong suit, but his strong suit was that he threw strikes, and he had a real good changeup. If you don't have velocity, you need to throw strikes, but pitcher's strikes as opposed to hitter's strikes right over the plate. Chris gave up quite a few homers and runs. But he did have a changeup so good that a hitter could look for it and still not get good wood on it.

Jeremy Affeldt was exciting to watch. Because of our lack of pitching depth, Jeremy probably got to the majors sooner than he would've with a first-division team. He was from Spokane, Washington, and signed right out of high school. Sometimes it helps to sign with a struggling team because your opportunity comes sooner. Jeremy learned at the big league level rather than applying his trade for a longer time in the minors. He was a student of the game, very professional, and had electric stuff. He just needed the experience of pitching to big league hitters and the innings to get better command of his pitches. He recently retired, and when you look at what he did in his big league career for the Royals, for the Rockies, and then the culmination of his career with the Giants and being a vital part of three World Championship teams, I'm really happy for him. And he's done charity work in Spokane. It couldn't happen to a better guy.

We had Mike MacDougal. Mac was a scout's dream; 6'7", 210 pounds. Tall and skinny as a rail, but with long, loose limbs, and Mac could run it up there pretty close to 100, with movement. Mac struggled with his body and command of his pitches. In the first half of the 2003 season, he got locked into the strike zone, and when you throw close to 100 with movement, you could almost get by with just one pitch. He had a slider to go with it, and his stuff was off the charts. He made the All-Star team. In the second half, his command started to desert him a little bit. His career wasn't as long as he would've liked, and the consistency wasn't there, but he was a scout's dream with his natural velocity.

D. J. Carrasco is an interesting story. There's a guy who should write a book. D. J. was released but didn't give up and played for some independent teams, and Pittsburgh saw him and signed him. He did well enough with an A-team that they took him to the Fall League, but they didn't put him on the 40-man roster, so in hindsight their mistake was taking him to the Fall League and exposing him to other teams. His performance was good enough to get the attention of the Royals, who took him in the Rule 5 draft at the winter meetings. I was thinking that this was a Cinderella story if he turned out to be any good. He didn't throw as hard as MacDougal, but he had a real loose arm, and a resilient arm that could throw daily with no drop-off in his stuff. That's hard to find and what makes relievers such a commodity. D. J. had amazing movement on his fastball. It was in the low 90s, not in the stratosphere with MacDougal, but he had much better command. He was in the big leagues too soon because we had to have him on the roster or else send him back to the Pirates.

D. J. wasn't afraid though. I remember in April he came into a game with runners on, and he went right after the hitter and gave up a sacrifice fly. I was impressed with his mound presence. It was almost like where a lot of kids are nervous and it takes time to get used to the big leagues, D.J. was the opposite. He was a guy who looked at where he had come from to playing on the biggest stage that there is, and it was like "give me the ball and let me get in on the action." He had the perfect makeup to be a big league reliever, he just didn't have the experience, but we knew in spring training that we had made a good acquisition. He had a nice career, and even played a few games in Japan. A real class guy and a great teammate.

Attack

The book wouldn't be complete without mentioning the infamous attack of September 19, 2002, at U.S. Cellular Field on the South Side of Chicago.

It was probably shown on ESPN and Fox Sports a thousand times. We were playing the White Sox towards the end of the year. We were both at the bottom of the division, both long out of the pennant race. The game didn't mean anything other than to be played and for development purposes for the guys that were brought up in September. It was a cold night, and I can't believe there were more than 10,000 people in the ballpark, let alone any by the ninth inning.

What I was told is that the father and son were in the right field bleachers and worked their way around. I think some ushers clocked out because they worked their way down to the first base dugout. The railing along the first base side going past the dugout is only three feet high. You just lift your leg like a low hurdle and you're on the field.

Michael Tucker had just made an out on a bunt back to the pitcher. Between pitches, I would often bend at the waist with my hands on my knees like an outfielder.

That's the last thing I remember because I got completely bowled over. I didn't know what happened because with my hands on my knees I didn't get a chance to put my hands down to brace my fall. My head just torpedoed into the ground. It was almost like an out of body experience. I think I was so stunned from the impact of my head ramming into the ground that I hadn't realized that I momentarily lost all my hearing. All I knew was that I was lying on my back and two guys were swinging at me, but they were missing.

Of course, I didn't know that they were drunk or on drugs. I just remember thinking in an instant, who are these guys, what are they doing on the field and why are they swinging at me? I wasn't angry. I was just so out of it. One of them totally cold-cocked me in the jaw, which turned out to be a plus because that got me out of being stunned. Then I was thinking that I was in trouble here.

I tried to kick the guy that was in front off so I could turn and defend myself against the guy on the left who hit me in the jaw. As I made a quarter-turn, I got hit all over again, and I had no clue that the second time it was by all the players on my team ganging up on these guys with me at the bottom of the pile.

I saw the veins bulging in their necks and their mouths were moving, but they weren't saying anything. Being at the bottom of the pile, I was so out of it, I had no clue what was going on. All I knew was that I was getting kicked in the groin and the shins. I realized after the fact that some of the players on the top of the pile who couldn't get to the guys were trying to kick them back, but some of their kicks were getting me. The whole thing was just bizarre.

When everything was separated, I got up and saw that I had blood on my hand. I got my hearing back and heard somebody say, "Hey, there's a knife. Pick it up." Because I saw blood on my hand, I started to probe my back and sides. I thought I must be in shock because I didn't feel it. I remembered watching a tennis tournament where a guy came out of the stands and stabbed Monica Seles.

Our catcher, Brent Mayne, held his hands up in front of me and said, "No, Tom. You're okay. You didn't get stabbed, you got a cut on your forehead." Right away I was totally relieved. I had an abrasion on my forehead, and that's where the blood came from.

The trainer wanted to escort me into the clubhouse, and reality kicked in. We were in the middle of an inning and I told him I had to coach first base. He told me that I really had to come inside. And then my face hurt. I put my hand up to the right side of my face, and it had ballooned out. I put my left hand on the other side and told him that he was right. I could feel that my face was swollen on the side that was compressed with 25 guys piled on top of me.

When we got inside, the trainers wouldn't let me look in the mirror. They didn't want me to be traumatized straight away by seeing the swelling, which went down real fast once the ice pack went on.

I felt guilty after the game because of the amount of security and police that came to interview me. Everybody wants to get away on the last day of the road trip. Guys want to get home and see their families. It's not that far of a trip from Chicago to Kansas City, but it was a night game so we were getting home late enough as it was. The questioning certainly delayed our flight. I didn't have anything to feel guilty about because I didn't do anything wrong, but it was just the idea that the team had to wait because of me. That was awkward.

When it happened, my oldest daughter, Kristin, was in a panic because she was watching TV, and the ticker said that first base coach Tom Gamboa was attacked during the game and stabbed. She told her siblings, but nobody could find out about my status until I reassured them.

Out of all the players, trainers, coaches and managers, one guy gets attacked and it happens to be me. Tony Muser joked the next day that "there are 900 people in the big leagues. The odds are one in 900 of someone being attacked. Gamboa, if you're involved, it's basically 50/50." Tony's one of the most sarcastic guys I've ever met in my life, but he was the first one to put it in perspective, once he realized I was okay.

I knew it would be on the news, but I was so naïve that I actually thought that everybody would move on the next day and turn the page. It would be back to business as usual. I was completely dumbfounded when we finished batting practice the next day and our media guy told me I was going to have to address the media. I asked him what for.

He said, "Are you kidding? We've got a whole room full of people here."

When I walked into the room, there were 75 people waiting. I recognized some of them from TV, and not just from Kansas City, but from other places. When I got to the podium, you could feel the tension in the room. I always respect that the media has a job to do, and I sensed the tension because these people don't know me. I don't know if there was fear of asking the wrong question as to how I was going to take it, so I decided to diffuse the tension.

I said, "It's like I'm today's Kato Kaelin." Everybody in the room laughed. It was my 15 minutes of fame. That broke the tension, and they realized I was going to be easy to talk to.

Later on, one woman told me that I answered the questions with such an easy attitude. I didn't do anything wrong. I didn't have anything to apologize for. I was doing my job and was a victim who happened to be in the right place at the wrong time. I was thankful I didn't get hurt. What I didn't know at the time was that I was going to lose a portion of my hearing in my right ear. I ended up getting tinnitus, a ringing in my right ear, which doesn't hurt but is a nuisance.

I was glad I had a platform with the media to make it clear what a great sports town Chicago was. Having worked for the Cubs for five years,

I made periodic trips to Wrigley as the minor league field coordinator, and I lived in downtown Chicago when I was the third base coach. Nobody who saw my attack should think anything negative about Chicago over the actions of two deranged people. I got a lot of complimentary messages from fans from the South Side of Chicago, saying that they were glad I understood what good fans they are. I didn't jump on the bandwagon to put a black mark on the city.

I did learn a lot about mass media. I was the last one of all the coaches to buy a computer. I was the last one to get rid of a flip phone. By my own admission, I'm always behind the curve. When the requests from our media guy came in, I accommodated everybody at first. I was on the *Today Show* with Matt Lauer and Katie Couric. I had to wake up at some ungodly hour to do a satellite TV thing with them. I was on a radio show in Los Angeles. I was cooperative, but then I told our media guy that enough was enough. I could see that this was becoming a distraction.

I walked into the clubhouse one day, and Joe Randa, our third baseman, said, "Wow. You've really made the big time."

I said, "What does that mean?"

Randa said, "You were on *Letterman* last night."

I said, "No, I wasn't. I think I'd know where I was."

Randa said, "No. You were on the top 10 on *Letterman*."

I thought it was a joke until one of the players put a piece of paper in my locker.

Top Ten Shirtless Father and Son Explanations

10. He was obstructing our view
9. Autographed Tom Gamboa baseball would be worth more if he were dead
8. We're sorry, you'll have to talk to our shirtless lawyer
7. You try staying in your seat during a White Sox-Royals game
6. Dr. Phil says fathers and sons form stronger bonds when they commit senseless acts of violence
5. When two shirtless idiots can't attack anyone they want, the terrorists have won
4. People do crazy things after nine beers
3. For generations our family has proudly beaten first base coach Tom Gamboa
2. Getting in shape for hockey dad season
1. Couple Mets players gave us some crazy weed, man

With my sense of humor, I read it. I'm always one for a good joke, even if it's at my expense. When I realized this was going national, I understood that this media thing was beyond my scope of imagination.

There was one article in the paper the next day talking to the dad. I think after the fact, he had to make something up and made a ridiculous statement that I got what I deserved for flipping them off. If he was talking about a different person, he might've been able to get away with a statement like that, except that my credibility throughout my career was so impeccable that anybody who knew me knew how ludicrous that was. I've spent a career not only with players but sometimes mentoring minor league managers and coaches in telling them that when they do get verbally abused, the worst possible thing you could do is let the fan know that he's got your goat, and that you're actually listening to what he has to say. If you totally ignore it, eventually they'll direct their attention elsewhere. They want feedback. To me, it's common sense.

I can honestly say that in my whole pro career and ten years of winter ball, I was nothing but courteous and respectful to the fans. Even in Latin America, when they'd throw stuff at me or onto the field when we weren't doing well. Cubs fans would occasionally throw salad tomatoes during a losing streak or if somebody I waved in was thrown out at home. I just let stuff roll off my back. I think part of being a professional is to stay focused on your job. The people pay for their tickets so I've never been one to counter back.

It came out later that the dad had called his sister and asked if she was watching the game on TV. When she said she wasn't, he told her to turn on the game because they were going to be on in the next inning. She didn't understand what he was referring to, but it was a pre-planned thing.

My questions were how and why me? When they climbed over the little railing next to the first base dugout, my back was turned and I was the closest one to them, so I was a convenient target to get the attention they were looking for. They had drugs or pills before the game and then had some beer once they got to the park. Either one is a recipe for disaster, but mix the two and that's what ends up happening.

The public address announcer says who is on the coaching lines, and nobody ever pays attention to that. Which they shouldn't because the game and focus is about the players. That night I could see all the cameramen near our dugout. They announced number 26, Rich Dauer, at third base and number 21, Tom Gamboa, at first base. I got a standing ovation from all the people in Kansas City, and all the camera flashes went off.

I had mixed feelings. I was certainly flattered. I took it that the ovation was their way of saying that they were glad that I was back on the field and okay. But it was embarrassing at the same time because ovations like that are supposed to be for Mike Sweeney or Carlos Beltran when they double in two runs or hit a homer. Coaches and fans are there for the players.

We're not there to be singled out. To be singled out for something that I didn't do, but was a victim of, was flattering and embarrassing. I felt that I had to step forward and tip my hat to acknowledge the fans.

Each night, people would be eating popcorn and drinking beer when they heard Rich Dauer's name, and then my name would be announced and all of a sudden there was instant recognition through no attempt on my part. It got to the point where I couldn't wait to finish our last home stand and finish the season on the road, only we went on the road and the same response would happen. That's where you're just at a loss as to what to do about it. I was so relieved to be on the road, and then in the top of the first inning I get a nice ovation. It's well-meaning on the part of the fans, but it was hard.

When does this go away? You're supposed to be anonymous when you're a coach, unless you're a former star like Mark McGwire or Barry Bonds. But most of the coaches are anonymous and they like it that way. They know their job is to be behind the scenes, mentally help keep players up through a slump, reassure their confidence, throw batting practice and hit fungos, which is what I enjoyed doing.

I didn't know how to get back to the anonymity of it. The games in Detroit and Cleveland became "there's the coach that was attacked."

There was one nice thing to end the season. When I was the field coordinator for the Detroit Tigers from 1987–1990, our first-round pick in 1987 was Travis Fryman. As the field coordinator, I spent a lot of time with Travis at rookie ball in Bristol, at Low-A and Double-A. Then I managed in 1990, and Travis was my shortstop at Triple-A. At the All-Star break, I took Travis and his girlfriend, who is now his wife, to dinner and told him how much I was going to miss because he was going to the big leagues the next day. That was a real thrill for me. I think he was expecting to go up in September, but he went up in July, never to be seen again in the minors. He went on to have a heckuva career with the Tigers and Indians. The last game of the season was the final game of his career. Travis sent the bat boy over with a bat before the game.

It was inscribed "To Tom Gamboa, From Bristol to the big leagues. Travis Fryman. Thanks for everything."

Boy, that made me feel old. As you get older, time goes by faster. In the blink of an eye, Travis is retiring and it seems like just a couple of years ago he was in Bristol. He got into coaching in the minors, and our paths have crossed as opposing managers. It's great to see him back in the game.

When the season ended and we flew back to Kansas City, Tony Peña told me that there were going to be some changes on the coaching staff and that I was going to be the third base or the hitting coach. On my drive from Kansas City to Palm Springs the day after the season, we hired Jeff Pentland as the hitting coach. Rich Dauer was let go, so I assumed I was the third base coach, and yet the day before I got back to California, the general manager called me to say that I was going to be in the bullpen for 2003.

It just seemed like it was a way to decrease my visibility. I can't blame them because you don't want to be a distraction. But in a sense, it was a demotion. There's a hierarchy. The third base coach has more prominence and responsibility than a first base coach. Not to undermine any of them, but in the hierarchy, going to the bullpen was basically going backwards. It was unfortunate for me because I think the attack had everything to do with that move being made.

Now it's April 2003. The Royals, coming off a last-place finish, were the hottest team in baseball. We started 16–3. Tony Peña did a fabulous job. He was a terrific motivator and had this unbelievable passion that permeated the team.

So we went into Chicago with a 10–1 record. I had a habit of going to the ballpark around noon, and I would run up and down the aisles from foul pole to foul pole in whatever stadium we were in on the road. When I finished, I saw the supervisor of Major League security who was one of the people I was involved with in the subsequent interviews after being attacked. He was right there on the field at one or two in the afternoon. We said hello, and I asked him what he was doing here.

He said, "Are you kidding? This is the first time that your team is back here since the attack."

I laughed and told him that was last season. "You guys don't really think lightning is going to strike twice, do you?"

He said, "Tom, we're going to make sure that it doesn't. We've beefed up the security for tonight."

I went to the locker room and thought about how crazy it was that they were going to have extra people at the game because of me. And because the bullpen in Chicago was out in right field, there was an extra security guard who walked me out to the bullpen and stayed there with me. I asked if this was necessary, and the guard told me that there was a security meeting earlier in the day and they had a zero-tolerance policy for this game.

After one of the innings ended, some college guys, who I'm sure had too much to drink, started a "Gamboa Sucks" chant. The more they chanted, the more people got involved with it. It got to a point where it was like a cheer at a college football game. I was sitting out in the open with my arms folded and my back to them. I wasn't going to give them the courtesy of turning around to look at them.

Mike DiFelice, who wasn't with us the year before, was sitting next to me. He said, "My God, what did you do last year to bring this on?"

I said, "Exactly what I'm doing now. Absolutely nothing."

The pitcher finished his warm-up tosses and the chant stopped. Then one guy yelled out at the top of his lungs, "Hey Gamboa, I fucked your mother last night, and she liked it!"

I could feel everybody's head turn towards me. I turned to all of our guys in the bullpen and said, "Now I'm really pissed. To think that my mom is apparently in Chicago, and she didn't even call me last night."

Everybody busted up. I just tried to make light of a situation that was really sad. When parents take their kids to the ballpark, that's not the kind of thing they want the kids to hear. I turned to the security guard, who was next to me, and said, "Just out of curiosity, when you say zero-tolerance, just exactly what does somebody have to do to get ejected tonight?" The poor guy didn't know what to do. You can't eject everybody in the bleachers, and you're not going to find the one guy who yelled.

That night there was not one, not two, but three different people who came out of the stands and ran around, trying to get their 30 seconds of fame. I just can't relate to what these people think about. The third was so drunk that he tried to tackle the first base umpire, Laz Diaz. The fan was so out of it that he was on the ground with his arms wrapped around Laz's legs.

Later that night, I got back to the hotel and watched the news. You hope they don't show that stuff because it just encourages other people to do that, in my opinion. Not only did they show this goofy guy trying to tackle Laz, but in the inset was my picture in the bullpen, televising my reaction of seeing it happen to someone else. Is this ever going to go away?

The next day before we took batting practice, there were media members who wanted to get my reaction. Again, I had mixed emotions. Part of me said that I have to respect it because they have a job to do. And if I shy away, then what am I doing? The other half was wondering when this was going to stop, because our team was 11–1 and the focus should be on the players. Once again, through no fault of my own, I'm detracting from the team.

Our media guy told me that whether it was now or later, I was going to have to answer questions. I asked Tony, and he told me to get it out of the way. After batting practice, Tony brought me into his office and closed the door. "Gambi, I just have one question. When is this going to stop so we can turn the page and focus on what's going on right now?"

I said, "Tony, just tell me what to do. I didn't ask them to come here. I didn't ask three guys to come out of the stands and run on the field. What do you want me to do? Should I just stay in Kansas City and not come to these three games?"

I didn't know what the answer was, and he didn't either. I certainly understood him being upset by it because it was taking away from our team. We're trying to win, and I'm answering questions about why three idiots came on the field. Anybody can see that's a distraction.

The coup de grace came later in the year. This one defies all odds. In early August, we went back to Chicago to play the White Sox. While we were shagging fly balls in center field I saw a media guy coming out, and I knew he was coming to talk to me. I had no idea why.

Just as batting practice ended, they opened up the gates and media people were literally running down by our dugout. What could possibly be going on now?

The media guy comes out on the field to let me know that of the 365 days in a calendar year, on that very day when our team was in Chicago, that was when the judge handed down the sentence. Now the media people came from the courthouse to the ballpark to get my reaction. We were in a pennant race, and now I had to take these questions and give my opinion of the sentencing.

The sentencing was ridiculous. The judge was very elderly. To say that he was compassionate would've been an understatement. His ruling was that people have to understand that this guy has a drug and alcohol problem that needs to be treated. In spite of a rap sheet that was unbelievably long and violating his parole, the judge just kept making excuses because of the drug and alcohol problem. He was given a few years of probation, which everyone thought was ridiculous.

Once that media session was over, Tony Peña basically read me the riot act. I took it but told him that he still didn't tell me what I was supposed to do. It's not like I manipulated things to have this guy sentenced when our team was here. What are the odds of that? We could've been in Cleveland, Detroit, Kansas City, or anywhere else in the country. If that was the case, I could've taken some phone calls from these people, and we would've never heard about it. We happened to be in Chicago, so naturally everybody wanted my reaction.

The Royals finished the 2003 season with a winning record for the first time since 1994, and everybody was brought back except me. The bullpen coach was let go. A coaching change is usually in the sports page under transactions. So-and-so was optioned out. So-and-so was called up from Triple-A. So-and-so was hired or fired. In my case, being let go as bullpen coach of the Royals made the front page of the *USA Today* sports section.

Me and Tony had gotten along great. We had history before Kansas City. During my years in Puerto Rico, we managed against each other in the Caribbean World Series. Tony was aspiring to be a major league manager and was managing Águilas in the Dominican league. He led them to back-to-back championships, and we managed against each other in 1997 and 1998. His team won both times, while we finished second. In 2000, I got my revenge at the Triple-A level in the Pacific Coast League. He was the Astros' Triple-A manger at New Orleans, and I was the Dodgers' Triple-A manager at Albuquerque. We beat up on them pretty good to win the central division.

When Peña took over for Muser, he had a big barbecue for all the coaches, and I met his family. I learned that Tony told his wife while he was in New Orleans, that one day he was going to get a big league job and he wanted this guy Gamboa on his staff. I had a reputation as an American who was bilingual and had spent ten years in Latin America managing perennial winners in winter ball. Like Tony, I had a reputation as a motivator who had high energy and aggressive teams.

I was a victim of circumstance. I couldn't have had worse luck, and this thing would keep coming up when we went to Chicago. Something I thought would be gone the next day never went away.

In 2005, Rafael Palmeiro waved his finger at congress and then failed a drug test. But after he failed the test, he was still an Oriole. Every town the Orioles went to, the press wanted to know what he had to say. It was a distraction. I sort of knew what he was feeling. Within a month, he was no longer with Baltimore. He at least brought it on himself. I never did anything wrong.

Even with all my experience, I couldn't get a job for the 2004 season. It was just weird. Finally, in the summer I got a call from Mexico to manage Permessio in the winter league.

The sad thing for me is that I've had over 40 years in professional baseball and yet, as my kids have told me, when I pass away the attack will be the first thing mentioned. Tom Gamboa, the coach who was attacked in Chicago in 2002, passed away yesterday. I'm one of the few people in this game who has managed pennant winners at the rookie league, low-A, high-A, Double-A, Triple-A and Latin winter ball. But I'll be forever known as the coach that was attacked.

I'm glad I have a sense of humor and can take it with a grain of salt. A few years later, a friend called me and said that I was the final answer on "Jeopardy!" And somebody actually got it right. I said, "The guy that got that right needs to get a life if he knew my name."

After the Attack

I couldn't get a job in 2004. When I got back from Mexico prior to the 2005 season, the Angels needed a Double-A manager. Abe Flores, the assistant farm director, was a big sponsor of mine who had worked at my camp many years before. Abe recommended me to Tony Reagins, who later became the Angels' GM but was the farm director at the time. Tony was from Indio, which is right near Palm Springs. Tony drove out to the desert, partially to see his family and partially to interview me. We had a two-hour interview, and he hired me on the spot to manage the Double-A team in Little Rock, Arkansas, in the Texas League.

It turned out to be a fun year for a lot of reasons. The team I had very soon became the team Mike Scioscia had in the big leagues. Although it's hard to go back from the majors to the minors, when you've got good talent it makes the year fun. Our catcher was Mike Napoli, who led the league in homers and RBI. Kendrys Morales was at first base. Alberto Callapso was the second baseman in the first half of the season, and when he went to Triple-A, we got Howie Kendrick from A-ball, and he could really hit. Erick Ayabar was the shortstop. Reggie Willits, who became a fourth/fifth outfielder with the Angels, was the center fielder. The pitching staff included Ervin Santana, Joe Saunders and Jered Weaver, who later became three of the five starters with the Angels.

The team was run by Bill Valentine, a former American League umpire. Bill was the longtime general manager and was known as Mr. Baseball in Arkansas. He was a cantankerous old codger and old-school in every sense of the word. With my personality and also being an old-school guy, I cut through the roughness. We hit it off and became great friends. There wasn't a homestand where Bill, his wife, and I didn't go out for dinner.

We played at Ray Winder Field, which was among the oldest parks used in professional baseball. You had to see it to believe it. Thank God for the people who came after me that they built a new ballpark after I left. Bill took unbelievable pride in Winder Field, like it was a child of his. None of my pitchers liked the mound. One day, all of my pitchers came out to the park early with tampers and shovels, and they were basically going to rebuild the mound. Valentine came out from his office, went into the stands, and saw everybody on the mound. Valentine, who was in his 70s, yells at the top of his lungs, "God dammit, you sons of bitches! Get off that fucking mound!"

I was always trying to mend fences between Valentine's relationships with the players. I told him, "Bill, these guys want to like you but they feel like you hate them." He was from a different era but when you got to know him, he had a heart of gold.

We won the pennant, but as much fun as it was, if you're in the big leagues you can justify being away from home for seven or eight months. It's tough to do that in the minors. Being part of a nice country club in the desert, I kind of longed for a roving job if I wasn't going to be in the big leagues.

The Angels treated me great, but Grady Fuson was the Vice President of the Padres and a friend and golf partner of mine, and he wanted me in San Diego as the outfield and base running coordinator. I also filled in as minor league hitting instructor, and we had this guy at Fort Wayne, Wil Venable, who I thought was the most gifted guy in the whole system. I spent a lot of time with Wil and his dad, Max, a former big league player and the Fort Wayne hitting coach. Wil went on to have a nice career with the Padres and had one big year where he hit 22 homers and stole 30 bases, which got him a nice contract.

Although he's a good outfielder and prolific base stealer, I don't think he ever reached his full potential as a hitter. In the minors he was an up the middle, slightly opposite field guy who had real good power. When he got to the big leagues, he was so concerned about pulling the ball and the power, his ability to use all the fields suffered, and his average suffered as a result. I wish I could've worked with Wil longer because we had a great rapport and he was a fun guy to work with.

Grady was a scout with the A's during the "Moneyball" era and was responsible for them getting guys like Barry Zito, Mark Mulder, Tim Hudson, Eric Chavez and Jason Giambi. Texas took him away and then he ended up in San Diego. I worked with him during my second tenure with the Padres. I was the field coordinator and oversaw six teams with three-man staffs. There were five rovers, so I had 23 people working under me. And I communicated with Grady a lot since he was my boss.

Something came up, and Grady wanted everybody to meet at the end of the day. I let the staff know that Grady wanted everybody to meet in the conference room at 5:00. So 5:00 comes and all of us are there except for Duffy Dyer, who was our catching coordinator. Grady asked me where Duffy was, and I told him that I told everyone about the meeting. Grady said, "Well, let's get him in here."

I immediately opened my flip phone and started hitting buttons. Grady goes, "what are you doing?"

I said, "You told me to get Duffy in here."

Grady said, "I know I did but what are you doing?"

I said, "How do you expect me to get him here? I'm dialing his number."

In front of everybody, Grady says, "You mean you don't have everybody's number programmed into your phone?"

Anybody that knows me knows that my computer skills, even with an iPhone, are not good. I'm just of the old generation. I looked at Grady and said, "Like I would know how to program numbers into my phone."

Grady goes, "Well, you're my right hand guy running this whole department. Are you trying to tell me that you have everybody's phone number memorized?"

I looked at Grady and said, "Well, of course I do."

He looked at me in disbelief, scanned the room and said, "What's Tony Muser's phone number?"

I said, "His home or his cell?"

Grady said, "I don't give a shit, just give me is number." I said the number, and Grady spun around, looked at Muse and asked if I was right. Muse said that I was. So Grady said, "What about Bob Cluck?" Bob was a special assignment pitching instructor. So I gave Grady that number. Grady asked Bob if I was right, and Clucky said that I was.

Grady said, "Well, what's my number?" So I told him his number. Grady looked at the whole room, put his hand to his forehead and said, "What are you, the fucking Rain Man?"

My son is a real genius, a professor at Dartmouth who has all 37 of Shakespeare's plays memorized. The one thing I can take credit for is that my son gets his photographic memory from me, only I never used mine in an educational sense. There's a lot of me that's like Forrest Gump. I'm naïve in a lot of ways. I used to assume that everybody could do that. I didn't realize that it was that big of a deal. But Grady was beside himself because I didn't know how to program number into my phone, but it was nothing for me to have the numbers of 24 staff members memorized. It certainly got a lot of talk over the next few days, especially from the younger guys who couldn't believe it.

I was with the Padres from 2006–2009, until new ownership came in and made changes. In 2010, I was replaced, but I was still under contract for the season so I got paid for not doing anything other than play golf. During the year I got a jury summons. Anytime I had ever gotten one, I had been out of state on the road in Arizona or Florida or in Puerto Rico for the winter.

Now I'm at home, and there was no way to get out of it because I was in Palm Springs. I went along to the selection with 200 or 300 other people. It was a murder trial, and the judge predicted that it would take five weeks. This was during the recession, so during the screening process all these painters, plumbers, and contractors were pleading that there was no way they could get five weeks off without going under. I was off for the year, and before I knew it I was juror number 11.

It took two days to pick the 12 jurors, and there was half a day left on day two. The judge, an older gentleman, looked at the clock and said, "Well, I think we're going to commence. We can get some of this done, or at least start it, today. Before we begin, does anybody have anything to say?"

I assumed all the hands would go up, and I looked around and I was the only one with my hand in the air. The judge looked at his sheet and said, "Mr. Gamboa, you have something?"

I said, in all seriousness, "Your honor, I'm smart enough to know that this guy is entitled to a fair trial." The defendant was in the room with all the lawyers. This was a real courtroom thing. I had never experienced this, other than my divorce, which nobody was there for. "But due to what we heard, the outcome is so blatantly obvious to me, I'm wondering what we're going to be spending five weeks doing here."

The judge leaned back in his chair, folded his arms and sarcastically said, "Mr. Gamboa, why don't you just enlighten me and my courtroom on how we're all going to be wasting our time."

They had established that I was a baseball coach in the interview process, and everybody in the courtroom was aware of it. I said,

> Your honor, I mean no disrespect at all but using my background as an example, we've been told, number one, that this is not the first, but the second DUI by this defendant. Nobody is disputing that. In my business, that would've been the first strike. Secondly, when this so-called accident occurred, we've been told that not one, not two, but three police cars were chasing this guy in excess of 90 miles per hour, and I know the speed limit on the highway is 40 and 50 depending on where you're at. Me and my friends, the few times anyone has been pulled over, when the

> siren goes on you pull up right and stop. And he didn't. To me that was the second strike. Thirdly, we've been told that in an attempt to evade the police, there was a fork in the highway, and at 90 this guy tried to make a quick veer to the left in hopes of throwing the police cars off, and in the process, lost control of his car, and went up over the curb and hit a palm tree and the passenger was killed. So therefore, strike three. If nobody's disputing the facts, it's three strikes and you're out. What is this going to be about?

The defense attorney stood up and, as if I'm the idiot, said, "Your honor, do you mind if I ask Mr. Gamboa a question?"

The judge leaned forward on his elbow and said, "Please do," as though I'm the one that's out of kilter here.

The defense attorney said, "Well Mr. Gamboa, what if over the next five weeks I was able to convince you that in my client's state of mind that he wasn't responsible for his actions?"

Then I got pissed. It was as if I wasn't in a courtroom. It was like I was in an argument with an umpire. I turned to the judge and said, "You're not going to make me answer a ridiculous question like this, are you?"

And the judge leaned back, folded his arms and said, "Mr. Gamboa, I can hardly wait for this answer."

I pointed my finger at the defense attorney and I said, "You know what? Regardless of the fact we're in a courtroom, you've actually pissed me off right now, because I for one am sick and tired of hearing about some guy that walked into a post office and killed seven people because of something that happened to him when he was ten. I think that we're all responsible for our actions all the time. I'm wasting everybody's time here. I know I'm voting guilty."

The judge looked at me and said, "Mr. Gamboa. Number one, nobody would ever accuse you of being a fence-straddler. And number two, you've given me a very entertaining story to tell my wife tonight at dinner. But that's not how we do things in our system. Everybody is presumed to be innocent until proven guilty and entitled to a fair trial. We're going to have to let you go."

When I walked out of the courtroom, the people that were sitting on the end of the rows were high-fiving me as I walked out as though I was speaking for what everybody was thinking. I was just being honest. I was just relating the facts.

Before leaving the courthouse, I went to the men's room and when I was coming out, the defense attorney was walking in. He said, "Mr. Gamboa, just a quick question since you seem to have all the answers. What would you have us do?"

I said, "Hey, I'm not an attorney. I've never done this before. But I do have common sense. I can see why the state of California is going bankrupt because of money that is just wasted. Five weeks are going on for something where the facts are just the facts. I would think that you would just plead guilty and throw it on the mercy of the court. I don't know what the penalty is supposed to be for what the guy did. But somebody died. It wasn't an accident. The guy was drunk when he was driving and has been before."

That trial went on for five weeks, it made the front page of our newspaper when it was over, and the defendant was found guilty of second-degree murder and got 35 years in prison. My friends thought it was funny that somehow I see everything in terms of a baseball game.

Mike Gillespie is like a brother that I never had. Mike was a coach for 20 years at USC and is currently at UC Irvine. His son-in-law, Chad Kreuter, played for me for two winters in Puerto Rico when he was trying to bridge that gap from minor league catcher with the Rangers to getting to the big leagues. He ended up succeeding his father-in-law at USC but was let go. His firing coincided with the making of "Moneyball." The director was Bennett Miller, who had been nominated for an Academy Award but being from Australia he didn't really know anything about baseball. Chad was hired as the technical adviser to make sure they got the baseball stuff right in the movie.

They filmed for a month at the Oakland Coliseum. They ended up coming to Southern California to film some of the flashback scenes at Casey Stengel Field, when scouts are watching a young Billy Beane. They needed an extra to play a scout, a non-speaking part that they had forgotten to cast. Chad told the director that one of his ex-managers had been a scout, and Chad called me and asked if I'd want to play one. I'd get extra pay, which was about $300 a day. I said sure. I thought it would be fun to see how a movie was filmed, so I gave up a day of golf to drive into Los Angeles. The field I went to was actually where I hit my first home run back in high school.

During the day, Chad mentioned to Bennett that I had really scouted Billy Beane. Bennett Miller came up to me and said, "You really scouted Billy Beane?"

I said, "Yeah. He went to Mount Carmel High School in San Diego." Bennett asked me what the conversation is like when a scout works out a player and when you meet him. When I told him, he just threw a few pages of the script into the air and told his assistant, "I like what he's saying better than what's in the script. Make this guy an actor."

An assistant director told me I'd have to fill out all this paperwork.

She asked me if I realized what just happened. I said, "Well I guess I'm going to speak a line or two." She told me that an extra makes $300, but if you speak even a word then it becomes a $1,000 a day. She said, "The way the union rules are, you're going to be double-dipping. We've already signed you as an extra so you're going to get paid the standard extra fee, and then you'll get another $1,000 for the speaking part."

She also told me that if my part didn't get edited out, not only would my name be in the credits but I would be eligible to join the Screen Actors Guild. I said that I had no interest in being an actor. When I got done signing all these papers, they gave me some clothes to look like a scout would look in 1980. I was going to change in the back of my Lexus in the parking lot. And the woman goes, "Oh no. I forgot to tell you, you have a trailer now." I said, "A trailer? For what?"

She said, "Well, when they're in-between scenes and you're not doing anything, you can sit in your trailer." She took me to this trailer with my name on it. This is just crazy. When they broke for lunch at noon, they have this big food truck and everybody takes their lunch break. Right outside the stadium was the city park, and I just sat on a bench by myself. I didn't know anybody there except for Chad, who was at the director's heels all the time.

While I'm sitting, some crew members came over with their food, and one guy asked if they could sit with me. I said, "It's not my table, of course you can." This one guy from wardrobe looks at me and said, "Can I ask you a question? Are you the real Tom Gamboa?"

I said, "I don't even know what that means but yeah, that's my name."

He goes, "This is so weird. We just came from filming the scene where the A's won their 20th game in a row, and you were the first base coach for the Kansas City Royals." I told him I was. He said, "The reason I know is because you were number 21, and the third-base coach Rich Dauer was number 26."

I said, "Good God, how would you know that?"

He said, "Because I had to make up uniforms for both of you guys." Then he turned to the other crew members and said, "How weird is this? We had a guy up in Oakland playing him and now he's in the same movie playing someone else." If you look at the credits, I'm listed as Scout Martinez. I was the so-called superscout with the Mets.

So in this flashback, I'm going to meet Billy Beane after he takes batting practice. So I'm standing right by the on-deck circle, and there's a guy standing next to me, I have no idea who he is, and there are all these camera and lighting crews setting up all these different things. Bennett Miller noticed me and said, "Tom, what are you doing here?"

I said, "Well, I was told to be here at 1:00." Bennett said, "We're not even close to ready to filming the scene yet. Get the hell out of the way for your stand-in."

I said, "For my what?" Bennett goes, "The guy next to you is your stand-in."

I look at the guy, and he has a paper on his back with my name on it. And as Bennett was walking away I said, "You gotta be shitting me." Bennett turned around and said, "What?" You could've heard a pin drop.

I said, "Well, it's no wonder why all these actors have such big fucking egos. I've been an actor for not even two hours, and I have a trailer and a stand-in." All the people were laughing. It was like "here's one guy that gets it." I was kind of making fun of the whole thing. We're all just people, but somehow the people in front of the camera get all this adulation.

So me and the area scout were watching him take batting practice, and the director told us we were supposed to look up and out as though Billy was hitting every ball out of the ballpark. They had the camera on a little railroad track, and there's one shot where my face is the only thing on the screen, and the camera is slowly coming on that track. I'm watching young Billy hit ball after ball out of the ballpark, and Bennett told me to just be myself because there were no lines. He wanted me to ad-lib.

So there's the crack of the bat, and I turn to the scout next to me and I say, "This motherfucker will be drafted in the first round."

I heard the director yell, "Cut! Cut!" I looked around, thinking there was some background noise or an airplane flew overhead, but Miller was looking at me. He goes, "Tom, Tom, you can't say that!" I didn't even know what I said. I looked at the guy next to me, who was actually a scout for the Rangers, and I asked what I had said. He was laughing and said, "You said 'motherfucker.'"

I said, "Well, I guess that's what I would say. They told me to be myself."

Bennett goes, "You can't say that on film. What else would you say?"

I said, "I don't know. Maybe 'son of a bitch'?" He said that was good. So on the second take, the camera zeroes in on me and I say, "This son of a bitch will be drafted in the first round."

And he said, "Cut. Print." All we did was two takes. At the end of the day, the assistant director came up to me and told me that Bennett wanted me for tomorrow. I hadn't planned on staying and only had the clothes I was wearing, but I grew up in LA and called one of my best friends. I said, "Hey, I'm going to take you out to dinner tonight and by the way, I'm crashing at your house."

The next day, we filmed the scene inside the house where the area scout and I were trying to sign Billy Beane. I had a few lines in there as well. I got paid for two days as an extra and two days as an actor, and to this day I occasionally get residual checks. They're not much, but for two days of work I could see why a lot of people want to be in that business. So that was the beginning, middle and end of my movie career.

I went back to the Angels in 2011, and I got a chance to manage close to home. I was with Inland Empire, which was a high-Class A team in the California League. Two months into the season, my mother was diagnosed with terminal cancer, and the oncologist said, "If I was in your shoes I'd be much more concerned with the 2012 baseball season rather than this one because of the limited time your mom's got."

I retired on June 1 to spend time with my mom. Although they gave her three to five months, I told her on the first day of my retirement, "Mom, I'm going to take you to so many movies, plays and concerts there's going to be no time for dying. That's not on the schedule." My mom lived 15 more months. We went to dinner and a movie six days before she passed. That'll probably be my greatest achievement: leaving baseball behind and spending quality time with her.

For whatever reason, I didn't really miss baseball even after my mom had passed. I was content to play golf, enjoy my country club style of living, and hang out with my friends. I took the clubhouse camaraderie of baseball and exchanged that with the clubhouse camaraderie at the country club.

In 2014, I was on my way to a golf tournament when Paul DePodesta, who was a vice president of the Padres when I was there, asked me to manage the Mets farm team in Brooklyn. I was very flattered that he called, but I didn't even hesitate in turning them down. I told him I had no interest, but he asked me to think about it for a week. Unbeknownst to me, he had called Grady Fuson, and during that week Grady and Ed Sprague, Sr., were asking why I wouldn't go back and were talking up all the pluses of baseball.

It got me to the point that when Paul called me back after the golf tournament, I said, "Paul, if I was you, I would want to hire a younger guy that had his future in front of him that you could mold and train to manage because if I were to do it, it would only be for a year or two." In a sense, I was turning the job down again.

Paul said, "No, we want a veteran guy like yourself who's been from the bottom to the top and a teacher." At that point I felt like it was meant to be, so I gladly accepted the job.

I had always had the misfortune of being in antiquated ballparks, and

With Hall of Fame manager Joe Torre before a Brooklyn Cyclones game, 2016. Torre, who led the Yankees to six pennants and four World Series titles, was one of the managers I admired (courtesy George Napolitano).

then after the team won they would get beautiful parks that I would never see in person. It happened in Stockton and it happened when I was in Arkansas. Ray Winder Field in Arkansas was the oldest pro park being used. If that's not where Doubleday invented baseball, it must've been close. The stench in the clubhouses and dugouts underground was awful, and we had to endure it for 70 games. The year after we won, they had a brand new state-of-the-art ballpark right on the river in downtown Arkansas. When I was with the Mud Hens, I managed in the godawful park we were in, and right after that they opened a new park. That was my M.O. Albuquerque got a new stadium after I left. On my way back from Kansas City one year, I stopped to see it. With all these travels I've had in the minor leagues, I felt cheated that I never got the benefit of the new.

Finally, at the end of my career, I got the benefit of the new when I was hired by the Mets to manage the Brooklyn Cyclones. For people that haven't been there, just go on the Brooklyn Cyclones website because the pictures are just beautiful. It's good from a player's standpoint and a fan's standpoint. The park is situated right off the ocean, and behind the left-field fence is one of the roller coasters at the famous Coney Island amusement park. Visiting teams find it a distraction that every three minutes the roller coaster is active. Behind the right field fence is the famous boardwalk and the ocean. I can't say left-handed batters like the park very much because the prevailing winds come right off the ocean, blowing in from right field. The park used to be a grass ballpark, but after Hurricane Sandy in 2012 it became an Astroturf field. The diamond is sunken and it's all Astroturf. Between the playing surface, the clubhouse, the managers' and coaches' offices, it's a big league stadium except it holds 7,000 instead of 45,000. It's been a pleasure to manage there. It's about 12 miles from Citi Field, so we get the benefit of new balls every day to take batting practice with, which is unheard of in the minors.

It's been a great place to develop young ballplayers. I tell the players to never take for granted the fact that they're getting an opportunity to play where they're playing. In my era, it wasn't like this at all. To come into pro ball and get a chance to play in front of 6,000 people a night in a state-of-the-art park with good lights and new baseballs for BP is something. I often think that this current generation has grown up as a generation of entitlement, which is a far cry from how I grew up. When we go to places like Connecticut, Batavia and Mahoning Valley, it's a wakeup call for them. I say, "Now you're back in more of my era. That's what I'm accustomed to."

The manager used to be the end-all. You were the manager, the substitute parent, the counselor, friend, grandfather. You were kind of all roles. With the advent of mental skills coaches in the 1980s, the mental part of the game was focused on more. One of my pitchers on the Brooklyn Cyclones in 2016 was Adam Atkins. He was a closer at Louisiana Tech and was used to closing games and having success. But he was having zero success with us, and ended up in a role of just pitching in one-sided games because he didn't have any confidence in himself, which was obvious. His performance didn't lend us as a staff to have any confidence in him. Finally, one night, I snapped at him. It was on purpose, to light a fire under him, because as a manager I felt I had pushed every other button there was to push, but we weren't getting any results. His fear of failure and lack of performance was just spiraling downwards. When I went home that night, I felt bad about getting on him although my intent was a good one. The next day I pulled him out of the lunchroom and told him we would take

Heading out to coach third at MCU Park in Brooklyn. I came out of retirement to work with the Mets single-A team, the Cyclones, for what turned out to be three seasons.

a walk for an hour, just around the warning track. I don't know how many times we walked around it, but we walked a lot. I was trying to get across that with the pressure he was putting on himself to be perfect, the failure was becoming a self-fulfilling prophecy. The moment he gave up a hit, he felt like he had failed again. The moment that he gave up a run, he felt like he had failed again. He wasn't allowing himself to perform. I told him how Greg Maddux didn't try to throw every pitch for a strike or else he'd be setting himself up for failure. He would try to throw two of the first three pitches of an at-bat for strikes because that way he would have some margin for error. If he throws a borderline pitch that isn't called for a strike he doesn't necessarily feel like he failed. It was a talk, not just to mend the fences, but to start with one small step to build confidence and to take the pressure off himself. And for any reliever to think, "If I'm not successful today, I need to have a short-term memory because I might be needed in the game tomorrow and then I will be successful."

His last seven outings were seven scoreless appearances.

Ejected in Final Game

I knew going in that 2016 would be my last season. We played 20 innings on opening night, and that set the tone for the season. We lost a ten-inning game on a walk-off in which we were no-hit. We lost a 17-inning game. We lost a 1–0 game where the run scored on a three-base sac fly. The season finally ended on Labor Day against the Staten Island Yankees.

In the fourth inning, our third baseman, Blake Tiberi, hit a roller up along first and the pitcher missed a tag. The plate umpire ruled safe, but the Yankees asked the umpires to confer and the base umpire, who was way over at short, overturned the call and I came out to argue. I didn't get close to being ejected all year, but I have zero tolerance when an umpire lies. His quote was, "I clearly saw the tag."

We were out of it, but if we're going to play a game, at least call it right. When they conferred and changed the call, and especially the guy lying and saying he saw the tag, I couldn't take that. "Clearly saw? From where you were standing? I'm closer to the play than you were and I could clearly see that when the pitcher swiped at him there was daylight between the glove and the player. So I know he was safe. I'm not leaving here till we get it right. We had it right the first time, you let them talk you into it and you think because they appealed he must've got him, and I'm not leaving here."

They were intimidated at that point, and they know I don't come on the field unless I know I'm right. Eventually, he said the call is going to stand. I said, "You must be fistfuckin' me up my ass." Then he threw me out and I threw him out, and all hell broke loose. I threw some helmets and bats on the field.

And that was my last game.

World Baseball Classic

My friend Jerry Weinstein has an extensive background in international baseball and was asked to manage Team Israel in the 2017 World Baseball Classic. The qualifying rounds, a four-team round-robin, were in Brooklyn, so he called me on a few occasions to ask about field conditions, winds and anything that could give him an edge. Israel was competing with Great Britain, Brazil and Pakistan for the 16th and final spot in the WBC.

The players didn't have to be from Israel but they had to have Jewish heritage. The coaching staff was Jewish although they didn't have to be, but bench coach Bob Kelley had to bow out because his mother-in-law was in hospice. Jerry asked me to stay in Brooklyn and be his bench coach, and out of respect for our 40-year friendship, I did it. The training camp was in Hudson Valley because it was the only stadium in the New York-Penn League with turf.

The best thing Jerry did for the team was at the end of our first practice. Jerry had the whole team sit in the dugout and had the guys who had been on the Israeli team in 2013 talk about what the experience meant to them. They had made it to the qualifier against Spain and had a 9–7 lead in the ninth inning but Spain scored three times to win. The last player to speak was right-handed pitcher Josh Zeid, who took the loss in the game that sent Spain to the WBC.

Number one, I'm not Jewish. Number two, I have no international baseball experience. I thought this was going to be a fun thing to help out my friend. But when Zeid spoke about what the experience meant to him and taking the loss in the final game, he got so choked up that it got everybody, including me, choked up, and I realized in an instant that this was way bigger than what I thought it was. A lot of these guys spoke from the heart about playing for their homeland and what it meant to them. And when Zeid spoke, you'd have thought the game happened the night before, it was that fresh in his mind. And that made an unbelievable impact on everybody.

It's one thing to climb a mountain or to try to win a baseball game, but when you have an underlying purpose and a cause involved, it just takes the event to a greater level. When we were receiving adulation as the tournament went along because the other teams were in the top 20 and we were 41st, we were compared to the Jamaican bobsled team and David vs. Goliath. We were definitely the Cinderella team of this tournament, which helped us because there was no pressure. There was everything to gain and nothing to lose. But we also knew we had a better team than we were given credit for.

We had two recognizable names: Jason Marquis, who pitched 15 years in the big leagues, started two of the three games in the qualifier, and Ike Davis, who hit 32 home runs one year for the Mets. We had a lot of 4-A guys, virtual no-names. We beat Great Britain 4–1 with Marquis pitching. Corey Baker pitched a terrific game and we beat a favored Brazil team managed by Barry Larkin 1–0. Then we had to beat Great Britain again to get into the WBC, and we beat them 9–2 with Marquis starting again and Zeid being a big factor. Brad Goldberg was our closer in the series and closed out the 1–0 win. But it was interesting that Zeid was a big factor in the 4–1 win and in the 9–2 win that was actually close for a while.

Israel qualified for the first time, and I was caught up in the excitement and had a great time. I thanked Peter Kurz, the president of the Israel Association of Baseball. I didn't plan on going to South Korea because I was just replacing the bench coach. Peter and Jerry told me that I was part of the staff and part of the team and that I was going.

We had a three-day training camp in Phoenix and had a couple of nice additions to the team. We got Sam Fuld, a former outfielder with the Cubs and Twins. And we added Met infielder Ty Kelly, who played a brilliant third base for us in the tournament.

To think that it was the top 16 teams and Israel made it to the final seven is something everybody who was a part of the team is very proud of. Zeid's speech set a motivating tone throughout the tournament. We had a close-knit team, and Jerry did a great job bringing it all together.

Israel was the lowest seed, and we opened playing against South Korea in Seoul in front of a capacity crowd, which to some extent put the pressure on them. The longer the game went on, I sensed that they were pressing, having to win at home and in a 1–1 game. Fortunately for us we got an infield single in the 10th inning to drive in the winning run. As fate would have it, there was Zeid pitching the ninth and tenth innings and getting the win.

Then we had to come back the next morning on very little sleep. As the home team we took batting practice at 8:15 and then came out swinging and beat Chinese Taipei 15–7. In less than 24 hours we were 2–0 while the Netherlands hadn't even played yet. We were guaranteed of advancing to the next round in Japan. We had two advance scouts who did a terrific job on the opposition, advising us where to put guys defensively and how to pitch to each batter. We would have a staff meeting each day. We were going to play the Netherlands, who were also 2–0 and going to Japan. Jerry said the meeting could be short because they were just playing for pride that day because the focus was on Japan. Peter mentioned that there was a lot of money at stake, and up to this point nobody knew anything about any money. Peter said that the game was worth half a million dollars. The winning team gets $1 million, second place gets $500,000, third place gets $250,000 and fourth place gets $125,000.

When MLB started the WBC it was to promote baseball worldwide and to develop baseball around the world, so that whatever money a team earned, half would go to that country for baseball development. So winning $1 million in Korea meant $500,000 would go to Israel in terms of building fields, installing lights, buying equipment, hiring coaches.

I moved from bench coach to third base because Jerry Narron, who had been coaching third, had to join the Diamondbacks because Arizona bench coach Ron Gardenhire had been diagnosed with prostate cancer.

We were coming off an off day while the Netherlands had played the day before—plus it was a day game after a night game for them. Once again, Marquis pitched well, we played our usual great defense and we beat the Netherlands 4–2. We had gone 3–0 in Brooklyn, 3–0 in Korea and had won two exhibition games in Korea. Then in the Japan pool, we beat Cuba 4–1, and that's when the baseball world was really stunned. Who are these guys who are 4–0 in pool play when they're ranked 41st in the world?

At a press conference someone asked Jerry if this was really Israel or U.S. number two, which was a compliment. Jerry came back and said that every player had qualified under Jewish heritage. We were one win away from making it to Los Angeles for the final four. Unfortunately, reality set in. We lost to Netherlands. There was no turning point. We lost 12–2. Then we played Japan in front of 57,000 fans in their home park, the Tokyo Dome. We played them scoreless into the sixth inning but they scored three in the sixth and five in the eighth. The coaching staff was proud that even entering the ninth down 8–0 and only having two hits, we scored three times in the ninth, which I think showed the character of our team. We didn't just throw in the towel.

It was terrific life experience for each and every one of us to see first-hand the passion the fans in Asia had, along with their respect for the opposition. I had never been to Japan and as I was waiting for my luggage a Japanese man looked right at me, pointed and said, "Movie star." I said, "No. I think you've mistaken me for somebody else." And then he said, "*Moneyball*." I laughed and said, "Yeah. I was in that movie. If you blinked or went to the bathroom you'd have missed my part." He told me he knew I was in the movie. I thought, Wow, what a small world.

The motel we stayed at was on a hill in downtown Tokyo, so when you were in the lobby you were still four floors above ground level, where there was a mall. One day I decided to get lunch and I'm walking with a handbag on my shoulder, and as soon as I started walking into this mall I could see out of the corner of my eye some guy following me, to the point that I stopped at a men's store just so that this guy would walk on by—but he didn't. He stopped and looked in the window. When I started walking, he started walking. It was lunchtime so it's not like I had any fear but I was aware that he was following me. I got on an elevator and he got on the elevator. I put my handbag on the floor and at that moment, the guy shoved a book and pen at me, and he had two old baseball cards of me to sign. I got the biggest kick out of it because it showed how respectful he was. In the States, people just come up to you, saying, Will you sign this ball, Will you sign this program? But this guy didn't want to bother me as I was walking and waited until I was on an elevator and put my handbag on the ground. In my mind it went from a stalking situation to nice autograph request.

I was hitting ground balls to the infielders in batting practice before the final game and I ended up with a brand new ball in my pocket. I guess subconsciously I knew this could be my last game and thought, What a way to go out, I wish I could give a ball to a kid. But in Japan, the fields are bordered with a net from pole to pole to protect the fans from any line drives, which is a good idea that they could copy in the States. As I was walking to the dugout I saw a kid with a cap and glove with his dad and they were the only two people in this one section by our dugout. I motioned to them and pointed up at the net, because obviously I don't speak Japanese. The father knew what I meant, so the boy stood up, I tossed the ball over the net and the kid caught it.

I had never done this, although I wish I had done it more. You just get preoccupied with yourself and the traveling. I used to rationalize it as the kids want autographs from the star players, not the coach. I was never rude to anybody, but I'm the first to admit that I avoided a lot of that. But actually little kids just want anybody who's in uniform.

It was like the MasterCard commercial: The look on the boy's face and his dad's smile were priceless. I immediately put my hands up like a stop sign and ran into the clubhouse to get my phone and went back to take a picture of them. I put it on Facebook, which was my only post during the whole trip. I posted that I gave the ball to a kid, and was there a better way for father and son to bond than at a ballgame? The next morning there were 230 likes and one of my friends said that I was one guy who got it.

And I thought, you know what? I went most of my career without getting it. You're so involved with the wins and losses and the road trips that only at the end am I getting it, what baseball is all about. This book started by explaining my passion for this game when I was 10. That day in Japan, I had been thinking this could be the last game I'm in uniform. Usually when I'm done hitting, I toss any balls in my pocket towards the mound. But for some reason, I thought I could find a kid to give it to.

I wasn't prepared for the look on their faces. It just didn't dawn on me that it was going to be a big deal to get a ball, even from an American coach they did not know. And then I remembered back when I was a kid, and the realization set in: Oh my God, I think I forgot what this is all about.

Epilogue

Just when you think you've seen it all or learned it all, you'll see something you haven't seen. I had never been a part of a triple play, either as a coach or player, offensively or defensively. Then it happened during my final season when the Cyclones turned one.

Not only is my career coming to an end, but I was a little piece of Cubs history, having worked for them for five years and, like many, I became a huge fan and watched every game in the 2016 playoffs and World Series. One of my close friends in baseball, Gary Jones, is the third base coach for the Cubs. We talked every other week from the first day of spring training, so I'm happy for him and I'm happy for the Cubs.

On Thanksgiving Eve, three years after I introduced Kristin to Todd Zeile, they got engaged. Todd went to high school in the area where I raised my kids, and actually went to the same high school as Kristin although they were nine years apart. I watched Todd play in high school but didn't really know him. But when he went to UCLA, Guy Hansen happened to be the pitching coach. Todd's parents belonged to a country club, and I met Todd by playing golf with him and Guy. Over the years, I got to know him a bit better, including when Todd was on the 1995 Cubs and I was a field coordinator.

The whole baseball fairytale is complete.

Index

CPSIA information can be obtained
at www.ICGtesting.com
Printed in the USA
BVHW042202301022
650728BV00007B/51

9 781476 667416